Impression Management in the Workplace

Wanting to create a favorable impression with others is a basic part of human nature in both work and personal life. In this book, Andrew J. DuBrin skillfully provides a guide to the effective use of impression management based on scholarly research and theory, with particular attention to practical application. He highlights not only impressions that individuals make, but those made by entire organizations.

Self-tests and questionnaires allow readers to pinpoint how they currently employ impression management techniques in their work lives. Each chapter includes a section on "Guidelines for Application and Practice" that provides real-world advice based on the theories and research outlined in the chapter.

With this book, students will glean the best methods for creating positive, career-building impressions in current and future positions.

Andrew J. DuBrin is a Professor of Management emeritus at the E. Philip Saunders College of Business at the Rochester Institute of Technology, where he has taught courses and conducts research in leadership, organizational behavior, influence processes, and career management.

Impression Management in the Workplace

Research, Theory, and Practice

Andrew J. DuBrin

Rochester Institute of Technology

Routledge
Taylor & Francis Group

NEW YORK AND LONDON

Publisher:	John Szilagyi
Development Editor:	Felisa Salvago-Keyes
Editorial Assistant:	Sara Werden
Production Editor:	Sioned Jones
Typesetter:	RefineCatch Ltd
Copyeditor:	Lisa Williams
Proofreader:	Sue Cope
Indexer:	Patricia Hymans
Cover Design:	Asha Pearce
Companion Website Designer:	Leon Nolan, Jr.

First published 2011
by Routledge
270 Madison Avenue, New York, NY 10016

Simultaneously published in the UK
by Routledge
2 Park Square, Milton Park, Abingdon, Oxon OX14 4RN

Routledge is an imprint of the Taylor & Francis Group, an informa business

© 2011 Taylor & Francis

The right of Andrew J. DuBrin to be identified as author of this work has been asserted by him in accordance with sections 77 and 78 of the Copyright, Designs and Patents Act 1988.

Typeset in Times New Roman and Helvetica by RefineCatch Ltd, Bungay, Suffolk
Printed and bound in the United States of America on acid-free paper by Edwards Brothers, Inc.

Library of Congress Cataloging in Publication Data
DuBrin, Andrew J.
   Impression management in the workplace : research, theory, and practice / Andrew J. Dubrin.
        p. cm.
   Includes bibliographical references and index.
   1. Career development – Psychological aspects. 2. Impression formation (Psychology) 3. Management – Psychological aspects. I. Title.
   HF5381.D8123 2010
   650.1'3 – dc22
   2009040064

ISBN13: 978-0-415-87173-0 (hbk)
ISBN13: 978-0-415-87174-7 (pbk)
ISBN13: 978-0-203-86571-2 (ebk)

To Stephanie

Brief Contents

Preface   *xiv*
Acknowledgments   *xvi*
About the Author   *xvi*

CHAPTER 1

The Meaning and Nature of
  Impression Management   1

CHAPTER 2

A Cybernetic Model of
  Impression Management   16

CHAPTER 3

Individual and Organizational
  Contributing Factors   38

CHAPTER 4

Substantive Approaches to
  Self-Presentation   60

CHAPTER 5

Surface-Level Approaches to
  Self-Presentation   80

CHAPTER 6

Being Impressive by Making
  Others Feel Good   101

CHAPTER 7

Self-Protection Techniques   118

CHAPTER 8

Impression Management for Job
  Search and Performance
  Evaluation   136

CHAPTER 9

Impression Management for
  Leaders   158

CHAPTER 10

Impression Management by
  Organizations   177

CHAPTER 11

Functional and Dysfunctional
  Consequences of Impression
  Management   195

Glossary   *207*
Notes   *210*
Index   *227*

Full Contents

Preface   xiv
   Purpose and Goals of the Book   xiv
   Structure of the Book   xv
   Companion Website   xvi
   Acknowledgments   xvi
   About the Author   xvi

CHAPTER 1

The Meaning and Nature of Impression Management   1
   The Origins of the Modern Study of Impression Management   2
   A Variety of Definitions of Impression Management   3
   Impression Motivation and Impression Construction   4
     Impression Motivation   6
      Motives for Impression Management and Self-Presentation   6
      Antecedents of Impression Motivation   8
      Impression Construction   9
   Ethical Considerations Associated with Impression Management   12
   Guidelines for Application and Practice   13
   Summary   14

CHAPTER 2

A Cybernetic Model of Impression Management   16
   A Brief Look at Cybernetic Theory   17
   The Basic Components of the Model   18
     Reference Goal: Desired Social Identity   20
      Activation of Identity Goal   21
      Goal-Based Interpretation   22
      Goal-Directed Motivation   23
   Feedback from Target   24

Actor Perception   25
Comparator   25
   Identity Enhancement and Identity Protection   26
   Identity Adjustment   27
   Identity Maintenance   28
Outcome Processing   28
   Script Processing   29
   Adjustment of Reference Goal   30
Actor Implementation   31
   Verbal Tactics   31
   Nonverbal Cues   32
Impact on Target   33
Practical Implications of the Model   33
Guidelines for Application and Practice   34
Summary   35

CHAPTER 3

Individual and Organizational Contributing Factors   38
   Individual Factors Contributing to Impression Management   38
     Self-Monitoring   39
     Machiavellianism   44
     Trustworthiness   45
     Extraversion   47
     Optimism   47
     Cognitive Skills   48
     Gender Differences   48
      Gender Differences in Communication Patterns   48
      Gender Differences in Profiles of Impression Management   50
   Dimensions of Organizational Culture Associated with Impression Management   50
   Situational Factors Contributing to Impression Management   53

*Contextual Variables Influencing
    Impression Management*   54
Social Network Centrality   55
Characteristics of the Target   56
Working Remotely   56
Guidelines for Application and Practice   57
Summary   58

CHAPTER 4

Substantive Approaches to Self-Presentation   60

Self-Presentation of Characteristics
    and Behaviors   60
Being Persuasive   60
Developing a Positive Reputation   63
Publicizing Personal Connections   65
Using Appropriate Humor   65
Being Civil and Humble   66
Managing Anger Effectively   67
Self-Presentation of Work
    Accomplishments   68
*Displaying Organizational
    Citizenship Behavior*   68
    How Concerns about Image Drive
        Citizenship Behavior   69
    Impression-Management-
        Relevant Characteristics of
        Organizational Citizenship
        Behavior   70
    The Potential Downside of Using
        Organizational Citizenship
        Behavior for Image
        Enhancement   71
Becoming a Subject Matter Expert   72
*Taking Credit for a Favorable
    Event*   72
*Providing Timely Progress
    Reports*   73
Making a Quick Showing   74
*Demonstrating the Ability to
    Multitask*   74
Avoiding Unfavorable
    Self-Presentation   75

Guidelines for Application and Practice   78
Summary   79

CHAPTER 5

Surface-Level Approaches to Self-Presentation   80

Clothing, Dress, and Appearance   81
Clothing and Dress   81
*Perceptions of Sexiness Based on
    Clothing*   84
*Perceptions of Appearance Based
    on Obesity and Complaints about
    Health*   85
*Height as a Contributor to Image
    Projection*   86
Business Etiquette   87
First-Impression Making   89
Nonverbal Impression Management   90
The Alpha Male or Female   92
Personal Branding   94
*The Personal Brand as a Professional
    Identity*   94
*Coaching Assistance with
    Branding*   95
*Strong Personal Brands for
    Businesspersons and Professional
    Athletes*   95
Guidelines for Application and Practice   97
Summary   99

CHAPTER 6

Being Impressive by Making Others Feel Good   101

Ingratiation for Enhancing Others   102
Why Ingratiation Is Important   102
Political Skill and Ingratiation   105
*An Executive-Level Study about the
    Effectiveness of Ingratiation*   106
*Flattery as a Method of
    Ingratiation*   108
    Making Other People Feel
        Important as a Form of
        Flattery   109

Mixing Mild Criticism to
  Increase the Effectiveness of
  Flattery   109
Self-Perceived Technical
  Orientation as a Variable that
  Influences Flattery   110
*Opinion Conformity as a Method
  of Ingratiation*   111
*Humor for Ingratiation and
  Enhancement of Others*   112
Political Correctness for Enhancing
  Others   113
Guidelines for Application and Practice   114
Summary   116

CHAPTER 7

Self-Protection Techniques   118
Self-Handicapping   119
Self-Esteem Protection   119
  *The Effects of Status on
    Self-Handicapping*   121
    Background Information about
      Status and Self-
      Handicapping   121
    Research Design and Results of
      the Study   122
  *Procrastination as
    Self-Handicapping*   123
  *Gender Differences in
    Self-Handicapping*   126
Damage Control   128
  Admitting Mistakes   128
  *Apologizing, Pardon Seeking,
    and Making Excuses*   129
    Apologizing and Pardon
      Seeking   129
    Excuses and the Self-Serving
      Bias   129
  *Recovering from a Major Error
    on the Job*   131
  Anger Control   132
Guidelines for Application and
  Practice   132
Summary   133

CHAPTER 8

**Impression Management for
Job Search and Performance
Evaluation   136**
Impression Management Related to
  the Job Interview   136
  *Impression Management Tactics
    Frequently Used during the
    Job Interview*   137
    Assertiveness   137
    Self-Promotion   137
    Ingratiation   138
    Entitlements and
      Enhancements   140
    Basking in Reflected
      Glory   140
    Opinion Conformity   141
    Excuses   141
    Justifications   141
    Apologies   142
    Falsification and Information
      Filtering   143
    Nonverbal Behavior   143
    Physical Appearance and
      Attractiveness   144
  *Situational Attributes that Influence
    the Choice of Impression
    Management Tactics*   145
    Attributes of the Interviewee   145
    Attributes of the Interviewer   146
    Attributes of the Situation   146
  *Candidate Self-Monitoring and
    Interview Ratings*   147
  *Impression Management versus
    Job Competencies in Determining
    Interview Ratings*   148
  *Post-Interview Impression
    Management*   150
Impression Management for Traditional
  and Video Résumés   150
  Traditional Résumés   151
  Video Résumés   151
Impression Management during
  Performance Evaluation   152

*Variables Influencing Impression
    Management for Performance
    Evaluation*   153
*Performance Blips and Ingratiation
    to Enhance Performance
    Evaluations*   153
Guidelines for Application and
    Practice   154
Summary   156

CHAPTER 9

Impression Management for Leaders   158

Projecting a Leadership Image   158
    *Acting Skills Required for
        Winning over an Audience*   159
        Connecting with the
            Audience   159
        Understanding and Exploiting
            Symbols   160
        Listening Empathetically   161
        Improvising   162
        Radiating Confidence   163
        Projecting Discipline and
            Toughness   163
        Honesty   163
    *Implicit Leadership Theories and
        the Projection of a Leadership
        Image*   164
    *Specific Influence Tactics for Projecting
        a Leadership Image*   165
        Leading by Example and
            Respect   165
        Exchanging Favors and
            Bargaining   166
        Making an Inspirational
            Appeal   166
        Consultation with Others   166
        Being a Team Player   167
        Practicing Hands-On
            Leadership   167
    Being a Servant Leader   167
Impression Management and Charismatic
    Leadership   169

*Definitions of Charismatic Leadership
    that Include an Element of
    Impression Management*   169
*Impression Management in the
    Service of Creating and Maintaining
    a Charismatic Identity*   170
    The Role of High Self-Esteem
        and High Self-Monitoring   171
    Desired Identity Images   172
*Specific Impression Management
    Behaviors*   172
Guidelines for Application and Practice   174
Summary   175

CHAPTER 10

Impression Management by Organizations   177

Corporate Image and Reputation   177
    The Theory of Corporate Image   179
    *The Construction of a Corporate
        Image*   180
    *Corporate Image and Online
        Reputation*   181
    Association with Celebrities   182
    *Sponsored Research to Enhance a
        Company Reputation*   182
Spin as Impression Management   184
Corporate Social Responsibility and
    Impression Management   185
    *The Meaning of Corporate Social
        Responsibility*   186
    Corporate Social Performance   187
    Social Responsibility Initiatives   187
        Expressing an Environmental
            Commitment   188
        Work-Life Programs   189
        Community Redevelopment
            Projects   189
        Acceptance of Whistle
            Blowers   190
        Compassionate Downsizing   190
Guidelines for Application and Practice   191
Summary   192

CHAPTER 11

Functional and Dysfunctional Consequences of Impression Management   195

Functional Consequences of Impression Management   195

Successful Outcomes of the Employment Interview   195

Improved Performance Evaluation and Supervisory Ratings   197

Career Advancement   198

Improved Relationships with Work Associates   199

Cooperative Behavior and Satisfaction within Teams   199

Enhanced Sales and Stock Price for the Organization   200

Dysfunctional Consequences of Impression Management   201

Ethical Lapses Including Faking, Lying, and Stealing   202

Diversion of Mental Resources   203

Engendering of Mistrust and Dislike of the Actor   204

Emotional Labor and Distress   204

Choking under Pressure   205

Guidelines for Application and Practice   205

Summary   206

GLOSSARY   207

NOTES   210

INDEX   227

Preface

Wanting to create a good impression on others is part of human nature both in personal life and on the job. It is difficult to be successful if you do not create a good impression on influential people. *Impression management* (IM) generally refers to how people control, or manage, the impressions others form of them. Among the hundreds of possibilities in the workplace would be to dress fashionably when visiting a client, and complimenting the presenter at a meeting.

Impression management in organizations, or the workplace, has received some attention in the professional literature for over 45 years, and has been a subject of interest to career advisors for about 75 years. As a popular subject, the topic of impression management in organizations is almost boundless, with about 22 million entries given to the subject for the best-known Internet search engines. However, entries for impression management in an Internet search could include almost anything to do with personal behavior and appearance, such as etiquette and hairstyle.

Some aspects of impression management are studied in a wide range of schools, from career schools (also known as vocational-technical institutes) to MBA programs, and doctoral programs. Almost all business schools offer some instruction in service courses or special seminars on managing one's impression well for purposes of a job search.

Purpose and Goals of the Book

The purpose of *Impression Management in the Workplace: Research, Theory, and Practice* is to provide a guide to the effective use of impression management, with as many strategies and tactics as feasible based on scholarly research and theory. The book is therefore a scholarly book, yet with an emphasis on application. The application emphasis is achieved primarily by presenting positive and ethical strategies and tactics for creating a positive impression in the workplace, including the impressions created by an entire organization.

Another goal of this book is to help overcome the perception that impression management is inherently manipulative, deceitful, and unethical. The subject of impression management needs to create a better impression. Nevertheless, our book includes discussions about negative and unethical forms of impression management.

Impression Management in the Workplace fills a niche as supplementary reading in courses and seminars in organizational behavior, power, and influence, and organizational politics. Researchers may be interested in the book as a source of additional research topics and hypotheses to pursue. Another major purpose of our book is to place an up-to-date focus and structure on the field of impression management in the workplace. *Impression Management in the Workplace* also has the purpose of emphasizing the importance of this field for managers and professionals working in a variety of settings.

As a consequence of the purposes and goals of this book, it has several potential audiences. First, students looking for research-based as well as practice-based ideas for creating a favorable impression should find this book useful. Similarly, managers and professionals who want to impress others favorably in the workplace would find the information in this book to be helpful. Third, scholars in the field might find the integration of research and opinion about impression management useful for their research. At the same time, some of the suggestions made in the book might serve as hypotheses for conducting more research. One example among dozens of possibilities is whether creating a *personal brand* really has a positive effect on job finding and career advancement.

Structure of the Book

To achieve its purposes and goals the book is divided into 11 chapters. Chapter 1 presents a description of the meaning and nature of impression management. We include a touch of history, definitions of the term, and a two-part model of impression management developed by Leary and Kowalski consisting of motivation for and construction of the impression. Chapter 2 digs further into the subject matter by describing the cybernetic model of impression management developed by Bozeman and Kacmar. This model helps the reader appreciate the complexity of impression management in the workplace.

Chapter 3 describes individual and organizational factors that contribute to or predispose people toward managing their impression. Among these many factors are the traits of self-monitoring and Machiavellianism, and a competitive organization culture. Chapter 4 is about self-presentation tactics for impression management that deal with focusing on the self, and focusing on work accomplishment. Two examples are developing a positive reputation, and becoming a subject matter expert. Chapter 5 is about surface-level self-presentation tactics such as clothing, dress, and appearance, and developing a personal brand.

Chapter 6 describes another vital aspect of impression management—enhancing the status of others including ingratiation along with flattery, and being politically correct. Chapter 7 is about self-protection techniques of impression management, including self-handicapping, excuses, and recovering from a major mistake. Chapter 8 describes the application of impression management for both job search and performance evaluation, one of the most researched topics about impression management. Chapter 9 is about how leaders use impression management to enhance their effectiveness, with a special emphasis on the link between charisma and managing one's impression. Chapter 10 deals with how corporations (or the executives within them) attempt to manage their images, through developing a corporate reputation, spin, and corporate social responsibility,

Chapter 11 ties much of the previous chapters together by describing the functional and dysfunctional consequences of impression management. Among the functional consequences are successful outcomes of an employment interview, and stronger relationships with work associates. Dysfunctional consequences of impression management include ethical lapses and choking under pressure.

The basic information for each chapter is based on scholarly research. However, the information is supplemented with some information from the business press and the author's judgment. Each chapter contains a section called "Guidelines for Application and Practice," followed by a thorough summary. The notes for each chapter appear at the end of the book.

Companion Website

To complement the material in the book, we have created a companion website, which provides useful resources for both students and instructors: an instructor's manual with sample test questions, PowerPoint lecture slides, and further resources. This material can be found at www.routledge.com/textbooks/9780415871747

Acknowledgments

A project as complicated as a textbook or scholarly book requires the cooperation of a group of dedicated and talented people. First, I thank the hundreds of managers, professionals, and students with whom I have discussed impression management. Thank you also to the manuscript reviewers who made a variety of general and specific suggestions that have been incorporated into this book. These professors were as follows:

Barbara Crockett, Maryville University; James Breaugh, University of Missouri–St. Louis; Berrin Erdogan, Portland State University; William Smith, Emporia State University; Sally Riggs Fuller, University of South Florida; John Kammeyer-Mueller, University of Florida.

Thank you also to the editorial and production staff at Routledge who helped make this book possible, as follows:

John Szilagyi, Publisher; Felisa Salvago-Keyes, Development Editor; Sioned Jones, Production Editor; Lisa Williams, Copy Editor.

Writing without loved ones would be a lonely task. My thanks, therefore, also go to my family members—Drew, Douglas and Gizella, Melanie and Will, Drake, Rosie, Clare, Camila, Sofia, Eliana, Carson, and Julian. Stefanie, the woman in my life, also receives my appreciation.

A. J. D.

About the Author

Andrew J. DuBrin is a Professor of Management emeritus at the E. Philip Saunders College of Business at the Rochester Institute of Technology, where he has taught courses and conducts research in leadership, organizational behavior, influence processes, and career management. He also served as department chairman and team leader in previous years. He received his Ph.D. in industrial/organizational psychology at Michigan State University.

DuBrin has business experience in human resource management, and consults with organizations and individuals. His specialties include leadership, organizational politics including influence tactics, and career development. DuBrin is an established author of both textbooks and trade books, and also contributes to professional journals. He has written textbooks on leadership, organizational behavior, management, and human relations.

Chapter 1

The Meaning and Nature of Impression Management

Wanting to create a favorable impression on others is a basic part of human nature in both work and personal life. In meeting with the public, the chief executive officer (CEO) wants to convince others that he or she is wise, hardworking, and trustworthy. When exiting from the cockpit to greet the passengers, the commercial airline pilot wants to project the impression of self-confidence, being in control, and exercising good judgment. The customer service representative listening to the problem you are having with an electronic device wants to project the feeling that he or she is a friendly, competent person who will take care of your problem. And, of course, some scammers want to convey the false impression that they have your best interests in mind while really trying to steal from you.

In fitting with the theme of this book, an instructive definition of **impression management** is the process by which people control the impression others form of them.[1] *Control* in this sense refers to managing, shaping, or adjusting. For example, a certified financial planner wants to ensure that clients and potential clients perceive her to be a trustworthy and knowledgeable person. Toward this end she might engage in such activities as referring to the large portfolios she has managed, and the fact that she holds office in an association of certified professional planners.

People in the workplace are particularly eager to create a positive impression because they want to attain such outcomes as developing allies, getting a raise, getting promoted, receiving a bonus, making a sale, avoiding being placed on the downsizing list, and being hired in the first place. Impression management is such a natural part of organizational life that it is considered to be a major component of organizational politics.[2] Furthermore, Edward J. Hegarty wrote many years ago that impressing important people is the objective of all company politics.[3]

Impression management often connotes creating a false impression, or hiding deficiencies. In contrast, the thrust of this book will be to focus on research, theory, and practice about creating impressions that help a person emphasize legitimate positive qualities. Another misperception about impression management is that it is largely aimed at superficial aspects of a person's impression, such as wearing expensive clothing and accessories, having their teeth whitened, and facial wrinkles removed. A more rigorous study of impression management suggests that deeper aspects of behavior, including logical thinking and persuasive skills, are part of managing your impression.

We begin our study of impression management by describing the modern origins of its study, representative definitions, along with the motivation behind creating impressions and how they are constructed. We also describe some of the ethical considerations associated with impression management. As with other chapters in this book, we also devote a separate section to applying knowledge about impression management.

The Origins of the Modern Study of Impression Management

The idea of people using conscious or pre-conscious techniques to facilitate others thinking positively of them probably goes back thousands of years. (*Conscious* in this context refers to being fully aware of what you are doing. *Pre-conscious* refers to almost automatic behavior not requiring much thought, such as braking when you see a red light.) Survival in prehistoric times might have been partially dependent on other prehistoric people thinking kindly of you. Projecting too strong a negative image might have resulted in being stoned. In approximately 1600, impression management became better known with the famous statement of William Shakespeare, written in *As You Like It*: "All the world's a stage, and all the men and women are merely players. They have their exits and entrances, and one man in his time plays many parts." Shakespeare's famous words are still quoted frequently in books and articles about impression management.

The modern-day roots of the scientific study of impression management are frequently attributed to sociologist Erving Goffman, who framed impression management with his dramaturgical model of social interaction.[4] In overview, Goffman views people as "actors" engaging in "performances" in various "settings" before audiences. The key task of actors or performers is to construct an identity. The impression a person creates is a major part of his or her identity.

The actors and the audiences interact to develop a definition of the situation which guides their behavior. Although not mentioned specifically by Goffman, much of this behavior takes place without much conscious awareness by participants. Imagine a CEO holding a town-hall meeting with hundreds of employees. The CEO appears somber and dignified because he has to announce further cost reductions, including worker layoffs, eliminating jobs, and closing several offices and plants. The image the CEO projects helps define the situation as quite serious. As a result, the usual joking and kidding that might occur at a town-hall meeting do not appear.

Goffman reasoned that the performance of people functioning as actors depends upon the characteristics of both the situations and the audiences present. Performing as actors on the stage of life, people attempt to control the images or identities they portray to relevant people in their environment. The end-states the actors hope to attain could be social, psychological, or material. Being perceived in a particular way could therefore lead to better interpersonal relationships, feeling better about yourself, or receiving higher compensation on the job.

Goffman, as well as other researchers, believed that controlling one's identity as it is portrayed to others can influence how situations are defined, and thereby establish expected norms, roles, and behaviors. (Goffman evidently credits most people with a high degree of insight into human behavior and political skill.) By interacting with and influencing situations and audiences (or the environment) actors can better position themselves to achieve their desired ends. Impression management is therefore goal-directed behavior.

Goffman also described the importance of self-presentation for defining the individual's place in the social environment, for establishing the tone and direction of an interaction, and for defining how roles influence performance. According to Goffman, self-presentation is influential in the construction of social reality. For example, if a person projects himself or herself as being intelligent and well informed during a meeting, a social reality of being given a key follow-up assignment to the meeting might be forthcoming.

Perhaps the most useful point of Goffman's complex analysis is that even seemingly innocuous actions might be aimed at showing a person in a favorable light. For example, an electronics repair technician might scratch the back of his head during a discussion of a customer problem. The head scratching is aimed at creating the impression that the technician is thinking deeply about the customer's problem.

In practice, Goffman's analysis would include a mutual funds sales representative dressing elegantly, and making reference to her MBA from an elite school during an investment seminar. Many members of the audience might be persuaded to believe that a credible mutual funds sales representative is therefore a wealthy and well-educated person, prompting them to invest in the funds she represents.

A Variety of Definitions of Impression Management

As mentioned above, impression management refers generally to the process by which individuals attempt to control the impressions others form of them. The object of an individual engaging in impression management is generally to have others form a positive impression of him or her. Yet some people are looking to form a negative impression. A soldier attempting to avoid combat duty, or who is seeking a medical discharge, might want to project the image of an emotionally unstable person, and therefore not suited for combat. A prison inmate might have been incarcerated for so long that when the time comes for parole or release he fears competing in the outside world. With the prospects of no employment, no housing, and no food, he decides to form the impression that he will return quickly to crime if released. So he makes statements to the prison officials and parole board about his likelihood of returning to crime.

Creating a negative impression can also take place within a work organization, in the form of *strategic incompetence*. The actor projects the impression of being incompetent with respect to a task in order to avoid being assigned the task. A person asked to take notes at a meeting might declare, "I am terrible at note taking," in order to avoid the responsibility.

Steven Crawley, a human resources executive, says the inability to perform certain tasks can be very helpful in avoiding the tasks a person does not want to perform. He claims that his proudest moment of strategic incompetence took place when the president of an automotive-parts manufacturer asked Crawley to organize the company picnic. Not liking to do party planning, he responded to inquiries with comments such as "How do you do that?" The responsibility for the picnic was soon assigned to another worker.[5] The link to impression management is that Crawley created a negative impression about his competence by pretending not to understand the task. (You might not think highly of Crawley's ethics.)

As explained by Mark R. Leary and Robin M. Kowalski, most scholars in the field have used the terms *impression management* and *self-presentation* interchangeably, yet some have distinguished between the terms.[6] For example, Barry Schlenker defined impression management as the "attempt to control images that are projected in real or imagined social interactions." He reserved the term *self-presentation* for images that are "self-relevant."[7]

The distinction between impression management and self-presentation can be important. A person might enhance the image of another person, such as through flattery. The flattered person then develops a more positive impression of the flatterer. Another consideration is that images may be managed by methods other than self-presentation. A person intent on developing a good reputation might ask somebody else in his or her network to *good mouth* him or her.

In general, the term impression management is broader and more encompassing than self-presentation. Given that most research on the topic has dealt with how people control the impression others form of them, it is difficult to avoid using the terms interchangeably.[8] Chapter 6 in this book focuses on techniques of impression management designed to enhance the status or good feelings of others, thereby facilitating a positive impression of the enhancer.

Figure 1-1 presents ten representative definitions of impression management. Enough consistency among these definitions exists to make the formal study of impression management viable. At the same time, the term *impression management* conveys enough meaning to facilitate communication about the topic. The common meaning is that the person takes action so that the target person or persons perceive him or her positively. (The slight exceptions about creating a negative impression are mentioned above.)

Impression Motivation and Impression Construction

Impression management is sufficiently complex to be described and analyzed in a variety of ways. In Chapter 2, we present a cybernetic model of impression management. Here we examine a two-component model of impression management developed by Mark K. Leary and Robin M. Kowalski that offers two major advantages.[9] The model provides a solid base for understanding other frameworks

Figure 1-1 Ten of Definitions of Impression Management.

1. The attempt to control the image that others form about an individual.[10]
2. *Impression management* (also called *self-presentation*) refers to the process by which individuals attempt to control the impressions others form of them.[11]
3. Impression management involves what we do to create and maintain the desired impression in others about ourselves.[12]
4. A person's systematic attempt to behave in ways that will create and maintain desired impressions in the eyes of others.[13]
5. Behaviors designed to influence the way in which a person is perceived by others.[14]
6. Impression management in organizations consists of strategic communications designed to establish, maintain, or protect desired identities.[15]
7. The activity of controlling information in order to steer others' opinions in the service of personal or social goals.[16]
8. A new form of social competence in organizations, which individuals employ to master organizational politics, facilitate better work relationships, increase group cohesiveness, avoid offending coworkers, and create a more pleasant organizational climate.[17]
9. Impression management is concerned with the behaviors people direct toward others to create and maintain desired perceptions of themselves.[18]
10. *Image management* is a leader's ability to project an image that is consistent with observers' expectations.[19]

for impression management. The same model offers insights into what makes for successful management of the image a person projects. The model is based on a synthesis of dozens of research studies as well as theorizing about impression management.

The general point of the model under consideration is that impression management involves two discrete processes: impression motivation and impression construction. Under certain circumstances, people become motivated to control how others see them. At a business networking gathering, for example, many people are motivated to project the image of a successful person whom other people would consider to be a valuable network member. Upon being motivated to create certain impressions, people may alter their behaviors to affect others' impressions of them. Altering behavior includes choosing the type of impression to create, and also deciding whether to create the desired impression through such means as self-description, nonverbal behavior, or props.

The person engaged in networking who is motivated to create a successful impression might then rehearse certain scenarios about how well connected he or she is to venture capitalists.

As outlined in Figure 1-2, the process of impression motivation is influenced by three primary factors: the goal relevance of the impression, the value of the desired

Figure 1-2 The Two Components of Impression Management.

Impression Motivation	Impression Construction
• Goal relevance of impressions • Value of desired goals • Discrepancy between desired and current image	• Self-concept • Desired and undesired identity images • Role constraints • Target values • Current or potential social image

Source: Mark R. Leary and Robin M. Kowalski, "Impression Management: A Literature Review and Two-Component Model," *Psychological Bulletin*, No. 1, 1990, p. 36.

goals, and the discrepancy between the desired and the current image. The process of impression construction is influenced by five factors: the person's self-concept, his or her desired and undesired identity images, role constraints in which the person is placed, the target's values, and the actor's perceptions of his or her current or potential social image.

Impression Motivation

People vary as to how much they are concerned about how others view them. Also, the same person does not always have the same level of concern about how he or she is viewed. A person waiting in line at a fast-food restaurant might be less concerned about the impression he or she creates than during an in-person tax audit or a job interview. Most of the time, people operate between these two extremes. According to Leary and Kowalski, people process others' reactions to them at a pre-attentive or non-conscious level. As a consequence, impression management for most people in most situations occurs automatically without much deliberate thought. Yet, as will be described throughout this book, there are many ways in which people deliberately go about managing their impressions to succeed in a given situation.

Motives for Impression Management and Self-Presentation

Before looking at the antecedents of impression motivation listed in Figure 1-2, it is helpful to examine several of the motives behind managing one's impression.

1. *Maximizing rewards and minimizing punishments*. A primary consideration is that people manage their impression for the same reason they engage in many other behaviors—to maximize expected rewards and minimize expected punishments. For example, during a meeting with potential investors the

aspiring entrepreneur wants to make a positive self-presentation in order to attract investors. Not receiving funding would be a punishment because the entrepreneur's efforts at launching the new company could be blocked without funding.

2. *Gaining power over others*. Self-presentation is also based on the desire to gain power over others. By creating a positive impression, it is possible to control the actions of others toward you in a favorable direction. The supervisor who creates a favorable impression will have an easier time inducing subordinates to work extra hard than a supervisor who creates a negative impression.

3. *Creating a public self in accord with the ideal self*. A subtle reason for impression management is to create a public self that is consistent with the ideal self. Many people have ideal images that go beyond their typical behavior. The ideal image might include believing that one is trustworthy, moral, and highly intelligent. To make others believe that this ideal image is valid, the person constructs a public image that might include references to trustworthy activities such as being a treasurer for a church, or an executor of an estate.

4. *Self-esteem maintenance*. Self-esteem maintenance can be a strong motive for positive self-presentation. Regulation of self-esteem through impression management works in two ways. First, the reaction of others to the individual may raise or deflate self-esteem. Self-esteem is elevated via compliments, praise, and other indicators of positive attitudes toward the person. As a result, many people attempt to create impressions that will bring about the types of positive feedback just mentioned. For example, an engineer having lunch with colleagues in the company cafeteria might casually mention that he just was granted a patent for a technology that supports a major company product. The positive feedback he receives will boost his self-esteem—at least temporarily.

   Second, self-esteem is affected by self-evaluation of performance and others' imagined reactions to the person. Even without explicit feedback from others, the person's subjective self-evaluation of performance can influence self-esteem. Assume that a marketing specialist makes a PowerPoint presentation about sales forecasts for her company's new noncarbonated beverage. Her evaluation is that the presentation was captivating, even if the people present offered no evaluation of her performance. Believing that she did a wonderful job, she gains in self-esteem. The reverse is also true—if the marketing specialist believes that her presentation was flawed, she might suffer a drop in self-esteem.

5. *Creating an identity*. Self-presentation is also a means of creating an identity. The person may engage in public behaviors that symbolize group membership. A person wanting to appear like a young business professional might walk through the office and streets occupied with a cell phone and personal digital assistant, and quite often carrying a bottle of water. The same person would

most likely wear business attire typical of business professionals in his or her field. Although the stereotyped behaviors just mentioned are superficial, they contribute heavily to identity creation.

The different motives for engaging in impression management described above will sometimes be satisfied by the same behavior. For example, documenting one's job successes to other people might (1) enhance rewards, (2) gain power over others, (3) create a positive public self, (4) boost self-esteem, and (5) create an identity.

Antecedents of Impression Motivation

Three central factors that determine impression motivation are outlined in Figure 1-1 and described next: the goal relevance of the impressions, the value of the desired outcomes, and the discrepancy between the person's desired and current social image.

Goal Relevance of Impressions The more the managed impression is perceived to be relevant to attaining a person's goals, the more strongly the person will be motivated to manage his or her impression. The goals in question relate to the motives described above, such as gaining power over others and boosting self-esteem. One factor determining whether a given impression management behavior is relevant is how public the behavior will be, including the probability that the behavior will be observed by others and the size of the audience. A worker seeking more self-esteem would be strongly motivated to impress others via a description of her work presented on a company blog because so many other employees would see the blog.

Another factor enhancing goal relevance is the extent of dependency on the target. When the person is dependent on others for valued outcomes, such as receiving a bonus, the impressions he or she creates are more important. The individual will therefore be more motivated to manage his or her impression. If a person's immediate manager has the authority to make bonus recommendations, he or she will be the recipient of considerable ingratiation.

The anticipated frequency of contact with the target will also help shape the relevance of impression management to attaining a goal. When people expect future interactions with another person, they are more likely to attempt to control how that person perceives them. A middle manager who anticipates periodic contact with the company CEO is likely to work hard at creating a good impression in his or her presence.

Personal characteristics can also influence how relevant impression management appears to be in attaining positive outcomes. A person with strong Machiavellian tendencies (a propensity to manipulate others) is likely to perceive creating the right impression as essential in attaining goals. Chapter 3 describes individual factors that predispose people toward impression management.

The characteristics of the target also influence how relevant impression management might be to attaining certain goals. In general, people are more motivated to manage their impressions for people who are powerful because the powerful person can help the actor attain an important goal, such as being promoted. A small-business owner would be more motivated to manage his impression for a loan officer in a bank than for a vendor, such as the manager of an employment agency for temporary workers. Correctly or incorrectly, the small-business owner reasons that the loan officer has a greater impact on the viability of his or her business. The goal in this situation is to raise enough capital to expand the business.

Value of Desired Goals A principle of motivation is that the more value a person places on a goal, the stronger will be his or her effort to pursue that goal. Effort invested in impression management will therefore increase with the value of the goals the individual hopes to attain. If a person believes that becoming a corporate executive is an ideal career outcome, and also believes that appearing charismatic will facilitate attaining the goal of becoming an executive, he or she will work hard at appearing charismatic.

Leary and Kowalski note that because the value of outcomes increases as their availability decreases, the motivation to engage in impression management is stronger when the desired resources are scarce. A CEO position is a scarce resource (only one per company), which triggers a higher frequency of impression management to work toward becoming a CEO.

Discrepancy between Desired and Current Image Impression management is also motivated by the person's real and ideal image, or the image that one would like to hold of oneself and the image one believes that others already hold. Most people have a range of images that they regard as acceptable to project. When the image falls outside that range, the person might be motivated to fine-tune the image. When the image falls within the range of acceptability, the person is less likely to be motivated to manage his or her impression.

People who believe they have failed in the eyes of others, as well as those who have been embarrassed, are more likely to want to change the image they project. A case in point was an executive who received feedback from the human resources director, as well as an office assistant, that he had developed a reputation for being too flirtatious toward young women employees. Two women had even complained that some of the executive's comments about their appearance constituted sexual harassment. The executive worked quickly to change the impression he created in respect to his interaction with women. His most effective tactic was to stop commenting on the appearance of women, except for the occasional comment, "You are dressed for success today." He would also make the same comment to men, when appropriate.

Impression Construction

The construction of an image is not simply based on making a handful of positive statements about yourself to others. Following the synthesis developed by Leary and Kowalski, we look at five determinants of impression content, or how images are constructed.

Self-Concept Many impressions that people attempt to create of themselves are accurate impressions that fit their self-concept. Furthermore, the self-concept is the primary determinant of the impressions people attempt to project to others for several reasons. First, most people are proud of certain aspects of their self-concept and therefore eagerly display these aspects at appropriate times. Also, impression management may be used to ensure that people are perceived accurately, such as a software engineer wanting to emphasize to coworkers that she has good interpersonal skills, and is not exclusively a technical person.

Second, self-beliefs serve to limit self-presentations by providing information regarding the probability that they can project particular impressions. If the software engineer just mentioned perceives herself as having good interpersonal skills, she might attempt to project the image of a person who gets along well with people. (A caution is that irrational people may not be constrained by their self-concept because it might be distorted.) Most people are hesitant to attempt to project images that are inconsistent with their self-concept because of concern about being able to pull it off.

Third, people who are uncomfortable with lying are hesitant to make claims about themselves, or project images that are blatantly inconsistent with their self-concepts. The same people might be willing to stretch their self-concept a little before believing they are lying. Job applicants, for example, will often project an image of capabilities that are a little beyond their true expertise. Personal websites are one job-related domain related to work life where positively distorted self-presentations are likely to occur. Exaggerating one's accomplishments on these websites is almost expected.

Desired and Undesired Identity Images Image construction is also based on how people would like to be and not be seen. People often convey impressions that are biased in the direction of their desired identities. A manager who wants to see himself as a good coach will frequently engage in behaviors that show an interest in helping others, such as asking subordinates questions about their progress, and making encouraging statements to them. People also manage their impressions to avoid fitting an *undesired* identity image—something a person does not want to be. The manager in question might avoid statements and behaviors that suggest he or she does not really care about the welfare of subordinates. For example, even when work pressures are high the manager would take the time to listen to subordinates.

Role Constraints The roles we occupy are typically a powerful force in establishing limits to the impressions we create. In addition to specific prescriptions for behavior, most roles demand that the role occupants appear to be a particular kind of person or possess certain characteristics. To illustrate, a chief financial officer (CFO) is supposed to be a person of high integrity who manages money prudently. It would be inconsistent with the CFO's role to brag about junkets to gambling casinos or having lost thousands of dollars in a risky investment. Executives in general who publicly deviate too far from their role expectations are subject to dismissal. Several male executives have been asked to resign in recent years because they were known to have sent romantic e-mail messages to young women employees. Similarly, when a married executive conducts an affair with a company employee, he or she might be asked to resign.

On the positive side, role constraints can propel a person into engaging in positive aspects of impression management consistent with the role. Visualize a customer service representative in a department store. Part of her role is to be helpful so she projects the image of being friendly and concerned while dealing with customer problems.

Target Values Substantial research indicates that people modify their public images to the perceived values and preferences of key people with whom they interact. In a company where top-level management demands heavy commitment to the job as well as a strong work orientation, many employees will project the image of total company involvement. Among their behaviors would be to brag about working at nights and on weekends, and not having taken allotted vacations. Conversely, when top-level executives favor work-life balance, employees are likely to talk about leisure activities and wonderful family vacations. The people who manage the impressions in question are not necessarily being deceptive. Instead, they are emphasizing different aspects of the self in order to match the target's values. For example, the person who brags about working nights and weekends might also have outside interests and take vacations yet does not brag about these activities in the presence of company executives.

At times people will present themselves in ways that are inconsistent with the target's values. They make these self-presentations for the purpose of irritating the target or displaying independence. By emphasizing an image the target disapproves of, the person achieves his or her goal of annoying the target. Assume that a financial executive believes that the company is spending too much money on frivolous new products that ultimately consume too many company resources, as well as losing money. In contrast, the head of research and development believes that the company must invest heavily in new products in the hopes that one or two will be major successes. To irritate and antagonize the financial executive, the head of research and development talks flamboyantly about new products in her meetings with the financial executive.

Current or Potential Social Image A final aspect of how the content of images is determined to be discussed here is how people think they are currently regarded by others and how they think they will be perceived in the future. A primary consideration is that people are reluctant to present themselves in ways that conflict with the information others have about them. To do so might arouse suspicion, and trigger being perceived as unauthentic. The knowledge others have about a person therefore constrains the image projected. A businessperson who was fined for insider trading might be reluctant to attempt to create the impression of a holier-than-thou individual. Instead, he or she might engage in impression management tactics to repair the damage, such as emphasizing that he or she has learned from the mistake in action and judgment.

Another twist on the impact of the current image on a person's style of impression management can occur when his or her accomplishments are well known. The person might feel compelled to modestly downplay the accomplishments in a show of modesty. A manager well known for having turned around a failing division of the company will often deflect personal credit and talk about the wonderful performance of the team.

Being perceived in certain ways can also make the person feel entitled to claim certain images. A person who has conformed to group norms for a long time will accumulate *idiosyncrasy credits* that allow the person to deviate a little from the norm in the future. A staid information technology specialist known for her conscientiousness might therefore return from a vacation bragging about 24 consecutive hours spent at a casino.

At times the ingredients to impression management will be influenced by how people think they will be perceived in the future. The possibility that people will learn certain information about them in the future affects the content of the self-presentation. A sales consultant might anticipate losing a major account by the end of the year. He might take a pre-emptive approach by explaining to his boss how hard he has worked with the customer to help the company avoid bankruptcy, but his efforts might not be successful.

In review, the model of impression motivation and construction developed by Leary and Kowalski identifies three central factors that determine impression motivation and five central factors that determine the mode of impression construction, as outlined in Figure 1-2.

Ethical Considerations Associated with Impression Management

Impression management in the workplace, as with other forms of organizational politics, often has ethical implications. An extreme example of unethical impression management would be attempting to impress others by pretending that your social network includes world-famous industrialists, athletes, and politicians. An example of ethical impression management would be keeping informed of current events and staying abreast of developments in your field in order to impress others with your knowledge and dedication. Most forms of impression management would fall between these extremes. One example would be exaggerating a little about how interested you are in marketing strategy when speaking to a marketing executive.

When evaluating the ethics of a particular approach to impression management, it is helpful to use a standard ethical screen. A representative ethical screen is the one developed by the Center for Business Ethics at Bentley University, which asks six questions to evaluate the ethics of a specific decision:[20]

- *Is it right?* This question is based on the deontological theory of ethics that there are certainly universally accepted guiding principles of rightness and wrongness, such as "thou shall not steal."
- *Is it fair?* This question is based on the deontological theory of justice that certain actions are inherently just or unjust. For example, it is unjust to fire a high-performing employee just so you can impress top management that you are cutting costs as much as possible?
- *Who gets hurt?* This question is based on the utilitarian notion of attempting to do the greatest good for the greatest number of people. If your approach to impression management hurts nobody, it is ethical from the standpoint of this question.
- *Would you be comfortable if the details of your decision or actions were made public in the media or through e-mail?* This question is based on the universalist principle of disclosure. Would you be willing to let others know that you blamed your poor performance with a client on a migraine headache you developed from drinking a contaminated energy drink?
- *What would you tell your child, sibling, or young relative to do?* This question is based on the deontological principle of reversibility, which evaluates the ethics of a decision by reversing the decision maker.
- *How does it smell?* This question is based on a person's intuition and common sense. For example, looking good by stealing someone else's innovative suggestion would "smell" bad to a sensible person.

As implied above, ethical issues that require a run through the guide are usually subtle rather than blatant, a decision that falls into the gray zone. For example, if you were applying for a position at Calvin Klein, would you purposely purchase some Calvin Klein clothing to wear to the interview?

Guidelines for Application and Practice

1. Managing your impression well at both superficial and deeper levels is a major factor in attaining career and personal success. Studying the subject of impression management and selectively applying the concepts are therefore of substantial potential benefit to your career.
2. Whether or not you believe that impression management is important, others will often judge you on the basis of the impression you create. Projecting a favorable impression, whether spontaneously or through conscious effort, is therefore to your advantage.
3. Your self-presentation is influential in creating a social reality. How you are perceived by others helps create circumstances. An example would be creating a sterling impression on a higher-level executive during a meeting, and subsequently being nominated for a new, higher-level position.

4. Almost any behavior can contribute to or detract from the image you project. Impressions of an individual can be generated by everyday, seemingly innocuous acts such as smiling at others, being helpful, and listening to another person.

5. A practical viewpoint of impression management is that you take actions to be perceived positively by the target person or persons.

6. To manage your impression effectively, it is helpful to understand the motivation behind your attempts at impression management. Among your motives might be maximizing rewards and minimizing punishments, gaining power over others, creating a public self in accord with your ideal self, maintaining your self-esteem, and creating a personal identity. The same behavior on your part, such as being an articulate speaker, might satisfy more than one of these motives.

7. As you go about constructing an image, keep in mind several determinants that may guide you in developing your image. The image should ordinarily fit your self-concept. Your self-beliefs, such as your analysis of your strengths and weaknesses, will often guide you as to the type of image you can project well. What you are the most proud of in relation to yourself should be incorporated into your self-presentation, such as taking pride in your advanced information technology skills. It is natural to incorporate into the impression you create your desired identity, or the way you would like to be known. Think through the role you occupy when creating an image. Your image works most effectively when it is consistent with your role, such as an employee assistance counselor projecting warmth and caring.

It is also helpful to project those aspects of your personality and talents that fit the key values and preferences of your audience. For example, when dealing with cost-conscious managers, emphasize some of your frugal work practices (if true). Should your accomplishments be well known, you will be perceived positively by many audience members when you do not incorporate bragging about these accomplishments in your image.

8. Before choosing a particular approach to impression management, reflect on its ethical merits. In this way, you are likely to engage in impression management that has enduring value.

Summary

Impression management refers to the process by which people control the impression others form of them. A positive impression often leads to important work-related outcomes such as getting a raise and being promoted. Impressions can be deep as well as superficial.

The modern-day roots of the scientific study of impression management are frequently attributed to Erving Goffman, who views people as "actors" engaging in "performances" in various settings before "audiences." The actors and the audiences interact to develop a definition of the situation which guides their behavior. The performance of people functioning as actors depends upon the characteristics of both the situations and the audiences present. Controlling one's identity as it is portrayed to others can influence how situations are defined, and thereby establish expected norms, roles, and behavior. Self-presentation also defines the individual's place in the social environment. Another declaration of Goffman is that even seemingly innocuous actions might be aimed at showing a person in a favorable light.

Impression management has been defined in a variety of ways, as presented in Figure 1-1. Impression management is usually for the purpose of creating a positive impression, yet some people go out of their way to look bad. The terms impression management and self-presentation are often used interchangeably, yet sometimes behaviors are directed at enhancing the impression another person creates in order to be liked. The common meaning of the definitions of impression management is that the person takes action so that the target person or persons perceive him or her positively.

The two-component model of impression management developed by Leary and Kowalski is summarized here. The model states that impression management involves two discrete processes: impression motivation and impression construction. The process of impression motivation is influenced by three primary factors: the goal relevance of the impression, the value of the desired goals, and the discrepancy between the desired and current image. The process of impression construction is influenced by five factors: the person's self-concept, his or her desired and undesired identity images, role constraints in which the person is placed, the target's values, and the actor's perceptions of his or her current or potential social image.

Among the motives for engaging in impression management are (1) maximizing rewards and minimizing punishments, (2) gaining power over others, (3) creating a public self in accord with the ideal self, (4) maintaining self-esteem, and (5) creating an identity. The different motives for engaging in impression management will sometimes be satisfied by the same behavior.

Managing your impression well at both superficial and deeper levels is a major factor in attaining career and personal success. Almost any behavior can contribute to or detract from the image you project. Impressions of an individual can be generated by everyday, seemingly innocuous acts such as smiling at others, being helpful, and listening to another person.

Before reaching a decision about using an approach to impression management that is not obviously ethical or blatantly unethical, seek answers to questions such as: Is it right? Is it fair? Who gets hurt? Would you tell your child, sibling, or young relative to do it?

Chapter 2

A Cybernetic Model of Impression Management

A useful framework for understanding impression management is that it is a control or cybernetic process. We have an ideal in mind of how we would like to be perceived, and we compare that standard to how we think we are currently perceived. We engage in certain behaviors to close the discrepancy between how we are perceived and how we would like to be perceived. The cybernetic perspective also assumes that we are rational, so we stay tuned to feedback that might tell us how well our impression management tactics are working. After receiving the feedback, we fine-tune our tactics to once again close the discrepancy between how we would like to be perceived and how we are perceived. With the modified set of impression management tactics in play, we then seek more feedback and fine-tune our behavior once again. The control process continues until we are satisfied with our approach to impression management.

Visualize Lisa, who is building a career as an international marketing professional. She wants to project the image of, and present herself as, a young professional who is committed to international business. As Lisa reflects on the image she creates, she is concerned that she does not distinguish herself from other young professionals aspiring to advance in international marketing. Lisa decides that she would be more credible—thereby projecting a stronger image—if she strengthened her Spanish-language skills. Following this conviction, Lisa works assiduously at becoming more fluent in Spanish. During business meetings and networking events, Lisa looks for an opportunity to display a little knowledge of Spanish.

At first, Spanish-speaking work associates appear somewhat unimpressed by Lisa's initiatives in the Spanish language. Consequently, Lisa invests more effort into speaking Spanish more fluently and with a better accent. With this fine-tuning accomplished, Lisa observes that both Spanish-speaking people and those who speak only English are more impressed with her second-language skills. Lisa receives feedback in essentially two forms: compliments about her Spanish speaking from work associates, and brief return conversations in Spanish from Spanish-speaking people. Lisa is now content that she has strengthened the image she projects of a credible international marketing professional. (Lisa also projects the image of a marketing professional in other ways, such as talking about international business and alluding to overseas trips she has taken.)

So far we have glimpsed how a cybernetic, or control, model can help us understand the process of impression management in the workplace. In this chapter we summarize the cybernetic model of impression management processes in organizations developed by Dennis P. Bozeman and K. Michele Kacmar.[1] We also provide additional explanation and examples for certain aspects of the model, and concentrate on its more applied and less esoteric aspects.

A Brief Look at Cybernetic Theory

Cybernetics can be regarded as a theory of information, communication, and control. Given that impression management is mostly about communication, cybernetics can therefore contribute to an understanding how people manage their impressions. At its core, cybernetics is concerned with the behavior and functioning of self-regulating systems. Cybernetic systems feature four components: a reference standard or goal, feedback, a comparator, and an effector. The *comparator* is the process by which the goal and feedback is compared. In everyday language, a comparator is an instrument for making comparisons. The *effector* is the process by which outputs or behavior can be altered. In the case of Lisa, her goal is to be perceived as a competent international marketing specialist. Her comparator is her cognitive evaluation of how close the feedback fits her goal, and her effector is her ability to concentrate more on improving her fluency in Spanish.

According to cybernetic theory, the person processes feedback from the environment by using a comparator to detect discrepancies between the reference standard (goal) and the feedback. In our example, Lisa is focusing on the aspect of her image as being bilingual to strengthen her overall image as an international marketing professional. The subtle feedback she receives about her Spanish-speaking ability helps her know if she has closed the discrepancy between her ideal and real image.

Three outcomes are possible: negative discrepancies, positive discrepancies, and zero discrepancies. Corrective action is likely to be taken when a discrepancy is negative because the person experiences a need for improvement. A positive discrepancy could also lead to improvement, such as a person who is trying to become more assertive discovering that he or she is perceived as being overly assertive, or aggressive. A zero discrepancy indicates that all is well and performance remains stable without taking corrective action.

A negative discrepancy indicates that the organism is not reaching the reference standard or goal. As a result, the organism or person adjusts his or her behavior via the effector to minimize the discrepancies. Lisa might intensify her efforts to become more fluent in Spanish through such means as finding more people with whom to speak Spanish regularly. Or, the person can adjust the reference goal downward to more closely align with the performance level noted in the feedback. Should marketing specialist Lisa interpret the feedback she is receiving as a sign of her inability to speak Spanish fluently, she might decide just to demonstrate a casual familiarity with the Spanish language and Latino culture. In this way her image as an international worker might be authenticated.

A positive discrepancy indicates that what the person attains (his or her output) exceeds the goal he or she was attempting to attain. A human being might make an adjustment because of the positive discrepancy or he or she might be content that performance has exceeded standard. The over-assertive person just mentioned might push back slightly on assertiveness. Over-performance is more difficult to visualize with Lisa. However, better-than-goal performance could include being perceived as having been raised in a Latino household, or being Latino herself.

Cybernetic systems have motivational implications. The actors in the system are goal oriented, with negative feedback guiding subsequent action toward attaining goals in the future. According to cybernetic theory, goals and the effort that follows are reflected in two principal activities: (1) effort directed toward gaining control of the environment and (2) effort directed toward getting the system or organism in tune with the demands placed by the environment. Assume that Ken, a manager, wants to project the image of a credible and trustworthy leader. He attempts to control the environment by acting and being trustworthy, for example following through on commitments he makes to subordinates, such as promising to find money for equipment purchase. Ken also analyzes what kind of behavior subordinates are likely to perceive as being trustworthy. A little questioning reveals that many other managers in the company have lied to workers about such matters as outsourcing being out of consideration. Ken will therefore be extra careful to be truthful about such matters.

Part of being perceived as trustworthy is to be perceived as authentic, or not phony. Authenticity is also gauged by feedback. As Rob Goffee and Gareth Jones explain, a leader cannot look in the mirror and say, "I am authentic." A person cannot be authentic acting alone. Authenticity is mostly defined by what other people see in you.[2] You can work at being authentic, yet feedback from others is required to know if an image of authenticity is being projected.

The Basic Components of the Model

Figure 2-1 presents the Bozeman and Kacmar cybernetic model of impression management. The model suggests that the motivation for impression management is linked most closely to the agent's perception of the difference between the **reference goal** and the feedback provided by the target. The reference goal is the actor's desired state of social identity, such as wanting to be perceived as a competent international marketing professional. These discrepancies are uncovered through the comparator. If the comparisons, or feedback, indicate to the actor that the image he or she wants to project is being achieved, the tactics being used presently will be continued. However, if a discrepancy occurs, the actor will search for other means of attaining the desired image. In a sense, the actor will develop another script. After the next tactic is selected, the actor will implement the behavior and wait for a reaction from the target. The reaction or feedback will be processed and then compared to the image the actor is seeking. The outcome from this comparison is significant because it creates the nature of the next step, leading to continuing interaction in the system.

Figure 2-1 A Cybernetic Model of Impression Management.

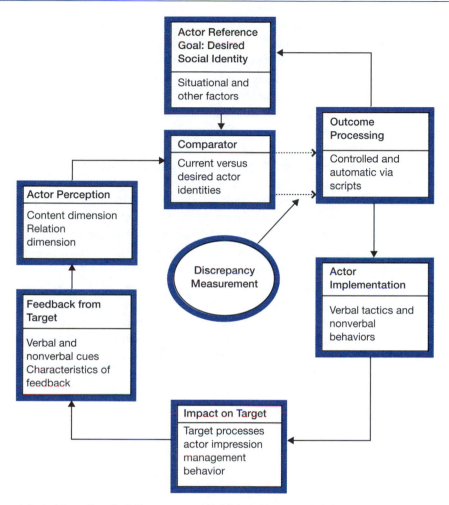

Source: Adapted from Dennis P. Bozeman and K. Michele Kacmar, "A Cybernetic Model of Impression Management Processes in Organizations," *Organizational Behavior and Human Decision Processes*, March 1997, p. 12.

The first part of the model can be illustrated by job interviewees, who are usually highly motivated to present positive images of themselves to interviewers. Quite often, competence to perform the job in question is a key issue to be tackled by the interviewee, and evaluated by the interviewer. To construct an image that conveys job competence, interviewees might use a script that focuses on self-promotion. Assume that the interviewer sends a message to the interviewee that he or she is impressed by the self-promotional information (the desired image to be projected). The interviewee will most likely continue to reinforce the positive image created by using other varieties of self-promotional tactics, such as enhancement or entitlement.

Enhancement refers to embellishing the positive aspects of a favorable outcome or accomplishment. *Entitlement* refers to increasing one's perceived role in or responsibility for positive outcomes or events, such as the interviewee explaining that he or she contributed an innovative idea that facilitated the team's success.

The opposite scenario is when the actor perceives that the initial self-promotion tactic backfired and the desired image projection is not achieved. The interviewee might attempt to adapt to the demands of the situation by seeking a more favorable evaluation by the interviewer. A typical tactic would be to qualify prior comments that may have appeared overly boastful by acknowledging the contributions of others to a positive outcome or event, such as team success. The interviewer's verbal and nonverbal feedback to the second tactic would then be used by the interviewee to evaluate whether or not the impression management tactic was effective. By using this additional feedback, the interviewee might be able to fine-tune his or her use of impression management for the rest of the interview.

As with most approaches to impression management, cultural factors can shape the extent to which self-promotion is advised. The job candidate for a position with an Asian company might engage in less self-promotion than if he or she were applying for a comparable position in an American company. The reason is that the typical American hiring manager values self-promotion and boasting about individual accomplishment more than does the typical Asian hiring manager.

The model depicted in Figure 2-1 assumes that impression management, whether conscious or unconscious, is a concern for the actor for several reasons. A major reason is that the interaction of situational factors, target characteristics, and actor individual differences has evoked an identity from among many possible identities that needs to be enhanced, protected, maintained, or adjusted. At the same time the perceived probability of being able to project this identity must be acceptable to the actor. An implication of the model is that impression management will occur only under certain conditions.

In the following pages the segments of the model are described individually. However, impression management really takes place in a dynamic, interactive manner, with the actor making fine adjustments as he or she goes along. Imagine yourself at a social networking event, such as a cocktail and dinner meeting. As you meet various people, you might automatically adjust your impression management tactics to adapt to the needs of individuals. If you meet an operations manager you might emphasize how impressed you are with the profit consequences of managing inventory well. If you meet a person who manages a non-profit agency, you might shift to a discussion of your charitable activities.

Reference Goal: Desired Social Identity

As suggested by Figure 2-1, the model is centered on the actor's reference goal or desired sense of **social identity**. The concept of social identity refers to an actor's identification with a specific grouping of people, such as team member, leader, or free agent. The social identity is both a dynamic and complex concept. By using target feedback, the actor can compare his or her desired social identity, or goal, to how he or she is perceived by the target. Any discrepancies that might exist between these two entities are noted and corrective actions taken if necessary. For example, a person might reflect, "It doesn't look as if I am being taken as a person of great accomplishment in my field. Maybe I should make more references to some of my best accomplishments."

Activation of Identity Goal

Although the model in question suggests one social identity goal for the purpose of impression management, in reality organizational members are likely to possess multiple identity goals they would like to attain. Different situations may call for different identities to be portrayed. For example, a sales representative might want to emphasize the identity of a problem solver and solutions finder in dealing with a client. During a meeting with peers, the representative might want to project the identity of a good team player. While meeting with superiors, he might aspire to attain an identity as an outstanding performer.

An important influence on the nature of the social identity portrayed to others is the specific aspects of the self-concept activated in a given social situation. Because the self-concept is multifaceted, different aspects can be relevant according to the situation. A colleague asking for technical assistance on a problem might trigger the helpful, nurturing part of a person's self-concept to emerge. In another situation, such as at a company retreat, the brasher, more ego-centered part of the same person's self-concept might be triggered into action.

Two processes especially linked to the self-concept are important for the motivation to engage in impression management. The motive to engage in self-enhancement stems from the actor's desire to increase or protect his or her self-esteem. Self-enhancing impression management occurs when an actor has a social identity goal that, if achieved, will enable the actor to bolster or protect his or her self-esteem or emotions related to the self. Self-enhancement motivation may also prompt the actor to select an identity that is not only more positive than his or her present self-concept, but also that can be reasonably claimed and achieved. An administrative assistant, for example, might attempt to project the identity of a person who influences the CEO in decision making because this identity is but a small stretch from what she is already doing.

Self-enhancing impression management involves separate discrepancies between the actor's self-concept and his or her desired social identity. First, the actor wants to be perceived by others in a more favorable light than is indicated by the current self-concept. Second, the motive of self-verification is derived from the person's desire to confirm his or her self-concept by receiving feedback about what others perceive to be his or her social identity. The person might reflect, "Do other people in my network see me as a builder of really cool websites?"

The motivation for impression management related to the self can be affectively or cognitively based. The actor might want to deal with feelings about the self, such as feeling more self-confident. Or, a cognitive process might come into play such as looking for feedback that he or she is perceived as a competent professional.

The particular identity the person wants to project is also influenced by situational factors, target characteristics, and individual differences among actors. Situational factors likely to influence the activation of a particular social identity include accountability, ambiguity, and the prospect of evaluation. A person who is accountable is likely to be more careful about projecting an accurate social identity. Ambiguity in the situation makes it more difficult to figure out which social identity to choose. Knowing that we will be evaluated is also a force for choosing a more accurate social identity.

The characteristics of the target likely to influence the activation of a particular social identity for impression management by the actor include prestige and reward power, as well as knowledge or familiarity with the actor. When the target is powerful, the agent is more likely to work hard at creating a positive impression. When the target knows the actor well, the latter might attempt to project a more accurate impression.

Individual differences will also influence the actor's tendencies toward impression management, as will be described in Chapter 3. For example, a person who is good at self-monitoring will be better able to create an impression to fit the occasion. The reason is that the high self-monitor knows how to "tell people what they want to hear." When visiting a manufacturing plant, a given corporate executive might emphasize how concerned he is about preserving manufacturing jobs and not sending them overseas. When meeting with outside financial analysts, the same executive might emphasize how hard the company is working to reduce costs.

Goal-Based Interpretation

The expectancy theory of motivation enters into the achievement of social identity goals. In brief, valence-instrumentality-expectancy (VIE) theory explains that human motivation is a function of the following: (1) the attractiveness of the value place on certain outcomes (valence); (2) the linkage of effort leading to a desired outcome; and (3) the perceived probability of being able to accomplish the task that leads to a reward. People will engage in a particular aspect of impression management if they feel they can pull it off, and if the impression management activity will lead to a valued outcome such as being promoted.

These components of VIE theory help determine whether a situation facing the actor is interpreted as an opportunity, a threat, or a relatively neutral situation that is not particularly an opportunity or threat. Part of the explanation is that individuals concerned with conveying a particular image or identity experience different emotional states depending on the importance of the goal of achieving (or avoiding) a desired (or undesired) image. At the same time the person automatically thinks of the expectancies involved in being able to create the desired image. Getting back to Lisa, she might be quite enthused about projecting the image of an international marketing professional, and she weighs the probability of being able to engage in such behaviors as speaking Spanish to certain network members. Lisa would probably also calculate automatically whether speaking Spanish would lead to the desired outcome of molding her impression as an international marketing professional.

Goal-Directed Motivation

As shown in Figure 2-1, the social identity the actor would like to achieve functions as the reference goal within the cybernetic model. At the same time, the perceived feedback from the target serves as the actor's current sense of social identity. The theoretical argument here is that we are who we are perceived to be by our audience. For example, if human resources manager Maggie is told by many of her targets that she is a caring and supportive person, Maggie develops the identity of a caring and supportive person.

After a specific social identity goal relevant to a given situation is selected, the key motivation to manage impressions in the situation stems from perceived discrepancies between the current and desired social identities of the actor. Inconsistencies between current and desired social identities lead to both behavioral and cognitive efforts to reduce the perceived discrepancies. These discrepancies may stem from two sources. One source is target feedback that is inconsistent with the actor's identity goal. The other source is the actor's selection or adjustment of an identity goal that creates an incongruity between the identity goal and the feedback in relation to the goal. Assume that Maggie wants to be perceived as caring and supportive, yet she receives e-mail messages from several targets that she behaved heartlessly in responding to their requests. Maggie would then be motivated to reduce the discrepancy by behaving in a more caring way toward employees. Or, she could make a cognitive adjustment by saying to herself, "No matter how hard I try to be kind, some employees cannot accept the reality that they cannot have everything they want."

Bozeman and Kacmar, the developers of the model in question, remind us that the discrepancies an individual finds between the actual and preferred social identities might be perceived as small or large. The pursuit of impression management goals is successful when the actor perceives zero or only minor discrepancies between the present and preferred social identities. In contrast, less successful impression managers will perceive large discrepancies between the current and desired social entities. An example of a failed impression manager would be Jason, a newcomer to a company who wants to be perceived as a talented professional, destined to be placed on a fast track for promotion. Unfortunately for his emotional well-being, he never receives feedback that he is regarded as an outstanding contributor.

In general, large discrepancies between goals and feedback have the greatest potential to motivate actors. However, the impact of the size of the discrepancy on motivation also depends on the actor's expectancies of being able to resolve the incongruity. Assume that Jason is confident that he can improve his image, and is strongly motivated to do so. He might hire a personal coach to help him showcase his talents more effectively.

Feedback from Target

To evaluate how much progress is made toward attaining the actor's true social identity, the reference goal must be known and feedback must be obtained. The nature of feedback must be explored because it is a major component of the cybernetic model.

The target can provide identity-relevant information that enables the actor to understand if the hoped for social identity has been attained. Also, feedback from targets can inform the actor about appropriate behaviors or necessary modifications that need to be made to the behaviors previously enacted. In reference again to Jason, he recognizes that he has not been receiving much positive feedback from his manager about being a person of high potential. The personal coach he hires serves as a source of information about what steps Jason should take to enhance his image. At the same time, part of the coach's professional role is to provide feedback to Jason about his image.

Research and wisdom suggest that actors who manage their impression must accomplish this feat without coming across as highly manipulative. To minimize projecting an image of being manipulative, it is effective to appear credible and not overly controlling. A frequent failing of people attempting to manage their impression is to behave inconsistently, depending on the situation. During a meeting with both superiors and subordinates present, a manager might make statements about how proud he is of the performance of his team, and how he admires their talents. Yet during meetings when superiors are not present, the manager might berate the same subordinates for their incompetence. As a result of this behavior, the subordinates perceive the manager as "phony" and "manipulative."

The feedback offered by the target is used by the actor to determine whether or not a positive interaction has taken place, thereby enhancing the actor's image. The feedback can take many forms. First, the target can furnish verbal cues that offer information to the actor about how he or she was perceived by the target. In addition to words, the actor will frequently receive nonverbal feedback. If the nonverbal feedback is consistent with the verbal feedback, the actor can be more confident that the verbal comments are an accurate reflection of the true feelings of the target. If the verbal feedback and nonverbal feedback are inconsistent, the actor recognizes that more work is necessary to project the right image. While giving a PowerPoint presentation, Maria might want to project the image of a data-savvy financial analyst with high potential. Assume that a few people at the meeting say something to the effect, "This is really useful information." Maria then checks the nonverbal feedback, such as the meeting participants leaning forward and their eyes widening. The nonverbal cues serve as useful feedback to Maria that she is projecting the image she intends.

Nonverbal feedback tends to be weighed heavily during episodes of impression management. One reason is that targets may feel uncomfortable giving negative feedback in words, yet they do not think of disguising their nonverbal feedback. Should Maria see considerable frowns and lateral head shaking during her presentation, she is likely to think that she is being perceived negatively in spite of verbal feedback to the contrary.

The actor who is behaving in accord with the model in Figure 2-1 must receive feedback if the process is to continue. If feedback is not available, the actor may ask evaluative questions about his or her performance. Sometimes feedback is not readily available because members of the target group think negatively of the actor's thoughts and behaviors, yet are hesitant to hurt his or her feelings.

The act of asking for feedback will often enhance the impression a person projects because negative perceptions will often be reversed. Asking for feedback is akin to asking, "How can I improve?" Targets are likely to think charitably of an individual who implies that he or she has weaknesses and has the courage to ask how to improve. One study suggested that managers who sought feedback from subordinates tended to receive higher ratings of managerial effectiveness.[3]

Actor Perception

The feedback from the target is filtered (processed) through the actor's perceptual processes and mechanisms. Goal-directed people selectively attend to and perceive information from their environment based on its relevance to their personal goals or intentions. If somebody receives feedback that is very far from what he or she wants to hear, the feedback might be shrugged off or treated with denial. Visualize a financial consultant (broker) working for an investment bank. She wants to create the impression of a consultant who has her clients' best interests at heart all the time. When a client accuses her of making many changes in her account just to generate commissions, the consultant gives the client a blank stare and continues with her presentation. The point is that in this scenario the feedback is too far removed from what the consultant wants to hear.

The feedback processed by the actor consists of the two major dimensions of content and relation, as shown in Figure 2-1. The communication dimension referred to as *content* relates to information and facts rather than the nature of the relationship between the people who are interacting with each other.

Actor competence is a major part of the content, such as the financial consultant being knowledgeable about investments. The communication dimension referred to as *relation* concerns how the people who are interacting are connected to each other, such as the similarity of the actor's views to those held by the target.

Comparator

A comparator in this sense is an instrument or mechanism for making a comparison. The actor's reference goal that is compared with the perceived target feedback produces discrepancies that may differ in three dimensions: magnitude (small versus large); direction (negative versus positive); and frequency (once versus continual) or not at all (zero discrepancies). The feedback is essential for the actor to choose a method that will lead to his or her desired social identity. Figure 2-2 illustrates how these impression management identity functions address the identity discrepancies in terms of both magnitude and direction.

The three strategic identity functions are (1) protection or enhancement, (2) maintenance, and (3) adjustment. The general purpose of identity protection, enhancement, and adjustment activities is to facilitate the actor attaining the social identity goal he or she seeks. Identity protection, enhancement, and adjustment functions are called upon to deal with larger discrepancies between the actor's social identity and the feedback from the target when the actor is strongly motivated to project a positive image. In contrast, identity maintenance activities help to provide a sense of consistency and stability to the actor's social identity by dealing with zero and small discrepancies.

The tactics included here in the section about comparators represent tactics of impression management, and therefore will be reintroduced at various places in this book.

Identity Enhancement and Identity Protection

When there is a negative discrepancy between the preferred social identity and what actually exists, the signal is emitted that the actor has failed to create the impression

Figure 2-2 Actor Identity Discrepancies and Corresponding Impression Management Functions.

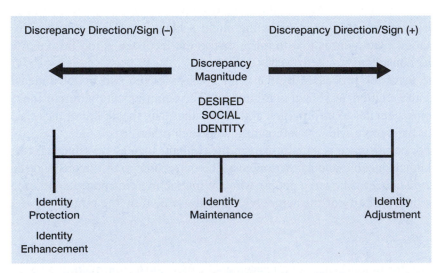

Source: Dennis P. Bozeman and K. Michele Kacmar, "A Cybernetic Model of Impression Management Processes in Organizations," *Organizational Behavior and Human Decision Processes*, March 1997, p.17.

he or she desires to create. Actors strongly motivated to create a particular identity will be more sensitive to these discrepancies, and will take action to reduce the discrepancies.

Identity enhancement activities are strategies and behaviors directed toward improving or advancing the actor's social identity as perceived by the target. The majority of these tactics are proactive in nature. Identity enhancement activities are most commonly associated with perceived opportunities to improve one's image as perceived by a particular target. Assume that an executive named Mark wants to improve the impression subordinates hold of him. He does so by demonstrating his competence on a variety of tasks and activities within the role of an executive, and also drops hints about his strong working relationship with the CEO. If successful, Mark will reduce or eliminate the perceived negative discrepancy between his current and desired social identities. Mark's perceptions are based on the feedback he has received from subordinates.

Identity protection activities are strategies and behaviors directed toward the prevention of damage or harm to the actor's social identity as perceived by the target. As a result, identity projection activities are often implemented when threats to an actor's social identity are perceived. In addition, activities geared toward identity protection are mostly reactive. Many executives in recent years have been accused of receiving backdated stock options, thereby guaranteeing them a large profit on the purchase of stock. Backdated stock options soon became perceived to be tainted with unethical accounting practices, and perhaps legal violations. To protect their images, some executives claimed they didn't know they were doing anything wrong in accepting these backdated stock options. They also claimed they were not familiar with the accounting issues associated with stock options. The contentions, or rationalizations, of the executives are offered to reduce the discrepancy between the image they want to project and their image as perceived by those who learn about the backdated options.

Identity Adjustment

According to cybernetic theory, it is possible for a positive discrepancy to occur between an actor's current and desired social identities. The positive discrepancy occurs when an actor's self-presentation behavior goes too far in creating a particular impression as perceived by the target audience. For example, a middle-age advertising specialist might want to project the image of being young and cool so as to attract clients who believe that youth is an asset in advertising. The positive discrepancy occurs when the advertising specialist is perceived to be immature and not serious. (Perhaps the body piercing went too far!)

At times the organizational actor will observe that a positive discrepancy is present—a situation in which the identity goal has been surpassed. Two reactions to the positive discrepancy can occur. One reaction is for the actor to be so pleased with the feedback from the target that he or she decides to move the identity goal higher to conform to the feedback. (Our advertising specialist might think, "I'm going for it. Why not be seen as totally young?") A second possibility is that the actor may view the over-attained goal as an undesirable discrepancy if the image projected is negative or difficult to maintain. Here, the advertising specialist might attempt to appear slightly older by dressing in less youthful clothing and using less youth talk.

Another consequence of a positive discrepancy is that the actor sets high expectations that he or she would prefer not to be maintained. Assume that Ken boasts about how much he is willing to do whatever is necessary to help his team through an emergency, including working nights and weekends until the emergency subsides. Ken's boss accepts his eagerness, but now assumes that Ken is willing to be assigned extra work whenever the department is under pressure. Ken must now soften his impression of being a totally devoted worker to avoid so much extra work. Perhaps he will now talk more about how much he values family life. An extreme approach for Ken would be to fail on some of the emergency work to avoid being chosen again for such an assignment.

Identity Maintenance

An actor's general sense of social identity is based on the self-presentations he or she made in the past as perceived by various targets. This typical social identity will often limit or trigger certain modes of self-presentation during interaction with targets who know the individual.

The actor feels somewhat obliged to behave in a way consistent with the image he or she projected in past interactions with others. In essence, the actor might feel uncomfortable acting too far out of character so he or she attempts to maintain a consistent identity. To stray too far from a typical identity might lower the credibility of the actor.

As shown in Figure 2-2, identity maintenance is used primarily to deal with small negative and positive discrepancies between the current and desired social identities. However, the actor also may use identity maintenance to enact his or her desired social identity even when no discrepancies are perceived. Stated differently, active managers of their impression may use identity maintenance activities as a way of reinforcing the identities they already worked hard to establish. A worker who has established the social identity of a creative person, will sometimes introduce a creative idea to the group just to remind people that he or she is still imaginative.

Many identity maintenance activities arise without conscious plotting by the actor. Instead, attempts at maintaining an identity are likely to occur outside of conscious awareness. For example, presenting creative ideas might have become programmed into the worker's behavioral repertoire.

Outcome Processing

Leading out from the comparator, or comparison between current versus desired identities, is the component of the model that deals with outcome processing.

The major function of outcome processing is to determine the effective responses for either reducing discrepancies or capitalizing upon desirable positive discrepancies. If the discrepancies are small or zero, the actor may simply resort to habitual actions to regulate his interactions with the target. Typically, the actor has a repertoire of tactics that have been used successfully in the past that is brought to each interaction.

If the current situation is perceived as similar to one encountered in the past, the actor uses this base of experience when figuring out how to respond. In similar situations, the actor may either duplicate the behaviors that have succeeded in the past or use them as general guides for current behavior when the present situation is similar in only some respects. Another approach is for the actor to purposely develop approaches to impression management designed to reduce any perceived discrepancies. When the situation is novel or unfamiliar a more conscious assessment of a variety of factors comprising the situation facing the actor needs to be undertaken in order to enhance, protect, or adjust the actor's identity.

Script Processing

Actors often use pre-established routines to cope with discrepancies. **Scripts** are mechanisms that facilitate efficient behavior by making easier the information processing demands of routines, and presenting guidelines for what type of behavior will work in a given situation. Scripts can be applied to processing information in either a controlled or automatic manner. When an actor is placed in a situation that is new to him or her, or when a large negative discrepancy is perceived, he or she is likely to engage in deliberate, conscious thought prior to interacting. In such cases, he or she may develop plans.

Imagine that Laura, an American industrial engineer, is sent to a factory in Beijing, China to discuss the outsourcing of a product line for her company. She wants to create a positive impression on the Chinese contingent, and at the same time she wants to exert her authority. She develops a plan for being both polite and authoritative at the same time because she believes that the Chinese culture values polite social interaction, yet also values authority. A *plan* here is a carefully constructed sequence of behavior, developed prior to interacting with a target. The plan is designed to enhance, protect, or adjust the actor's identity goals. Over time the plans can become scripts because the actor reasons that if a plan worked once, it might be repeated in a similar future situation.

In some situations the actor may not be able to develop a plan prior to certain image-threatening situations. Instead, when placed in the novel situation, an actor may use **script development**. The development of a script requires intentional processing of the most useful interpersonal signals when placed in a situation in which existing scripts do not appear to fit. Developing a script is an act of improvisation to meet the demands of a unique situation to compensate for not having developed a plan prior to entering the situation. Suppose that Laura had not developed a plan before visiting Beijing. While attending a dinner meeting prior to the next day's business meeting, she makes observations about the behavior of her Chinese work associates. She carefully looks for both verbal and nonverbal indicators of what type of behavior on her part elicits a positive reaction, such as gentle bowing when being introduced to another person. Laura also recognizes that she elicits a positive reaction when she mentions that she works quite closely with the vice president of operations at her company. As a result, Laura develops a script on the spot that includes polite behavior as well as references to formal authority.

Another relevant aspect of script processing is that actors are capable of modifying scripts that do not achieve the goal of reducing or eliminating the discrepancy between the desired and perceived image. Visualize an actor who wants to convey the image of being highly intelligent, but repeats a large number of stale facts. Targets become annoyed rather than impressed, so the actor develops another tactic to appear intelligent. Instead of presenting rehearsed facts, he offers a penetrating analysis of topics under discussion.

Script modification can also take place through *script tracking*, or finding an alternative path within the same script. Tracking is typically used when only a small discrepancy exists between the actor's current and desired social identities. Imagine an impression manager who in the past has created a positive image by casually mentioning the many postcards and letters he has received from famous people. Gradually, he finds that he receives a blank stare from his targets when mentioning these old-fashioned communication modes. So he tracks his script to now mention e-mails, instant messages, "Tweets," and video clips he has received from famous people.

Adjustment of Reference Goal

At times, even when the identity tactics of enhancement, protection, and adjustment are called into play, the actor still falls short of attaining the preferred social identity. (The identity functions are the tactics of enhancement, protection, and adjustment.) Consequently, after the attempts to attain a specific identity goal fail many times, the person engaging in impression management may decide to modify his or her reference goal. This process is indicated in Figure 2-1 by the arrow emerging upward from the outcome processing component into the reference goal. An example would be an actor who, after numerous failed attempts to develop a perception of competence, decides that being viewed as dependable might be a more attainable and reasonable goal.

Another possible outcome is that the actor may experience a pattern of positive discrepancies. The feedback offered by the target indicates that the actor has achieved a stronger impression on a particular dimension, such as competence, than was originally planned. If the actor views the positive discrepancy as desirable, and thinks that he or she can keep up the high performance, the actor might adjust the identity goal upward. An example would be Carol, a media specialist within a company who happens to be highly proficient at repairing virus damage to desktop computers. After helping a few people in the office one time with virus damage, Carol is viewed as highly proficient in helping out during virus attacks. Carol enjoys this upgraded identity goal, so she continues to refine her skills in combating computer viruses, and in helping work associates.

Actor Implementation

Actor implementation refers to the person managing his or her impression presents this behavior to the audience. At this stage of the model, the actor's observable verbal and nonverbal cues related to impression management behavior are produced. The verbal tactics and nonverbal cues are linked to the identity functions of enhancement, protection, and adjustment.

Verbal Tactics

As shown in Figure 2-3, the major verbal tactics of impression management can be categorized in terms of their orientation: content or relation. *Content-oriented* messages are typically about the actor and contain information dealing with his or

Figure 2-3 Strategic Identity Functions and Corresponding Behavior Tactics.

Strategic Identity Function	Content-Oriented (Actor)	Relation-Oriented (Target)
Identity enhancement	Self-promotion	Intimidation
	Entitlements	Ingratiation
	Enhancements	Other enhancement
	Exemplification	Opinion conformity
	False modesty	Favor doing
	Self-presentation	Pro-social (helping) behavior
Identity protection	Disclaimers	Apologies
	Self-handicapping	Restitution
	Accounts	Ingratiation
	Excuses	Favor doing
	Justifications	Opinion conformity
Identity adjustment	Self-deprecation	Noncompliance
	Opposing images	Opposing images
	Strategic failure	Supplication (asking for help)
	Self-handicapping	

Source: Dennis P. Bozeman and K. Michele Kacmar, "A Cybernetic Model of Impression Management Processes in Organizations," *Organizational Behavior and Human Decision Processes*, March 1997, p. 22.

her attributes and actions. *Relation-oriented* messages are typically more about the target as well as the relationship between the two people. Many of the behaviors listed in Figure 2-3 will be described at various places in this book.

These impression management tactics are also categorized in terms of the identity functions of enhancement, protection, and adjustment. As described previously, *enhancement* refers to strategies and behaviors directed toward improving or enhancing the actor's social identity. *Protection* relates to preventing damage or harm to the actor's social identity, and *adjustment* refers to resolving positive discrepancies between an actor's current and desired social identities.

The top section of the second column of Figure 2-3 presents tactics which are content oriented and focus on the actor, and which serve to enhance the identity of the actor. For example, self-promotion focuses on the actor, with little attention paid to the target. The top section of the third column contains tactics that are both target and enhancement oriented. The focus of these tactics is to improve upon the relationship between the actor and the target. Ingratiation, including flattery, is a major tactic in this category because it includes messages designed to increase the positive affect for the actor, thereby enhancing his or her identity.

The middle section of the second column contains impression management tactics that focus on the actor and enable him or her to protect or preserve his or her current social identity. Making excuses is one example used to protect the identity. A person who is late for a meeting and does not want to project the impression of being irresponsible might later send an e-mail describing a major traffic problem that made him or her late. An apology is an identity protection tactic because it focuses on the relationship with the target.

The bottom sections of the two columns in Figure 2-3 include impression management tactics that can be used to adjust one's social identity. These tactics will typically be called into play when the person managing his or her impression believes that the reference goal has been surpassed. A sample tactic that would focus the attention on the actor would be self-handicapping (pointing to a fault that could dampen performance). In this case, the actor would be trying to lower the target's expectation of him or her by indicating that he or she might not be able to sustain the overachieved reference goal. For example, the actor might say, "Please don't think that I can continue to come up with great ideas for cost cutting. I'm really not that talented with operations."

Nonverbal Cues

Nonverbal behavior is a major contributor to the impressions created when people interact with each other. Image consultants who coach clients on how to dress, adjust their posture, and cultivate their voice are well aware of the importance of nonverbal behavior in projecting an impression. Also, nonverbal cues act either to complement or contradict the verbal messages that are part of impression management. A rudimentary example is that a good impression is created if you greet a target with the statement "I am so glad to meet you," and reinforce your statement with a smile and a warm handshake. Even voice inflection can reinforce the image, by saying "I am *soooooo* glad to meet you." (Voice inflection is considered nonverbal behavior even though it is related to words.)

Impact on Target

As shown in Figure 2-1, the actor's impression management behavior initiates cognitive processing (or thinking) by the target after he or she observes the actor's self-presentation. This cognitive processing is followed by the target's response, as indicated in the component of the model referred to as "feedback from target." The impact on the target is thus a cognitive process that mediates the target's feedback on the actor's impression management activities.

The feedback from the target will not always be an accurate reflection with respect to how the target feels. For example, the target might dislike the actor's attempt at ingratiation through overdone flattery, yet might smile politely. Or conversely, the target might enjoy the flattery but would feel embarrassed in saying something to the effect, "You make me feel great."

In the model under consideration, the more important element in influencing the actor's self-presentation efforts is the target's observable responses—the feedback the actor receives. The actor derives both verbal and nonverbal cues as to the relative success or failure of impression management attempts from the target's observable behavior reactions. Recall Lisa, the international marketing specialist who wants to use her Spanish-speaking skills to enhance her impression. Lisa will feel she is on the right track when she receives target responses, such as "Cool," "You really are bicultural," and "I can understand why you pursue international marketing."

Practical Implications of the Model

The central core and most applied aspect of the model stems directly from cybernetics theory: our behavior is strongly directed by the feedback we receive when the feedback is compared to the identity goals we seek. From an actor's perspective there are several important factors. First, the actor should carefully assess which tactics of impression management related to a specific identity function fit the feedback from the target. (Again, the identity functions are identity enhancement, protection, and adjustment. Each identity function has related tactics, as shown in Figure 2-3.) Taking this factor into account will facilitate an actor using tactics that are focused more upon the content dimension, the relation dimension, or a blend of the two dimensions. An example here would be an actor interested in using identity enhancement to build a good relationship with the target. Observing that the target is the type of person who always likes to be right, the actor might use the tactic of *opinion conformity*.

Second, the model also indicates that organizational actors need to be aware that their presentations of self to targets, particularly familiar ones, should not stray too far from the scripts that have been established during previous interactions. The general "character" that one has established in prior interactions will be the standard against which current "performances" will be judged. In short, the actor should be on guard against acting out of character because to do so can result in a loss of credibility.

Third, nonverbal behavior plays a major role in impression management. When we are forming an impression of another individual, nonverbal cues often receive more weight than verbal statements. Another factor is that targets often establish nonverbal expectations of actors with whom they are familiar. As a result, the consistency of nonverbal behavior during interactions with familiar people enhances credibility. To illustrate, a relatively somber individual who suddenly smiles frequently might appear to be faking his or her mood.

The cybernetic model also has implications for targets, particularly with respect to the key role of feedback. Managers might use feedback to reinforce desirable job behavior, and to decrease or extinguish undesirable behavior. For example, if an unproductive subordinate relies too heavily on ingratiation the manager might ignore the behavior or provide content-oriented feedback that focuses the subordinate back on the job.

Guidelines for Application and Practice

1. A major consideration in managing your impression is to seek both verbal and nonverbal feedback about the impression you are attempting to create. Compare the feedback you receive to the image you are trying to project. If you observe negative discrepancies, look for ways to develop tactics that will strengthen your image. For example, assume that you are trying to project the image of being a highly knowledgeable specialist within your field. To accomplish this desired state, you frequently tell people how knowledgeable you are. The feedback you receive appears bland and neutral. You might modify your tactic by presenting actual examples of difficult technical problems in your discipline that you have solved.

2. To manage your impression, it is helpful to first have a clear picture of what image you would like to project, or your *social identity*. For example, are you trying to project the image of a strong team player, a leader, or a person who works best as an individual contributor? It is conceivable that you will have different social identities depending on the given situation.

3. Effective impression management requires motivation, meaning that there has to be a good reason to engage in impression management. A good question to reflect on is "How much would I value the payoff from successfully managing my impression?" For example, if effective impression management might lead to a promotion, how much do you value that promotion?

4. Another way of being motivated to manage your impression well is to use feedback to gauge how far you are from achieving your desired identity goal. If the discrepancy is large, you will have to work extra hard at attaining your

goal. An example would be an individual who wanted to speak impressively working with a voice coach to improve his or her speech patterns. Having more facts at hand would also help create the right impression.

5. When attempting to measure how well you are achieving a particular identity goal, observe carefully the nonverbal feedback you receive. For example, if you want to project the image of a person with high integrity and trustworthiness, scrutinize the facial expression of your targets when you tell them something important. Nonverbal expressions such as a quizzical gaze or rolling eyes could suggest that you are not yet communicating a high degree of trustworthiness.

6. A desired social identity works much like a broad goal you are attempting to achieve when managing your impression. When the discrepancy is large between the desired and actual social identity, think of using identity protection, identity enhancement, and identity adjustment. Identity maintenance is used for small discrepancies between the desired social identity and the identity as revealed by feedback. Figure 2-3 presents specific tactics under each category, and many of these tactics will be described in later chapters of this book.

7. After a desired social identity has been achieved, it will be necessary to maintain that identity in the future. Otherwise, the desired social identity will be lost. You might regard identity maintenance as refreshing your image periodically.

8. Developing a *script* for impression management means that you plan how you will deal with an upcoming situation in which you want to create a particular impression. It can be helpful to rehearse these scenarios with a camcorder.

Summary

Impression management can be considered a control or cybernetic process. Cybernetic systems feature four components: a reference standard or goal, feedback, a comparator, and an effector. Environmental feedback is processed by the organism through the comparator in order to detect discrepancies between the references standard (goal) and the feedback. Three outcomes are possible: negative discrepancies, positive discrepancies, and zero discrepancies. When faced with a negative discrepancy, the person adjusts his or her behavior via the effector to minimize the discrepancies. Or the reference goal might be adjusted downward. A positive discrepancy indicates that the output is greater than the reference goal, possibly leading to a downward adjustment of the image created.

Cybernetic systems have motivational implications. Goals and the effort that follows are reflected in effort directed toward controlling the environment and effort directed toward aligning the system (or organism) with environmental demands.

The cybernetic model posits that the motivation for impression management is primarily a function of the perceived discrepancies between the feedback from the target and the reference goal. These discrepancies are uncovered through the comparator. Impression management takes place in a dynamic, interactive manner, with the actor making fine adjustments as he or she goes along.

The model is centered on the actor's reference goal or desired state of social identity, or identification with a particular social category. Organizational members are likely to possess multiple identity goals they would like to attain. The specific aspects of the self-concept activated in a given social situation influence the social identity portrayed to others. The motive to engage in self-enhancement stems from the actor's desire to increase or protect his or her self-esteem. The particular identity the person wants to project is also influenced by situational factors, target characteristics, and individual differences among actors.

The components of VIE (or expectancy) theory help determine whether a situation facing the actor is interpreted as an opportunity, a threat, or a relatively neutral situation. People will engage in a particular aspect of impression management if they feel they can pull it off, and if the impression management activity will lead to a valued outcome.

The desired social identity of the actor serves as the reference goal of the model. After a specific social identity goal relevant to a given situation is selected, the key to the motivation to manage impressions stems from perceived discrepancies between the current and desired social identities of the actor. In general, large discrepancies between goals and feedback have the greatest potential to motivate actors.

The target can provide identity-relevant information that will allow the actor to determine whether or not his or her desired social identity has been achieved. Also, feedback from targets can inform the actor about appropriate behaviors or necessary modifications that need to be made to previous behaviors. Impression managers must be careful to make the modifications without appearing too manipulative. Both verbal and nonverbal feedback should be observed. Asking for feedback will often enhance the actor's image.

The feedback from the target is filtered (processed) through the perception processes and mechanisms of the actor. Goal-directed people selectively attend to and perceive information from their environment based on its relevance to their personal goals or intentions. The feedback is essential for the actor to choose a method that will lead to his or her desired social identity. The three strategic identity functions are (1) protection or enhancement, (2) maintenance, and (3) adjustment. Strategic identify functions are called upon to deal with larger discrepancies between the actor's social identity and the feedback from the target when the actor is strongly motivated to project a positive image. Identity maintenance activities help to provide a sense of consistency and stability to the social identity by dealing with zero and small discrepancies.

A negative discrepancy between current and desired social identities indicates that the actor has not achieved the desired impression. Identity enhancement activities are strategies and behaviors directed toward improving or advancing the actor's social identity as perceived by the target. Identity protection activities are strategies and behaviors directed toward the prevention of damage or harm to the actor's social identity.

A positive discrepancy may occur between an actor's current and desired social identities. One reaction is to be pleased with the feedback of the target, leading to an upward adjustment of the reference goal. Another reaction is that the actor sets high expectations that he or she would prefer not to maintain. Identity maintenance is used primarily to deal with small negative and positive discrepancies between the current and desired social identities.

The major function of outcome processing is to determine the effective responses for either reducing discrepancies or capitalizing upon desirable positive discrepancies. In similar situations, the actor may either duplicate the behaviors that have succeeded in the past or use them as general guides in relatively similar situations.

Actors often use pre-established routines, or scripts, to cope with discrepancies. In some situations the actor may not be able to develop a plan prior to certain image-threatening situations. Instead, the actor develops a script when placed in a novel situation. The script can be modified, including script tracking, or finding an alternative path within the same script. After numerous failed attempts toward goal attainment, the actor may decide to adjust his or her reference goal. A series of positive discrepancies may lead to an upward adjustment of the identity goal.

The major verbal tactics of impression management can be categorized in terms of their orientation, as listed in Figure 2-3. Content-oriented messages tend to focus on the actor and involve information that reflects upon his or her qualities and behaviors. Relation-oriented messages tend to focus more on the target and the relationship between the actor and the target. These impression management tactics are also categorized in terms of the identity functions of enhancement, protection, and adjustment. Nonverbal behavior is also a crucial determinant of impression formed during face-to-face encounters. The impact of impression management tactics on the target is a cognitive process that mediates the target's feedback about the impression management activities. At times the feedback will not accurately reflect how the target feels.

Chapter 3

Individual and Organizational Contributing Factors

Workers at all levels from entry-level associates to executives vary considerably in how much interest and skill they have in managing their impression. At one extreme are workers who are forever concerned about their image, even to the point of worrying that they are not carrying the latest model of laptop computer, cell phone, or personal digital assistant. At the other extreme are workers who do not care what kind of impression they create, such as the store associate who chews gum and engages in a personal phone conversation while serving a customer.

Organizations also vary in terms of how much impression management takes place, and how much is desired. At one extreme might be a highly political organization where most members continually attempt to impress each other. At the other extreme might be a laid-back organization in which seniority is almost the only basis for promotion, and almost nobody cares about impressing anybody.

In this chapter we examine some of the research-based factors that help explain why individuals and organizations vary so widely in the emphasis placed on impression management. This information is important because much of the professional and popular literature about impression management does not place much emphasis on individual differences in impression management. Also glossed over is the fact that impression management is more suited to some organizational settings than others.

In this chapter we look first at factors within individuals that predispose them to engaging in impression management. We then look at characteristics of the organization, along with the specific situation, that prompt organizational members to manage their impressions. Another possibility is that you might have an organization filled with people with a propensity toward impression management. The result would be an organization characterized by impression management, even if this high frequency of impression management is attributed much more to individuals than the organization itself.

Individual Factors Contributing to Impression Management

Individual differences are a major influence on the extent to which a person engages in impression management, as well as his or her skill in projecting the desired image. Here we describe how impression management is influenced by five personality factors: self-monitoring, Machiavellianism, trustworthiness, extra-version, and optimism. We also touch upon how cognitive skills and gender differences contribute to impression management. Although gender differences are a group, not an individual factor, gender differences can function like an individual difference.

Here and in most of the other chapters in this book, we present a variety of tactics or approaches to impression management that vary in terms of their support by empirical research (or actually gathering data and facts). Tactics and approaches not supported by empirical research can be quite important, even though supported mostly by anecdote and opinion. A good example is that many experienced executives believe that sending handwritten thank-you notes creates a good impression, and this author believes strongly that this opinion is correct. However, it would be difficult to find an empirical study demonstrating the impression management value of handwritten thank-you notes.

Figure 3-1 classifies the individual factors related to impression management in terms of their research support.

Self-Monitoring

A major personality factor in determining the extent to which people manage their impression is their propensity to shape their behavior in terms of what they perceive the target would prefer. As a personality factor, **self-monitoring** refers to the observation and control of expressive and self-presentational behaviors.[1] Actors with a strong tendency to self-monitor are alert to situational cues that guide them in the presentation of what they believe to be appropriate behavior in a variety of situations—even if these behaviors are not a good fit with their inclinations. In contrast, actors low in self-monitoring typically display behaviors that are congruent with their inner feelings and beliefs, even at the risk of offending another person. The high self-monitor is sometimes referred to as chameleon-like because of his or her tendency to change colors to fit the situation.

As with all human traits, the trait of self-monitoring creates a predisposition to act in a particular way. A person who scores high on the trait of self-monitoring will

Figure 3-1 Individual Factors Contributing to Impression Management Classified by Amount of Research Support.

Trait or Behavior Well Supported by Research	Trait or Behavior Supported More by Anecdote and Opinion
Self-monitoring	Trustworthiness
Machiavellianism	Extraversion
	Optimism
	Gender differences in communication style

behave in such ways as attempting to please others. The quiz for measuring the self-monitoring trait is presented in Figure 3-2.

Here is an example of how self-monitoring might work in practice: Jenna, a materials manager who lives in New Jersey, is attending a company meeting at headquarters in Boston, Massachusetts. Jenna has visited Europe several times, and found England to be her least favorite European country. She perceives prices in England to be too high, and the people to be too smug. At the headquarters meeting,

Figure 3-2 The Self-Monitoring Scale.

Instructions: The statements below concern your personal reactions to a number of different situations. No two statements are exactly alike, so consider each statement carefully before answering. If a statement is *true* or *mostly true* as applied to you, circle the "T" next to the question. If a statement is *false* or *not usually true* as applied to you, circle the "F" next to the question.

(T) (F) 1. I find it hard to imitate the behavior of other people.

(T) (F) 2. My behavior is usually an expression of my true inner feelings, attitudes, and beliefs.

(T) (F) 3. At parties and social gatherings, I do not attempt to do or say things that others will like.

(T) (F) 4. I can only argue for ideas which I already believe.

(T) (F) 5. I can make impromptu speeches even on topics about which I have almost no information.

(T) (F) 6. I guess I put on a show to impress or entertain people.

(T) (F) 7. When I am uncertain how to act in a social situation, I look to the behavior of others for cues.

(T) (F) 8. I would probably make a good actor.

(T) (F) 9. I rarely seek the advice of my friends to choose movies, books, or music.

(T) (F) 10. I sometimes appear to others to be experiencing deeper emotions than I actually am.

(T) (F) 11. I laugh more when I watch a comedy with others than when alone.

(T) (F) 12. In groups of people, I am rarely the center of attention.

(T) (F) 13. In different situations and with different people, I often act like very different persons.

(T) (F) 14. I am not particularly good at making other people like me.

(T) (F) 15. Even if I am not enjoying myself, I often pretend to be having a good time.

(T) (F) 16. I'm not always the person I appear to be.

(T) (F) 17. I would not change my opinions (or the way I do things) in order to please someone else or win their favor.

(T) (F) 18. I have considered being an entertainer.

(T) (F) 19. In order to get along and be liked, I tend to be what people expect me to be rather than anything else.

(T) (F) 20. I have never been good at games like charades or improvisational acting.

(T) (F) 21. I have trouble changing my behavior to suit different people and different situations.

(T) (F) 22. At a party, I let others keep the jokes and stories going.

(T) (F) 23. I feel a bit awkward in company and do not show up quite as well as I should.

(T) (F) 24. I can look anyone in the eye and tell a lie with a straight face (if for a right end).

(T) (F) 25. I may deceive people by being friendly when I really dislike them.

Scoring and Interpretation: Give yourself one point each time your answer agrees with the key. A score that is between 0 and 12 would indicate that you are a relatively low self-monitor; a score that is between 13 and 25 would indicate that you are a relatively high self-monitor.

1.	F	9.	F	18.	T
2.	F	10.	T	19.	T
3.	F	11.	T	20.	F
4.	F.	12.	F	21.	F
5.	T	13.	T	22.	F
6.	T	14.	F	23.	F
7.	T	15.	T	24.	T
8.	T	16.	T	25.	T
9.	F	17.	F		

Source: Mark Snyder, "Self-Monitoring of Expressive Behavior," *Journal of Personality and Social Psychology*, No. 4, October 1974, pp. 528–537.

Jenna is introduced to Garth, the head of materials management of the English affiliate. To create a good impression, Jenna invests several minutes talking about the *positive* aspects of her visit to London. She even talks about the magnificent growth in property values through 2007 (a positive side of high prices), and the great pride of Londoners (a positive side of smugness). Jenna does not believe that she is lying, but that she is helping the visitor from England feel good about his visit to Boston.

When self-monitoring of behavior translates into lying, it would almost always be regarded as unethical. Here is an extreme workplace scenario in which self-monitoring to the point of lying might not be considered unethical: A man in tears turns in his 1990 Chevy Blazer to the auto salvage dealer. The SUV has been driven

275,000 miles, and is badly dented and rusted. The salvage specialist nods in sympathy and says, "I can see why you love her. She's a beautiful old vehicle." (Our salvage man is telling the Blazer owner what he wants to hear to ease his emotional turmoil.)

Mark C. Bolino and William H. Turnley examined how self-monitoring is associated with impression management. The research was conducted with two different samples of business students enrolled in a course in organizational behavior. A key research issue was the type of impression management tactics favored by high self-monitors.[2] Participants completed a self-monitoring scale similar to the one presented in Figure 3-2. They also completed a Machiavellianism scale which will be mentioned later in this chapter. Participants also completed a scale measuring five dimensions of impression management: ingratiation, self-promotion, exemplification, supplication, and intimidation, defined as follows:

1. *Ingratiation*. Seeking to be viewed as likeable by flattering others or doing favors for them.
2. *Self-promotion*. Seeking to be viewed as competent by touting personal abilities and accomplishments.
3. *Exemplification*. Seeking to be viewed as dedicated by going above and beyond the call of duty.
4. *Supplication*. Seeking to be viewed as needy by showing their weaknesses or broadcasting their limitations.
5. *Intimidation*. Seeking to be viewed as intimidating by threatening or bullying others.

Figure 3-3 provides more insight into these standard impression management strategies. Note that if used in excess, or inappropriately, each strategy can have a negative consequence, as shown in the far-right column. Figure 3-4 provides the specific behaviors associated with each of the five strategies.

Figure 3-3 Impression Management Strategies and Associated Image Outcomes.

Strategy	Representative Behaviors	Desired Image	Undesired Image
Ingratiation	Flattery, favor-doing	Likeable	Sycophant
Self-promotion	Performance claims, boasting	Competent	Conceited
Exemplification	Going beyond the call of duty, appearing busy	Dedicated	Feels superior
Supplication	Asking for help, playing dumb	Needy	Lazy
Intimidation	Making threats, displaying anger	Intimidating	Bossy

Source: E. E. Jones and T. S. Pitman, *Toward a General Theory of Strategic Self-Presentation* (Hillsdale, NJ: Lawrence Erlbaum, 1982), p. 249.

Figure 3-4 The Impression Management Scale.

Respond to the following statements by thinking about "how often you behave this way."

Self-Promotion
1. Talk proudly about your experience or education.
2. Make people aware of your talents or qualifications.
3. Let others know that you are valuable to the organization.
4. Make people aware of your accomplishments.

Ingratiation
1. Compliment your colleagues so they will see you as likeable.
2. Take an interest in your colleagues' personal lives to show them that you are friendly.
3. Praise your colleagues for their accomplishments so they will consider you a nice person.
4. Do personal favors for your colleagues to show them that you are a friendly person.

Exemplification
1. Stay at work late so people will know you are hardworking.
2. Try to appear busy, even at times when things appear slower.
3. Arrive at work early to look dedicated.
4. Come to the office at night or on weekends to show that you are dedicated.

Intimidation
1. Be intimidating with coworkers when it will help you get your job done.
2. Let others know you can make things difficult for them if they push you too far.
3. Deal forcefully with colleagues when they hamper your ability to get your job done.
4. Deal strongly or aggressively with coworkers who interfere in your business.
5. Use intimidation to get colleagues to behave appropriately.

Supplication
1. Act like you know less than you do so people will help you out.
2. Try to gain assistance or sympathy from people by appearing needy in some areas.
3. Pretend not to understand something to gain someone's help.
4. Act like you need assistance so people will help you out.
5. Pretend to know less than you do so you can avoid an unpleasant assignment.

Source: Mark C. Bolino and William H. Turnley, "Measuring Impression Management in Organizations: A Scale Development Based on the Jones and Pittman Taxonomy," *Organizational Research Methods*, No. 2, 1999, pp. 187–206.

In addition to completing the scales, the students participated in a semester-long research project conducted in small groups. To measure the outcome of impression management, students rated other group members in terms of their desirability as a group member. An examination of the relationship between self-monitoring and impression management indicated a notable contrast in impression management styles among high and low self-monitors. Three profiles of impression management were observed:

1. *Positives*. Individuals who used relatively high levels of ingratiation, self-promotion, and exemplification, but used supplication and intimidation less frequently.
2. *Aggressives*. Individuals who used relatively high levels of all impression management tactics.
3. *Passives*. Individuals who used relatively low levels of each tactic.

High self-monitors were more likely to be positives (63% of high self-monitors were classified as positives). Low self-monitors made less frequent use of positive tactics (42% of low self-monitors used positive tactics). The interpretation is that high self-monitors—those who are sensitive to how they are seen by others—tend to emphasize more positive impression management tactics. In contrast, low self-monitors were more likely than high self-monitors to be placed in the aggressive or passive clusters. Low self-monitors made up 60% of the aggressive cluster of tactics, and 60% of the passive cluster.

The researchers interpreted the findings to mean that high self-monitors did not necessarily engage in more impression management tactics across the board. Instead, they tended to emphasize those behaviors they thought would lead to a favorable impression. We add the interpretation that high self-monitoring predisposes individuals to be more sensitive to the type of impression management tactics they are using in order to project the best image of themselves.

A partial explanation of why people engage in self-monitoring is that they are seeking approval. Essentially, if you "tell people what they want to hear" you will receive their approval. Actors with high approval needs tend to be concerned about being accepted and fear being rejected.[3] A finance specialist visiting a manufacturing plant might therefore be prompted to say to targets, "If it weren't for you guys, our company would have nothing to sell, and I wouldn't have any company money to manage." In seeking approval from financial managers, the same specialist might make the statement, "We could get a bigger return on investment if we could lower our manufacturing costs, such as by global outsourcing."

Machiavellianism

As part of the same study just described, the relationship between impression management tactics and Machiavellian tendencies was studied. **Machiavellianism** is the extent to which individuals behave manipulatively, hold cynical views of human nature, and have a generally low regard for conventional standards of morality.[4] Research suggests that Machiavellianism is likely to be positively correlated with the use of impression management. The association is likely to be stronger when the intent of impression management is to deceive others. In contrast, when high self-monitors use impression management, the aim is more probably to please others.

The results of the study reported above supported the idea that a person's level of Machiavellianism can be an antecedent to impression management tactics. Manifest differences were found in the patterns of impression management tactics employed by high Machiavellians and low Machiavellians. The majority of the aggressive group was composed of people with high Machiavellian tendencies (55%). Unexpectedly, the high Machiavellians also comprised the majority (54%) of the passives cluster. In contrast, low Machiavellians made up 56% of the positives—those who placed more emphasis on ingratiation, self-promotion, and exemplification.

In summary, compared to low Machiavellians, high Machiavellians tended to be either aggressive or passive in their use of the five impression management tactics. In contrast, low Machiavellians tended to emphasize the more positive impression management tactics. High Machiavellians are more likely to use impression management tactics that more immediately benefit themselves.

The researchers concluded that Machiavellianism is not necessarily related to the amount of impression management used by individuals, but instead to their willingness to engage in more risky, and perhaps more deceptive forms of impression management. An example of a Machiavellian personality using a deceptive form of impression management would be a certified financial planner alluding to the idea that she was in personal contact with a famous investor. She might also drop the hint that she had become a multi-millionaire using the investment strategies she provides clients—even though her net worth was really not so impressive.

Another way a person with strong Machiavellian tendencies might engage in unethical impression management is to give the impression that he or she is offering the target an opportunity to join a special group. The target is therefore manipulated into believing that he or she can become elite also by joining the group, such as becoming part of a special investment group. Bernard Madoff, one of the major fraudulent investment managers of all time—along with many of his associates—led victims to believe that only a select group of *friends* were being invited to participate in some of his investments. Madoff, and his associates, therefore created the untrue and unethical impression that they were being kind to their targets.

Trustworthiness

For many organizational actors, an important goal of impression management is to be perceived as trustworthy. At the same time a person who is perceived as being trustworthy and honest will have an easier time creating a desired impression. Trustworthiness is therefore both a goal, and an antecedent (or contributing factor) to impression management. In this context, **trust** is defined as a person's confidence in another individual's intentions and motives and in the sincerity of that individual's word.[5] The person who is trusted, and therefore perceived as being trustworthy, will have an easier time projecting other aspects of his or her desired image.

Research and opinion suggest that certain trust builders help a person create an image of trustworthiness. Exhibiting these behaviors will both create a favorable impression, and serve as a base for creating a favorable impression with respect to other aspects of behavior (such as having high job competence or a strong social network).[6] Several of the suggestions apply mostly to workers in managerial and leadership positions.

- *Make your behavior consistent with your intentions.* Practice what you preach and set the example. Let others know of your intentions and invite feedback on how well you are achieving them.
- *Be a problem solver.* When your organization or organizational unit encounters a problem, move into a problem-solving mode instead of looking to blame others for what went wrong.
- *Honor confidences.* One incident of passing along confidential information results in a permanent loss of trust by the person whose confidence was violated.
- *Maintain a high level of integrity.* Build a reputation for doing what you think is morally right in spite of the political consequences.
- *Tell the truth in ways people can verify.* It is much easier to be consistent when you do not have to keep patching up your story to conform to an earlier lie. An example of verification would be for a group member to see if the manager really did attempt to buy new conference room furniture as he or she said.
- *Admit mistakes.* Covering up a mistake, particularly when everybody knows that you did it, destroys trust quickly.

It takes an organizational actor a long time to build trust, yet one brief incident of untrustworthy behavior can permanently destroy it. People are usually allowed a fair share of honest mistakes. In contrast, dishonest mistakes quickly erode a person's credibility and effectiveness. An example of a dishonest mistake would be receiving a kickback from a supplier or engaging in insider trading. It would take a long time to project a positive image after having been caught making the mistakes just mentioned.

Part of a leader's role is to be perceived as someone who can create sensible visions. Yet before workers will buy into a vision, the leader first has to be trusted. Shirley W. Bridges, the chief information officer of Delta Air Lines, gives an illustration of how the process works in these words: "People don't buy into a vision, they buy into a leader—then they buy into the vision. So if you haven't built trust throughout the organization, then no matter what you stand up and tell the people, they're not going to buy into it. They've got to buy into you first."[7]

Extraversion

A basic personality factor that contributes to a willingness and propensity to engage in impression management is extraversion, often identified as one of the five major personality factors composing the human personality. **Extraversion** reflects the quantity or intensity of social interactions, the need for social stimulation, self-confidence, and competition. Traits associated with extraversion include being sociable, gregarious, assertive, talkative, and active. An outgoing person is often described as extraverted, whereas introverted persons are described as reserved, timid, and quiet.

Visualize the scenario of a job fair. An extraverted person would feel natural initiating contacts with employer representatives as well as other potential valuable contacts at the fair. The same person would also feel comfortable making a one-minute self-presentation to serve as a quick introduction to company representatives. As a result, the job seeker would create a positive impression. In contrast, an introverted person at the fair who did not take the initiative to speak to employer representatives or other potential network members would probably create a poor impression.

As with most personality traits or factors, if extraversion is carried to the extreme, it could creative a negative impression. People who are inappropriately outgoing, such as talking too much and smiling too frequently, risk creating a negative impression among more diffident people.

Optimism

Optimism refers to a tendency to experience positive emotional states, and to typically believe that positive outcomes will be forthcoming from most activities. The anticipation of positive outcomes may sometimes depart from reality. The other end of the scale is *pessimism*—a tendency to experience negative emotional states and to typically believe that negative outcomes will be forthcoming from most activities. Optimism versus pessimism is also referred to in more technical terms as positive affectivity versus negative affectivity, and is considered a major personality trait.[8]

The potential link between optimism and impression management is that optimistic people are more likely to believe they can project their desired image. As a result, they are more likely to engage in impression management. In comparison, pessimists are less likely to believe that impression management will have a positive impact so they do not make a deliberate effort to attain their desired identity goal. An optimistic entrepreneur might attend a meeting with potential investors and think, "I know I can dazzle these venture capitalists with the merit of my idea and my personal qualities." His or her pessimistic counterpart might think, "With so many other entrepreneurs chasing the same investors, I doubt I can make a good impression."

Cognitive Skills

Managing an impression well usually requires good cognitive skills or mental ability for several reasons. First, the actor has to be perceptive enough to read the feedback about how he or she is perceived. For example, an actor might need to decipher whether a target's smile means that he or she is impressed, or he or she is being condescending. Second, to be effective in projecting an image, an actor must develop a script to work in a particular situation. In one situation, the actor might be trying to project a positive impression to highly technical workers. In another situation, the actor might be trying to project a positive impression on workers who emphasize interpersonal skills rather than technical skills.

As explained by Bozeman and Kacmar, script development—or modifying a script to suit the occasion—requires a heavy cognitive load.[9] To enhance, protect, or adjust his or her identity goal, the actor might have to make rapid shifts in response to feedback cues. The actor might reflect, "My target does not appear particularly impressed at the moment. What facts about me or my company can I refer to that will create a more favorable impression? What am I saying or doing that is not working?"

Another facet of having cognitive skills is having insight into situations that will help a person recognize that a good impression would help make the situation more favorable for him or her. Many job applicants have disqualified themselves in recent years by wearing athletic shoes with a suit while being interviewed for a professional position, such as industrial sales representative. Even more widespread is the practice of receiving or initiating cell phone conversations, or text messaging, during a job interview. A higher degree of insight or social sensitivity would have been helpful in avoiding these blunders.

Gender Differences

Gender differences are another possible contributing factor to impression management. Similar to Machiavellianism, however, gender differences might contribute to the type of impression management tactics chosen rather than to whether or not impression management is practiced. Here we look at two aspects of potential gender differences in tactics of impression management: communication style differences, and research about profiles of impression management.

Gender Differences in Communication Patterns

Observations have been made about stereotypical differences between men and women in communication patterns or styles. Cultural stereotypes of this nature refer to representative differences and perhaps hold true for slightly more than one-half the population. The communication style differences most relevant to impression management are as follows:[10]

1. *Women prefer to use conversation for rapport building.* For most women, the intent of conversation is to build rapport and connections with people. Women

are therefore more likely to emphasize similarities, to listen intently, and to be supportive. Women would therefore be more likely create a positive impression by making an effort to connect with the target.

2. *Men prefer to use talk primarily as a means to preserve independence and status by displaying knowledge and skill.* When most men talk, they want to receive positive evaluation from others and maintain their hierarchical status within the group. Men are therefore more oriented to giving a *report*, while women are more interested in establishing *rapport*. Men would therefore be more likely to attempt to impress targets through knowledge display.

3. *Women are more likely to compliment the work of a coworker, whereas men are more likely to be critical.* A communication problem may occur when a woman compliments the work of a male coworker and expects reciprocal praise. Women would have an edge here in creating a good impression through ingratiation.

4. *Men tend to be more direct in their conversation, whereas women emphasize politeness.* Women are therefore more likely to frequently use the phrases "I'm sorry" and "Thank you," even when there is no need to express apology or gratitude. For example, a supermarket manager notices that the store has suddenly become busy. She would therefore say to a store associate unpacking boxes, "I'm sorry, Pedro, but we've become busy all of a sudden. Could you please open up a new lane up front? Thank you." A manager who is a stereotyped male might say, "Pedro, we need you to open a line up front, pronto. Put down the boxes and get up there." Following this stereotype, men actors would attempt to build a positive impression by being direct and decisive. In contrast, women actors would attempt to build a positive impression through politeness.

5. *Women tend to be more conciliatory when facing differences, whereas men become more intimidating.* Again, women are more interested in building relationships, whereas men are more concerned about coming out ahead. When facing differences, women actors might attempt to creative a positive impression by being conciliatory. Men actors, in contrast, might be intimidating rather than attempt to create an image of compassion.

6. *Men are more interested than women in calling attention to their accomplishments or hogging recognition.* In one instance a sales representative who had already made her sales quota for the month turned over an excellent prospect to a coworker. She reasoned, "It's somebody else's turn. I've received more than my fair share of bonuses for the month." In some instances men might create a positive impression by emphasizing accomplishments, yet in other instances their quest for recognition would detract from being a team player.

7. *Men tend to dominate discussions during meetings.* One study of college faculty meetings found that women's longest turns at speaking were, on the

average, of shorter duration than men's shortest turns. A possible explanation here is that women are still less assertive than men in the workplace. During meetings, men might attempt to create a positive impression by being dominant, whereas women might attempt to create a positive impression by being reflective and nodding their head in agreement.

Gender Differences in Profiles of Impression Management

Returning to the study conducted with organizational behavior students, several gender differences were found in the preference for tactics of impression management. The most striking gender differences were found with the passive and aggressive clusters. Among women, 35% were placed in the passive category and 21% were in the aggressive category. In contrast, only 11% of men were placed in the passive category, and 34% were in the aggressive category. An overall trend was for women to be more likely to report using low levels of all impression management tactics. Males, however, were more likely than their female counterparts to be aggressive (individuals who used relatively high levels of all impression management tactics). Fewer gender differences were found with respect to the positive strategy (individuals who used relatively high levels of ingratiation, self-promotion, and exemplification, but used supplication and intimidation less frequently).

In interpreting these gender differences it is helpful to note that fewer gender differences were found between men and women using the positive strategy. Specifically, 55% of men and 44% of women favored this approach.[11]

Dimensions of Organizational Culture Associated with Impression Management

Individual dispositions may play a major role in determining whether workers engage in impression management. It is also important to recognize the influence of the organization and the setting in facilitating or discouraging impression management. In this section we look at selected aspects of the organizational culture that can influence the frequency and type of impression management. In the following section, we describe several more direct, or situational, factors associated with impression management in the workplace. However, the distinction between a cultural factor and a situational factor is not always clear cut. One reason is that cultural factors create situational factors, such as high pressure for results demanded by a manager being influenced by an organizational culture dimension of high productivity.

As familiar to most readers, **organizational culture** is a system of shared values and beliefs that influence worker behavior. The organizational culture profoundly influences the extent to which impression management takes place. A highly competitive firm such as a Wall Street investment bank, with loads of people competing for advancement, might place more emphasis on impression management as well as other forms of organizational politics. Workers throughout the organization will make frequent use of impression management, such as ingratiating themselves with powerful people at every opportunity. In extreme contrast, workers at a home for assisted living might be much less competitive, and the impression management tactics utilized would be implemented in low-key style. For example, a frequent ingratiating tactic might be to do small favors for a coworker such as helping him or her scrape snow from the windshield of his or her car in the parking lot.

Here we look at several dimensions, or components, of organizational culture that influence the presence of impression management. The more of these dimensions that favor political behavior are found to be present, the more impression management is likely to take place. Also, organizational culture is said to mediate impression management in the sense that in some organizational cultures impression management is more acceptable. The dimensions described here help explain why some cultures breed more impression management.[12]

1. *Power struggling.* Several organizational theorists, including Jeffrey Pfeffer and Charles Perrow, see organizations as environments in which individuals and groups struggle for limited resources.[13] Given that most organizations are hierarchies, the dimension of struggling for power is likely to be present to some extent in most organizations. The more pronounced the value, the more impression management will be present—because making a good impression can help a person acquire and retain power. Although few senior-level managers are likely to admit that struggling for power is a key corporate value, the struggle for power might be recognized by most workers. Some of the excesses of the corrupt Enron Corporation of the past have been attributed to an environment in which the struggle for power prompted managers and financial analysts to seek ever more creative ways of making money.

2. *Fear.* Most organizational theorists would not classify fear as a value. Nevertheless, a culture characterized by fear of being punished or fired triggers considerable political activity, including impression management for the sake of self-protection. During Carly Fiorina's five-year reign as CEO of Hewlett-Packard (HP), many workers feared either being downgraded for poor performance or losing their jobs. In her first several years in office, 17,900 employees lost their job. Fiorina worked 16 hours per day herself, and expected HP employees to work much harder than they had done in the past. A company veteran said, "Employees are now viewed as assets or tools, no different than machines or buildings." As part of the climate of fear, Fiorina instituted the concept of automatically firing the bottom 5% of performers.[14] At one point workers marched outside an HP facility carrying signs, much like pickets. Two of the placards read, "Fire two instead of 15,000" and "Carly's dream is a nightmare for workers."

3. *The importance of human interaction.* Edgar Schein, a pioneer in the scholarly study of organizational culture, observes that organizations make a variety of assumptions about how people interact with each other. Some facilitate interaction among people, while others regard it as a distraction.[15] When interaction among workers is welcome, political behavior is more likely to be positive, such as creating a good impression for the sake of creating allies. When interaction is regarded as a distraction, impression management tends to be more limited in scope, such as covering up one's mistakes.

4. *Trust and respect for the individual.* The more an organization values trust and respect for the individual, the less prevalent is negative political behavior such as the need to create a false, positive impression. For many years, the HP Way was the dominant cultural dimension at Hewlett-Packard. It was a code of behavior established by founders Bill Hewlett and Dave Packard. The first sentence of the code states, "We have trust and respect for the individual."[16] Partially as a result of this value, HP was not regarded as a highly political environment. During the reigns of Carly Fiorina and then Mark Hurd, about 30,000 HP workers have been downsized, leading to a weakening of the cultural dimension of trust and respect. As HP has returned to high prosperity, including reclaiming its lead in personal computers, trust and respect for individuals is making a comeback at the company. As a consequence, more emphasis is placed on relationship-building approaches to impression management.

5. *Organizational heroes and heroines.* Organizations tend to have role models who personify the value systems demonstrating what the organization defines as success. The heroic figures are often members of upper management, but they could also be other figures, such as a sales representative who made a giant sale that saved the company from financial peril or an information technology specialist who rescued the company from a giant virus attack.[17] The positive political consequence of heroes and heroines is that some workers may attempt to engage in behavior and performance that is so highly valued, thereby creating an impression that they think is valued. However, the negative side is that some workers may attempt to become heroic figures instead of taking care of more mundane responsibilities such as responding to inquiries from small customers or assisting others with routine software problems.

6. *Individualistic versus collectivistic culture.* In an individualistic culture more people may attempt to generate the impression of an independent and self-reliant individual. In contrast, in a collectivistic culture, more political actors will work toward generating an image of a person who displays politeness and harmony.

The general point about the dimensions of culture just described is that the organizational culture through its various dimensions can foster both positive and negative approaches to impression management. A strong culture will have a bigger effect than a weak culture, and a strong culture is difficult to change. For example, a strong culture might heavily influence what types of behavior and appearance are required to create a positive impression. An example is Paychex Inc., a national payroll and human resources outsourcing firm. Anything less than a highly professional demeanor and clothing creates a negative impression. Also workers are expected to pay full attention in meetings, without side conversations or glances at e-mail and text messages.

Situational Factors Contributing to Impression Management

Here we examine the role of four situational factors contributing to impression management, as outlined in Figure 3-5: contextual variables, social network centrality, characteristics of the target, and working remotely.

Figure 3-5 Situational Factors Contributing to Impression Management.

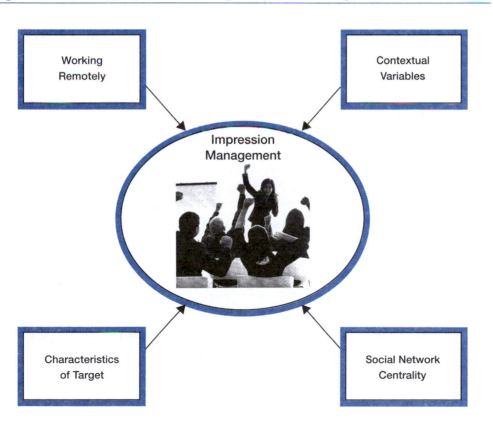

Contextual Variables Influencing Impression Management

The context or setting is important in understanding why people are likely to engage in impression management, with the four contextual variables presented next being particularly important.[18] You will observe that contextual variables are quite close in meaning and effect to dimensions of organizational culture.

1. *Power relations in the organization.* The more power managers have over workers in the organization, the more likely the workers are to engage in impression management. Greater power also implies more dependency on the power figures, so impression management seems all the more important. Similarly, in an organization that endorses the cultural value of power distance (more respect for authority) workers will think it is more legitimate to impress their superiors.
2. *Limited economic and political opportunities of subgroups.* Impression management may be more common in societies with limited economic and political opportunities. In the organization this could mean that minorities might engage in more impression management because they are relatively less powerful.
3. *Culture-specific codes.* A national culture that emphasizes harmonious interpersonal relationships may encourage members of that culture to manage their impressions. An example is that impression management among Latinos may be attributed to a culture-specific Latino script known as *sympatia* (the need for behaviors that encourage smooth interpersonal relations).
4. *Occupational status.* Individuals in low-status jobs are more likely to use impression management toward their superiors in order to improve their conditions. Although this generalization may be true, many people in relatively high-status positions, such as corporate professionals and middle managers, regularly use impression management to gain advantage. The use of glitzy PowerPoint presentations to impress the boss or members of higher management illustrates this point.

In practice, a combination of these contextual factors and the cultural factors mentioned above will augment the impression management activity within the organization. For example, a country or regional culture that emphasized politeness and civility combined with a collectivistic culture could readily result in workers presenting themselves to others cordially. Companies in rural areas are therefore predisposed to a culture in which workers attempt to impress each other with care, concern, and politeness. The reason is that many people in rural America value harmony with friends, family, and neighbors, and also have collectivistic values.

Social Network Centrality

Where a person is placed within a social network can contribute to the extent of his or her impression management activities. As researched and explained by Zoe I. Barsness, Kristina A. Diekman, and Marc-David L. Seidel, access to a large network of interpersonal ties in an organization may facilitate effective impression management. The reason is because such a network serves as a conduit through which individuals can obtain useful information.[19] Having a smaller number of contacts may not only reduce exposure, but also reduce access to information and resources. As a result it may be more difficult to impress others, particularly with respect to presenting the image of being well connected.

More central subordinates (those in the middle of a network) may enjoy greater confidence in managing impressions assertively because they have access to information gathered though a large network of organizational ties. In turn, this information is used to gauge their managers' receptiveness to influence, or when and how that influence might most effectively be exercised. The actors in question will therefore perceive greater opportunity to manage impressions assertively. An example will help clarify this abstract argument. Hugo, who is well connected at a beer distributorship, makes his own observations about how to make a positive impression on his boss—and therefore exert influence. In addition, he speaks to and has e-mail exchanges with people in his network to learn what type of information is likely to influence his boss. Hugo learns that the topic of consolidation of distributors is a major concern to his boss, so he gathers information on this topic to introduce in conversations with his manager.

As a result of these observations, the researchers in question investigated whether or not social network centrality is positively associated with impression management tactics directed at the supervisor as well as the job. A scale was used to measure impression management among 98 workers at an Internet commerce firm. Supervisor-focused behavior included ingratiatory and other-enhancement job behaviors directed at supervisors, such as giving them compliments. Job-focused behaviors included self-enhancement activities, such as making their supervisors aware of their accomplishments.

Social network centrality was measured by having employees look down an alphabetical list of company employees, and place checkmarks against the names of people they knew, and with whom they interacted regularly. Based on these checkmarks, the researchers constructed a matrix of familiarity networks.

Analysis of the data indicated that social network centrality was positively associated with job-focused impression management. However, centrality was not associated with supervisor-focused impression management. More central subordinates used job-focused behaviors more frequently than their peers who were not so well connected in the network. We can conclude that being well placed in a company social network contributes to at least one important form of impression management—making the manager aware of job accomplishments.

Characteristics of the Target

A basic principle of communication as well as impression management is that the characteristics of the audience, or target, must be taken into account. If the target views the impression management tactics as appropriate, the actor will create a positive impression. If the audience views the behaviors as inappropriate, the attempts at impression management will be perceived unfavorably. Gardner and Martinko observe that desired impressions tend to produce favorable audience responses, whereas unwanted impressions are more likely to result in negative responses.[20]

A practical example of the importance of understanding the target is to size up the person's need for approval. If past behavior suggests that the target is approval hungry, an effective way to create a good impression is to offer approval. Flattery is a recommended tactic when the target has a strong need for approval. A case in point is Mickey Drexler, now the CEO of J. Crew, yet long associated with Gap. Drexler fancies himself as an extraordinary merchandising talent. Many other influential people also recognize his merchandising talent. Associated with his talent, Drexler is a micromanager about the smallest details associated with retailing, including shirt colors and type of buttons.[21] An effective way of impressing Drexler is to offer sensible suggestions about potential products, yet at the same time appeal to his ego about being a "retailing genius."

Another important target characteristic that influences which impression management tactics have the best chance of success is cognitive skill. More intelligent targets will often be more influenced by more intelligent approaches to impression management, such as making a thoughtful, fact-filled presentation about job accomplishments.

Yet another important target characteristic for the purpose of impression management is an actor's communication style. It is best to communicate with the target in his or her preferred manner in order to create a positive impression. Among the many possibilities are preferences for one of the following: (1) frequent e-mail updates during the course of a week, (2) occasional telephone conversations to supplement e-mail messages, (3) instant messaging throughout the day, (4) text messaging, or (5) PowerPoint presentations to communicate any item of importance.

Working Remotely

People who conduct their work away from the traditional audience lack the advantage of regular face-to-face contact as a medium for impression management. Remote workers in the Internet commerce company mentioned above in relation to network centrality were clearly aware of the risks of reduced visibility. As a consequence, they dealt with these risks through the use of supervisor-focused and job-focused impression management.

In the study, remote work was defined as the proportion of time a respondent spent working in a different location than his or her superior. All respondents divided their time among the primary work location, on the road, and at home. A significant finding was that the greater the proportion of time spent working remotely, the more frequently the subordinate engaged in impression management. An implication of this finding is that workers have an intense desire to create a positive workplace image. The workers appeared to be concerned that if they did not inform their managers of their effort and performance, their performance would not be seen or acknowledged.

A representative comment by a remote worker in the study was, "How can my boss evaluate me? My boss is missing out. She can't see me in action."[22] This worker illustrates that being a remote worker contributes to the tendency to engage in impression management.

Guidelines for Application and Practice

1. To effectively manage your impression, it is important to engage in some degree of self-monitoring. It is possible to self-monitor without sacrificing your beliefs or being dishonest. The recommended approach is to figure out your target's interests, perhaps by careful listening during your conversation. You then reflect on what aspect about yourself you could truthfully emphasize that would fit the target's needs and interests, and convey that information to your target.

2. When building your toolkit of impression management tactics, keep in mind five of the best researched: ingratiation, self-promotion, exemplification, supplication, and intimidation. Use the tactic or tactics that fit the occasion, but recognize that supplication and intimidation are likely to be perceived negatively by many targets.

3. Exhibiting Machiavellianism can backfire when managing your impression because Machiavellianism can prompt a person to engage in risky and deceptive forms of impression management. For example, a Machiavellian might make false statements about himself or herself that will later be discovered.

4. Being perceived as trustworthy is an important goal of impression management. At the same time, it is easier to engage in impression management if you are perceived as trustworthy. It is therefore advantageous to develop a reputation of trustworthiness through such means as making your behavior consistent with your intentions.

5. Being extraverted and optimistic can make it easier to create a positive impression. Although it is not easy to change core personality traits, at least a person can emphasize extraverted and optimistic aspects of their personality in order to facilitate a good impression.

6. Rather than manage your impression by intuition and common sense alone, it is helpful to use your cognitive resources to size up the situation, including carefully observing the feedback you are receiving. The feedback will often help you fine-tune your approaches to impression management.

7. In an organizational culture characterized by power struggles, it may be necessary to engage frequently in impression management in order to gain your fair share of power. In contrast, in an organizational culture characterized by trust and respect for the individual, it may be less necessary to engage in impression management—particularly in attempting to project false impressions.

8. Being at the center of a social network in an organization may help you obtain useful ideas for job-focused impression management, such as self-promotion.

9. Sizing up your target is an essential part of effective impression management. One key aspect of behavior to look for is the strength of the need for the approval of the target. Ingratiation will usually work effectively with targets who have strong need for approval.

10. If you work remotely, such as being a telecommuter most of the time, engaging in impression management becomes all the more important. Your supervisor may not have much opportunity to observe your effort or your work, so he or she needs to be reminded of your contributions.

Summary

Individual differences are a major influence on the extent to which a person engages in impression management, as well as his or her skill in projecting the desired image. Self-monitoring is a major personality factor in determining the extent to which people manage their impression. Actors with a strong tendency to self-monitor are alert to situational cues that guide them in their self-presentations—even if these behaviors are not a good fit with their inclinations.

A study found that high self-monitors tend to be positives—those who used high levels of ingratiation, self-promotion, and exemplification, but made less use of supplication and intimidation. Low self-monitors were often aggressives (those who used high levels of all the impression management tactics studied), or passives— those who used low levels of the tactics. The need for approval often contributes to self-monitoring.

Machiavellianism contributes to impression management, with low Machiavellians emphasizing the more positive tactics. In contrast, high Machiavellians are more likely to use impression management tactics that immediately benefit themselves. Also, high Machiavellians are more willing to engage in more risky and deceptive tactics of impression management.

Trustworthiness is both a goal and an antecedent of impression management. The person who is trusted, and therefore perceived as being trustworthy, will have an easier time projecting other aspects of his or her desired image. Extraversion and optimism both contribute to a willingness to engage in impression management. Managing an impression well usually requires good cognitive skills, for reasons such as being able to read feedback, and developing a script for impression management.

Gender differences in communication patterns might underlie gender differences in the use of impression management tactics, with women focusing more than men on building relationships. A study found that an overall trend was for women to be more likely to report using low levels of impression management tactics. Men were more likely to make use of all the impression management tactics studied. However, men and women did not differ much in the use of positive impression management tactics.

The organizational culture profoundly influences the extent to which impression management takes place. For example, a highly competitive firm prompts more people to engage in impression management. The culture dimensions of power struggling and fear lead to more use of impression management. An emphasis on human interaction may lead to positive uses of impression management, as will trust and respect for the individual. Other dimensions of organizational culture influencing impression management include organizational heroes and heroines, and an individualistic versus collective culture.

Contextual variables that influence impression management include (1) power relations in the organization, (2) limited economic and political opportunities of subgroups, (3) culture-specific codes, and (4) occupational status.

Social network centrality facilitates impression management because such a network serves as a conduit through which individuals can obtain useful information. A study showed that social network centrality was positively associated with job-focused (but not supervisor-focused) impression management.

Characteristics of the target represent another situational variable for impression management. A major example would be the strength of the target's need for approval. Working remotely also influences impression management, with a study showing that the greater the proportion of time spent working remotely, the more frequent the use of impression management.

Chapter 4

Substantive Approaches to Self-Presentation

Up to this point we have described many of the best-researched tactics of impression management, including the popular taxonomy of impression management tactics developed by Jones and Pitman: self-promotion, ingratiation, exemplification, intimidation, and supplication.[1] It is important to recognize, however, that the art of impression management goes far beyond a handful of well-researched tactics. In this chapter we explore impression management further by describing a number of tactics labeled *substantive* or *deeper level* because they go beyond making a favorable appearance. Most of the tactics to be described require a reasonable amount of cognitive skill. The following chapter describes more superficial-level techniques of impression management. *Superficial* refers literally to the surface, and the surface can be quite important, such as in making a positive first impression.

The techniques of impression management described in this chapter are separated into two categories for convenience: those that focus on self-presentation of a person's characteristics and behaviors, and those that focus on work accomplishment. We also describe briefly tactics that should be avoided because they create a negative image.

Another perspective on understanding the approaches to self-presentation described in this chapter is to classify them as to whether they are based mostly on research versus those supported more by anecdote and opinion. These differentiations are presented in Figure 4-1.

Self-Presentation of Characteristics and Behaviors

A major thrust of managing your impression is to demonstrate or imply that you possess characteristics and behaviors that make you both a person of worth and a contributor to the department, team, division, or organization. Figure 4-2 lists the characteristics and behaviors presented in this section of the chapter.

Being Persuasive

Persuasiveness is both an influence tactic and a tactic of impression management because people who are persuasive are generally perceived positively.[2] As with all tactics of impression management, the needs and perceptions of the target define

Figure 4-1 Classification of Self-Presentation Approaches According to Basis of Support.

	Well Supported by Empirical Research	Supported More by Anecdote and Opinion
Self-presentation of characteristics and behavior	1. Being persuasive 2. Developing a positive reputation 3. Using appropriate humor	1. Publicizing personal connections 2. Being civil and humble 3. Using apologies, excuses, and pardon seeking 4. Managing anger effectively
Self-presentation of work accomplishments	1. Displaying organizational citizenship behavior 2. Being a subject matter expert	1. Taking credit for a favorable event 2. Providing timely progress reports 3. Making a quick showing 4. Managing anger effectively 5. Demonstrating the ability to multitask

Figure 4-2 Self-Presentation of Characteristics and Behaviors.

1. Being persuasive
2. Developing a positive reputation
3. Publicizing personal connections
4. Using appropriate humor
5. Being civil and humble
6. Managing anger effectively

whether a given tactic is effective. Some people do not want to be *persuaded*, and would therefore not be impressed by persuasiveness.

Persuasive communication is a broad topic which you have most likely studied elsewhere. Robert B. Cialdini has synthesized knowledge from experimental and social psychology about methods for getting people to concede, comply, or change. A brief overview of Cialdino's six principles of persuasion is helpful in understanding some research-based knowledge about how to persuade other people, therefore enhancing your image.[3]

1. *Liking: People like those who like them.* You have a better chance of persuading and influencing people who like you. Emphasizing similarities between you and the other person and offering praise are the two most reliable techniques for getting another person to like you. A persuasive statement might therefore be "I can see that the two of us are both dedicated professionals. If you could lend me a little of your expertise on market forecasting, I could get my project completed more quickly."

2. *Reciprocity: People repay in kind.* You can often influence and persuade someone else to behave in a particular way by displaying the behavior first. If you want another person to behave ethically toward you, it can be helpful to take the initiative to behave ethically first. For example, a sales representative who wants to persuade his manager to award him the full commissions he merits might be extra careful to turn in thorough and honest travel and expense reports.

3. *Social proof: People follow the lead of similar others.* Persuasion can have high impact when it comes from peers. This is one reason why messages sent by *friends* on social networking sites often have such high impact. One way to implement this principle of persuasion is to enlist the help of a person's peer in selling him or her an idea, such as making use of a new technology that you think will help the group.

4. *Consistency: People align with their clear commitments.* People need to feel committed to what you want them to do. After people have taken a stand in favor of a position, they prefer to stay with that commitment. Suppose as a team leader you want your team members to find ways to use less energy in your department. If the team members talk about their plans to reduce energy consumption, and also post their plans on a company website, they are more likely to follow through.

5. *Authority: People defer to experts.* Because people really do defer to experts, the action plan here is to make the people you are trying to persuade aware of your expertise. In many fields it is possible to obtain certification in addition to formal education that enhances your credentials. A well-recognized certification of this nature is the Project Management Professional. Having such certification would help the project leader or member convince others about professional and technical issues.

6. *Scarcity: People want more of what they can have less of.* If people think a resource is scarce, they will often be convinced to act quickly to obtain this resource, as in the advertising gimmick "While supplies last." One way to apply this principle is to persuade people by using information not readily available to others. The supervisor might say, "I have some preliminary safety data. If we can be accident free for just three more weeks, we will have the best safety record in the plant." (Of course, if the supervisor fabricates information, he or she will soon be discovered and will lose credibility for later attempts at persuasion.)

The developer of these principles explains that they should be applied in combination to multiply their impact. For example, while establishing your expertise you might simultaneously praise people for their accomplishments. It is also essential to be ethical, such as by not fabricating data to influence others.[4]

Persuasiveness also enhances a person's image because it helps get work accomplished in the modern organization, in which the cooperation is needed of many workers over whom one lacks formal authority. According to the research of Erin White, managers say they increasingly must use influence—rather than commanding others—to accomplish their own work. This trend has come about because of shorter hierarchies and the erosion of barriers among divisions. Managers frequently work with peers where lines of authority are unclear or do not exist.[5]

The unsophisticated approach to persuasion is to focus on the self, with frequent references to one's own talents. A more sophisticated approach that ultimately creates a more positive impression is to focus on the needs of the target. Jerome Clark, a vice president of the T. Rowe Price Group, Inc., a financial services firm, observes: "Your audience will be appropriately me-focused. The key when it comes to persuasion is to know what the benefit is to your prospective client or even to management within your company. Internally or externally, the same factors come into play."[6]

Persuasiveness, as with most impression management tactics, should take into account cultural differences. Being cognizant of how others in a particular culture behave is always helpful. For example, in attempting to persuade British people it is best not to be overbearing or to overstate your case because British people in general prefer less extravagant terms. In attempting to convince a group of professionals from England it might be better to say, "I think my idea has merit," than "I've got a fabulous, can't-miss, suggestion."

Developing a Positive Reputation

Organizational actors who build a good reputation create a positive impression. At the same time, creating a positive impression helps build a good reputation. Building a good reputation is also important for being powerful, and being powerful, in turn, creates a positive impression. Robert Green notes in *The 48 Laws of Power*:

> Reputation is the cornerstone of power. Through reputation alone you can intimidate and win; once you slip, however, you are vulnerable, and will be attacked on all sides. Make your reputation unassailable. Always be alert to potential attacks and thwart them before they happen. Meanwhile, learn to destroy your enemies by opening holes in their own reputations. Then stand aside and let public opinion hang them.[7]

A reputation can be framed as what other people think of you, including the extent to which other people inside and outside the organization think you are competent. Your behavior, including your written, spoken, and nonverbal communication, contributes to your reputation. Being known as a high performer is the most important contributor to being perceived as competent. Being perceived as competent often requires being visible, such as your name appearing frequently on internal communications, including an intranet. Being assigned to task forces and committees can also enhance a person's reputation as being competent.

A sampling of specific factors that contribute to a person's reputation in the workplace is presented in Figure 4-3. The sampling can only be illustrative because anything a person does, or does not do, might contribute to his or her reputation.

Developing a good reputation is another example of how national and organizational culture can influence the effectiveness of a tactic of self-presentation. In a collectivistic culture and company, it would be more effective to develop a reputation for facilitating group accomplishment (such as being an outstanding team player) than to develop the reputation of individual accomplishment.

Figure 4-3 A Sampling of Determinants of a Person's Reputation in the Workplace.

1. Building good relationships is a major contributor to building a reputation. A good reputation follows a good relationship for both individuals and the total organization. A positive reputation is likely to develop from each party trusting the other. Commitment is also important in the form of each party believing that the relationship is worth the investment of time and money. Also important is the satisfaction that stems from each party feeling that its positive expectations have been met.

2. "Actions speak much louder than words." What you actually accomplish carries more weight that what you say about yourself or your work.

3. Take on a difficult project without being asked. Take the initiative to ask, "What can I help with?" It is also helpful to take on a project that others are avoiding, such as updating an out-of-date database. (See the discussion of organizational citizenship behavior later in the chapter.)

4. Use tact and diplomacy when offering opinions. Being gentle in your criticisms helps avoid the reputation of being an overly critical, disrespectful person.

5. Keep some separation between professional and personal relationships. For example, to maintain a good relationship as a professional, avoid being too candid about your personal life when having lunch with coworkers.

6. Show a healthy degree of independence in your work. Ask for help when needed, but do not develop the reputation of somebody who cannot figure things out for himself or herself.

Source: Peggy Simcic Brønn, "Relationship Outcomes as Determinants of Reputation," *Corporate Communication: An International Journal*, No. 4, 2007, pp. 376–393; Caroline Potter, "Building a Good Reputation at Work," http://hotjobs.yahoo.com, 2007, accessed October 2, 2008; "Building a Relationship Consistent with Your Career Goals," http://www.mindtools.com, accessed June 30, 2009.

Publicizing Personal Connections

A widely used technique of impression management is to inform others of connections you might have with influential people. As explained by Cialdini, a typical approach to using personal connections is to proclaim a positive link to a favorable other.[8] The approach consists of boasting about one's link to an accomplished person. Among the ways this can be accomplished legitimately are to (1) refer to a joint project with the accomplished person, (2) talk about having been his or her subordinate or boss, and (3) mention shared social activities with him or her. Observe that being specific about the positive link goes beyond simply mentioning that you know a person with a favorable reputation.

Publicizing connections can also be used to establish links between the actor and the target. A sales prospect might say, "My family and I spent last weekend at our home on the Jersey shore." Hoping to create a favorable impression, the actor responds, "My grandparents have a home on the Jersey shore also. I love the place."

A variation of publicizing personal connections is the slightly devious impression management technique of claiming association with prestige figures or prestigious institutions.[9] *Name dropping* is the term often associated with this technique. In a workplace with high ethical standards, publicizing personal connections—particularly when exaggerated—would be frowned upon. The association with prestige figures and institutions is used in many ways, including the following:

- A brand manager who wants to be regarded more positively by his manager might say, "At lunch today with Alice (the CEO), she thought my ideas for promoting our new product were really exciting."
- Wanting to impress superiors in the company, a middle manager adds to her credentials in the company database: "Studied at the Darden School, University of Virginia." Her "studying" consisted of taking a weekend seminar in a management development program.
- A business process consultant attempting to build a good relationship with the unit manager to which he is assigned says, "Both your COO (chief operating officer) and many others at Fortune 500 companies think that this program can save a manufacturing division half a million dollars per year."

The link between prestige associations and reputation is that the targets may believe that a person with strong connections made these contacts based on having a good reputation.

Using Appropriate Humor

Another approach to bolstering an impression is to make effective use of humor. The rationale is that most targets believe that having an effective sense of humor is a positive quality that requires a reasonable degree of imagination and cognitive skill.

Ineffective use of humor, such as telling sexist, racist, or gross jokes, or strongly insulting others, is likely to project a negative image. Humor as used by leaders has been the subject of considerable serious inquiry. The same findings would apply to most organizational actors who want to make effective use of humor. Here are a few recommendations based on this research:[10]

- People who occupy high-status roles joke at a higher rate than those of lesser status and tend to be more successful at eliciting laughter from others. (Many public figures attempt to develop a reputation as having a good sense of humor by appearing on *Saturday Night Live*.)
- Self-enhancing humor (building up your self) facilitates the leader's acquisition of power from superiors by increasing the leader's appeal.
- Self-defeating (self-effacing to the extreme) humor is negatively related to power, and may lead to the perception that the leader is too playful and not serious.

Aggressive humor can be used to victimize, belittle, and cause others some type of disparagement—and will lead to negative outcomes such as stress and counter-hostility among group members. (No surprise to readers here.)

Being Civil and Humble

A useful tactic for creating a favorable impression is to avoid or minimize negative behaviors widely practiced by others. Based on research and opinion, at the top of this list would be civility and humility. Being civil makes the actor stand out because many people believe that crude, rude, and obnoxious behavior has become a national problem. A poll of nearly 800 U.S. workers found that 10% witnessed incivility every day on the job, and 20% said they were direct targets of incivility at least once a week.[11] Examples of incivility include the following:

- A salesperson makes sarcastic comments about another employee in front of a customer.
- A coworker initiates phone calls or sends text messages while listening to a presentation at a meeting.
- One worker continues to respond to e-mail or text messages while another is talking to him in person.
- A person whistles or sings constantly in the office (an intensely annoying behavior for many people).[12]

Civility toward subordinates is effective in creating a good impression with them. Terry Bacon, chief executive officer of a human resources consulting group, says:

Employees are not looking for a boss who is a fun-loving, back-slapping buddy. What they want is a professional, respectful manager who is honest, fair and has a strong work ethic. They don't want caring and emotional support, either. What they want is respect and honesty. People should be treated like human beings, not human resources.[13]

Civility toward subordinates has also been linked to positive outcomes for the employer. According to Linda Kaplan Thaler and Robin Koval, leaving a good impression on workers by smiling, offering compliments, sympathy, kind gestures, and little gifts will create a desire in others to work with the manager. The manager will also have better feelings about himself or herself. "Positive impressions are like seeds," the authors contend—"they spread and grow."[14]

Part of being civil is humility, or being humble at the right times. Humility includes the admission that you do not know everything and cannot do everything. A leader who is generally self-confident, but sprinkles confidence with humility, is likely to create a positive impression. Humility includes admitting your mistakes to team members and outsiders. A leader, upon receiving a compliment for an accomplishment, may explain that the group deserves the credit. The case for humility as a leadership trait is made strongly by Stephen G. Harrison, the president of a consulting firm, in his comment about how the definition of great leadership has changed: "Great leadership is manifested or articulated by people who know how to understate it. There is leadership value in humility, the leadership that comes from putting people in the limelight, not you. Great leadership comes from entirely unexpected places. It's understatement, it's dignity, it's service, it's selflessness."[15]

Amy Woods Brinkley, the global risk executive at Bank of America, uses humility to help manage her impression. She says, "It's very important to operate with a confident humility. I certainly don't mean meekness. In many cases, you have to be extremely bold. But you must understand what you know and what you don't know, and pull in people to fill gaps."[16] The process of pulling in people also contributes to a good impression because being asked your opinion is flattering.

Civility increases in effectiveness when applied to workers from a polite culture. For example, professional-level workers in India particularly value appreciation of their good work. The worker who wanted to create a good impression with Indians would therefore look for ways to express genuine appreciation.

Managing Anger Effectively

Understanding how to manage anger and other emotions well is a contributor to impression management. Effective use of emotion is the subpart of emotional intelligence referred to as **self-management**—the ability to control one's emotions and act with honesty and integrity in a consistent and acceptable manner.[17] The organizational actor who throws temper tantrums, swears at subordinates, or cries uncontrollably creates a poor impression. At the other extreme, a person who is emotionally flat also creates a poor impression because he or she is likely to be perceived as bland, uninvolved, and uninterested.

Crying on the job has typically been associated with creating a negative image, suggesting that the crier lacks emotional toughness and control. Nevertheless, showing an occasional tear can enhance a person's image. Stephanie Shields, a psychology professor, observes that, although women still report crying more frequently than men, it has become more socially acceptable since the 2001 terrorist attacks for women and men to cry in a few select situations. The death of a colleague, as well as other tragedies, is a situation warranting a few tears in the workplace. George Merkle, a credit-counseling executive, notes that some managers perceive tears as a natural side-effect of the emotional investment required by many jobs. In the medical field, showing empathy for patients might lead to tears.[18]

Self-Presentation of Work Accomplishments

Another broad category of impression management is to emphasize those aspects of the self most directly related to accomplishing work. Imagine a product design specialist who is managing her impression. For her to use the tactics of impression management already described, she might engage in such behaviors as persuasiveness, talking about her connections, and using humor effectively. To use the tactics to be described here, the design specialist would engage in such behaviors as going beyond the call of duty, becoming a recognized specialist within the company, and taking credit for a breakthrough design. The tactics of self-presentation of work accomplishments are listed in Figure 4-4.

Displaying Organizational Citizenship Behavior

In a meritocracy, a highly effective way to create a positive impression is to step outside one's job description to help coworkers and the company. You become admired for going beyond the call of duty. **Organizational citizenship behavior** is "individual behavior that is discretionary, not directly or explicitly recognized by the formal reward system, and that in aggregate promotes the effective functioning of the organization."[19]

According to its original conception, organizational citizenship behavior has five dimensions. These dimensions are important here because all of them can contribute to the image of individual projects if practiced sensibly and in moderation. The five dimensions of citizenship behavior are as follows:

Figure 4-4 Self-Presentation of Work Accomplishments.

1. Displaying organizational citizenship behavior
2. Being a subject matter expert
3. Taking credit for a favorable event
4. Providing timely progress reports
5. Making a quick showing
6. Demonstrating the ability to multitask

1. *Altruism* refers to behaviors directed at helping a work associate, such as a supervisor or manager.
2. *Generalized compliance* is the label for general employee conscientiousness that goes beyond enforceable work standards, such as those contained in a job description.
3. *Sportsmanship* (or *sportspersonship*) refers to tolerating nuisances on the job, including dealing with an inconvenience without complaining.
4. *Courtesy* refers to informing others before taking actions or making decisions that would affect their work.
5. *Civic virtue* behaviors refer to the active participation and involvement of workers in company affairs, such as attending meetings, and company parties, responding to e-mail and instant messages, and staying abreast of organizational issues.[20]

Although organizational citizenship behavior may appear to be altruistic, Mark Bolino suggests that such behaviors may be impression enhancing and self-serving.[21] The organizational actor does well for himself or herself by doing good for the organization. We concur with Bolino's analysis, and much of the information in this section is based on his theorizing.

How Concerns about Image Drive Citizenship Behavior

Organizational citizenship behavior is generally thought to be aimed at helping others, yet it is also possible that the motive underlying citizenship behavior is to foster a good impression. A prime example is that volunteering for special assignments and helping others may provide workers with opportunities to show off their talents and knowledge, leading to an enhanced image. Similarly, individuals may help others in order to convey the impression that they might also require help on occasion—the tactic of supplication. Organizational citizenship behavior can also be used as part of the intimidation tactic. For instance, if employees are aware that their coworkers cannot stay at work late, they might stay late themselves or threaten to work late. Because they can make their coworkers appear less dedicated in comparison, employees might use such tactics to intimidate their coworkers.

Impression management theorists argue that a primary human motive is to be viewed by others positively, and to avoid being viewed negatively. Engaging in organizational citizenship behavior is an effective means of achieving favorable attributions. The motivation for engaging in such behavior may be both self-enhancement and an authentic desire to help the organization. For example, a woman might go beyond her job description to find ways for the company to save energy. She might want to impress others with the good deeds, yet at the same time she really does want to save her company money as well as help protect the physical environment.

Bolino theorizes that impression management motives moderate the relationship between organizational citizenship behavior and work-group or organizational effectiveness. Specifically, the relationship between citizenship and effectiveness is weaker when organizational citizenship behaviors are motivated by impression management concerns. The weaker link to effectiveness might take place because the person who is more intent on impression management might not put as much legitimate effort into the supplementary (extra-role) tasks he or she performs. One reason for the lesser effort is that the worker concerned with impression management might be distracted from the task at hand. A specific example here is that a worker who volunteers to join an energy-reduction task force just to look good might show up at meetings, and make only superficial efforts to contribute.

Recent research also suggests that impression management motives can contribute to citizenship behavior in a positive way. Adam M. Grant and David M. Mayer investigated how prosocial (helping others) and impression management motives relate to affiliative citizenship behavior. *Affiliative* citizenship behaviors are activities directed toward maintaining the status quo by promoting and supporting work processes and relationships that already exist. Citizenship behaviors of this type help bring stability to the organization. Two studies about this aspect of impression management and citizenship behavior were conducted with close to 800 working supervisor-subordinate teams in a variety of settings. Supervisory and coworker ratings were used to judge citizenship behavior, and questionnaires were used to measure motives for prosocial behavior and impression management.

The first study found that impression management motives strengthened the positive association between prosocial motives and affiliative interpersonal citizenship behaviors in two nonprofit organizations. Workers intent on creating a good impression and who had prosocial motivation were more likely to help maintain the status quo in a helpful way. The citizenship behaviors were rated by supervisors. The second study found that impression management strengthened the positive association between prosocial motives and citizenship behavior among a diverse sample of employees. Supervisor and coworker ratings were used to evaluate affiliative citizenship behavior in the second study.[22]

Impression-Management-Relevant Characteristics of Organizational Citizenship Behavior

A practical consideration is how characteristics of organizational citizenship might be linked to impression management. Bolino describe five possibilities:

1. *Type.* Certain types of organizational citizenship behavior are more image enhancing than others. For example, in organizations that value cooperation, *altruism* behaviors will probably be the most image enhancing.
2. *Target.* Citizenship behaviors directed at certain individuals may be more effective at attaining the actor's image-enhancing goals. For example, helping an immediate manager or a higher-ranking manager might do more for one's image than helping a coworker.
3. *Audience.* The status of the citizenship observers, and how many observers are present, may affect the image-enhancing potential of the organizational

citizenship behaviors. Citizenship behavior witnessed by a large number of powerful people is likely to facilitate setting impression management goals more than if such behaviors are witnessed by an individual person of low status. Volunteering to help repair hurricane damage might fit here, assuming that people in power later observed the heroics on a video recording.

4. *Timing.* Displaying organizational citizenship behavior when it counts the most may increase the image-enhancing potential of the behavior. For instance, staying late will probably be highly valued in general. However, staying late when a critical assignment is due is likely to have a stronger impact for image enhancement.

5. *Magnitude.* The drama associated with a given act of organizational citizenship behavior is likely to influence its image-enhancing potential. Coming to the office during a crippling snow storm is likely to enhance a person's image more than lending another worker a cell phone.[23]

The general point of the above list is that acts of organizational citizenship behavior vary in their contribution to creating a positive impression. To make effective use of citizenship behavior for purposes of impression management, the above factors should be taken into account.

The Potential Downside of Using Organizational Citizenship Behavior for Image Enhancement

According to the analysis of Diane M. Bergeron, too much effort invested in organizational citizenship behavior may have negative career consequences. A worker might therefore be cautious about relying too heavily on organizational citizenship behavior as a tactic of impression management.

The general point of the theorizing in question is that organizations tend to reward employees based on good job performance. Because task performance is part of an employee's job description or role, positive job performance is assumed to lead to positive outcomes such as good performance evaluations, salary increases, bonuses, promotions, and the avoidance of being downsized. In contrast, because organizational citizenship behavior is usually not prescribed in a worker's role or job description, it may not be rewarded as is task performance. Bergeron's position is that a fixed increment of task performance has a higher likelihood of reward than might a comparable increment in citizenship behavior.

To circumvent this dilemma it is best for the organizational actor to engage in forms of organizational citizenship behavior that are less time consuming, such as being courteous and friendly. Being courteous and friendly can be accomplished while doing other more strictly task-related work.[24]

Another potential downside of using organizational citizenship behavior as a strategy or tactic of impression management is that the behavior may lead to role overload. Bolino and Turnely studied the initiative-taking aspect of organizational citizenship behavior with a sample of 98 couples. As measured in the study in question, initiative related to the extent to which employees come into work early or stay at work late, volunteer for special projects, check e-mail or voice-mail from home and on vacation, and so forth. Ratings of individual initiative were provided by the worker's spouse or significant other.

The study found that higher levels of individual initiative are associated with higher levels of employee role overload, job stress, and work-family conflict.[25] Job stress, in turn, can lead to lowered job performance, which can reflect negatively on the worker's image. The state of being highly stressed may lead to negative changes in physical appearance that detract from superficial aspects of a person's image.

Becoming a Subject Matter Expert

Becoming a subject matter expert on a topic of importance to the organization is an effective strategy for creating a good impression as well as gaining influence.[26] Being a subject matter expert is also useful as an impression management tactic because it facilitates being able to persuade others. Managers who possess expert knowledge in a relevant field and who continually build on that knowledge can get others to help them get work accomplished. Many leaders use expert knowledge to create a positive image as well as influence others. Small-business owners, in particular, rely on being subject matter experts because they founded the business on the basis of their product or technical knowledge. For example, the head of a software company is usually an expert in software development. Being an expert is useful in creating the right image for outsiders such as potential recruits, customers, and investors.

Steve Jobs is an extraordinary example of a subject matter expert because of his heavy involvement in many product developments at Apple Corp. and Pixar over the years. The aura of being a brilliant marketer and technology whiz is based on his subject matter expertise. The negative aspects of Jobs' image, such as being a control freak, impatient, verbally abusive, and needlessly insulting, are based on his personality characteristics, not his expertise.

Taking Credit for a Favorable Event

A major tactic of self-presentation of work accomplishments is to take credit for a favorable event. Stephen P. Robbins uses the term *acclaiming* for this tactic, defined as an explanation of favorable events by the individual which maximizes the positive implications for the individual.[27] A basic example would be for a product manager to take credit for the growth in sales of a product since he or she was appointed to the position.

A major weakness of the tactic of taking credit for a favorable event is that most people recognize that favorable events in an organization are team accomplishments, and therefore the individual should not receive too much credit. An exception is that

CEOs often take credit for growth in profits and stock prices during their tenure. Similarly, a CEO's image is quickly downgraded when profits and stock prices plummet during his or her tenure.

In general, taking credit for a favorable event is more likely to enhance a person's image when he or she takes some credit, but also shares credit with the team. A mortgage officer at a bank who wanted to take credit for the bank unloading a bunch of high-risk mortgages might therefore say: "During the last quarter my strategy for selling our worst-performing mortgages worked quite well. However, without my team of dedicated and talented specialists, we could never have pulled it off."

Taking undue credit for a favorable event, including taking credit for the ideas of subordinates, can quickly damage a manager's reputation. Such behavior creates an image of being unethical.

Providing Timely Progress Reports

A challenge in most organizations is to find an effective way of promoting yourself to your immediate manager, thereby enhancing your image. Business writer Cheryl Dahle contends that managers who recognize and reward employees are relatively rare. The person wanting to be noticed, and create a favorable impression, must therefore take the initiative to keep the boss informed about developments of merit.[28]

Regular progress reports are viewed as a good basic approach to keeping the manager informed. Ideally, a manager or professional-level worker has a list of specific goals that stemmed from a recent performance review, or a set of projective objectives to track. Under these conditions, the boss can be sent a memo informing him or her when each goal is accomplished. When a list of goals does not exist, the person can send reports listing outcomes rather than tasks. An example of an outcome would be: "Our website is now updated so customers can pay by credit card, debit card, PayPal, or bank account number."

Listing outcomes is more important than activity because accomplishments create a stronger impression than do activities leading to accomplishments. For example, a manager may not care much that a person spent 65 hours in one month on business development. What is more impressive is that three new clients were added, and a fourth one is pending. The report can be adapted to the needs of the target, including e-mails, Word documents, text messages, and voice-mail.

A more subtle approach to filing progress reports is to have regular, informal conversations with the manager about accomplishments. Peggy Klaus observes that storytelling can be an image-enhancing way of communicating accomplishments. She advises, "When we talk about the accomplishments of someone we adore and are proud of, we tell a story. We include the context, the drama, the challenge—all these interesting tidbits. And then when we go to talk about ourselves, we forget these skills. We slip into a monotone and deliver a laundry list."[29]

Making a Quick Showing

A well-established tactic for making a favorable impression related to job accomplishments is to display job competence in a first or other early assignment. A display of dramatic results can help gain acceptance for one's efforts or those of the group. Once a person has impressed management with his or her ability to solve that first problem, he or she can look forward to working on problems that will bring greater power. A staff professional might volunteer to spruce up a company website to make it more appealing. After accomplishing that feat, the person might be invited to join the e-commerce team.

Making a quick showing is a positive impression management tactic for two primary reasons. First, many targets are impressed by speed in the form of rapid results, so the actor who produces results quickly is viewed positively. Second, most organizational cultures value workers accomplishing tangible results. The more rapidly these results are evident, the more favorable will be the person's image.

On the flip side, *not* making a quick showing will sometimes result in a manager being fired in less than a year. Two of dozens of possible examples in recent years are that Adobe Systems Inc. and Sears Holdings Corp. both fired chief financial officers within six months because the officers were unable to attain outstanding results quickly.[30] (However, we do not know what other errors in impression management these executives made.)

Demonstrating the Ability to Multitask

Many people are impressed when an organizational actor either brags about multitasking, or engages in multitasking in their presence. From a technical standpoint, *multitasking* refers to engaging in two or more tasks simultaneously. Another interpretation of multitasking, however, is that the person is involved with two or more projects or large tasks, even if they are performed sequentially. For example, a person might be assigned to two task forces that do not meet at the same time, or the same person might be the CEO of two companies. A highly publicized example is Carlos Ghosn, who is the chief executive officer at both Nissan and Renault. To be in charge of one or more projects or companies contributes to an image of major accomplishment.

Multitasking on simultaneous tasks in the workplace takes such forms as the following: a manager dashing from one brief discussion to another while consulting a BlackBerry or other model personal digital assistant; a staff member sending or receiving text messages while attending an in-person meeting; and a manager sending and receiving cell phone messages while attending a videoconference.

Showing the ability to multitask illustrates an impression management tactic that offers some positive consequences, yet also has substantial negative consequences. One negative consequence from a human relations standpoint is that multitasking is perceived as rude by many targets. Reading e-mails on a BlackBerry while in conversation with others tends to diminish the importance of the person physically present. Similarly, talking on a cell phone while entertaining a client in a restaurant will be perceived as rude by some clients.

The negative cognitive consequences of multitasking are considerable for most people. David E. Meyer, the director of the Brain, Cognition and Action Laboratory at the University of Michigan, notes that when people attempt to perform two or more related tasks at the same time or alternating rapidly—instead of doing them sequentially—two negative consequences occur. Errors increase substantially, and the amount of time to perform the task may double.[31] Also, according to new research about the brain, few people can concentrate on more than four tasks at once.[32]

Personal finance advisor and television personality Suzie Orman is a strong advocate of avoiding multitasking when doing serious work. As a celebrity, Orman appears to be highly image conscious. She prides herself on her ability to focus on one thing at a time and adhere to her agenda. She says, "The people who multitask, I think, do everything to mediocrity at best. While they are getting a lot done, they are getting it done in such an inefficient way that they usually have to do it over again."[33]

Avoiding Unfavorable Self-Presentation

The thrust of this book is to describe tactics, and supporting research and theory where possible, that facilitate creating a positive impression. An exception, as mentioned in Chapter 1, is that creating a positive impression is not always a person's goal. At times people deliberately want to create a negative impression for purposes such as avoiding additional responsibility. Also, an actor might want to create a negative impression or fake illness in order to receive a higher disability payment or remain on disability payments longer. Our focus in this section is on unintentionally creating a negative impression. The actor wants to be perceived positively by targets, but lacks the sensitivity to recognize that he or she is creating a negative impression.

As just implied, an important strategy for creating a positive impression is to avoid creating a negative impression. If reversed, any tactic described in this chapter or throughout the book could create a negative impression in many situations. For example, if making a quick showing creates a positive impression, making a slow showing would create a negative impression. Situational factors, including the organizational culture, heavily influence whether a given behavior will create a negative impression. Multitasking during meetings is a prime example. In some organizations, such as many high-tech companies, it is considered acceptable behavior to use a laptop computer or consult a BlackBerry during a meeting. An example is that the former CEO of Xerox Corp., Anne M. Mulcahy, admits to glancing at a BlackBerry on her lap while others are speaking at a meeting. At other organizations, such behavior is considered to be unacceptably rude. Alan Mullaly, the CEO of Ford Motor Company, insists that participants at a meeting avoid the use of electronic devices during business meetings.

The possibilities for creating a negative impression are almost unlimited, yet have received little attention from scholars, possibly because what constitutes a negative image is often obvious. Speech is one of the many areas in which negative images are readily created. Diane DiResta, a speech pathologist, who operates her own communications consulting firm, describes the importance of effective speech in these terms:

> If you want to get to a certain level, especially in a professional environment like most businesses, you have to project the right image. You have to speak the way people you aspire to be speak. Your speech is related to status.[34]

In recognition of the fact that the possibilities for creating a negative impression are almost unlimited, Figure 4-5 lists a sampling of behaviors that would most likely create a negative impression in many work-related situations. The negative tactics are loosely organized into self-presentation of characteristics and behaviors, and self-presentation of work accomplishments. People with good insight and social sensitivity would typically be able to avoid these negative behaviors and faux pas.

Figure 4-5 Tactics for Attaining Negative Self-Promotion.

Almost any insensitive deed or statement can contribute to a person's negative impression. A sampling of such deeds and behaviors is included in this table.

Self-Presentation of Characteristics and Behaviors
1. Mumbling, placing the hand over the mouth, and using no facts while trying to persuade another person.
2. Making negative self-statements, such as "I'm certainly not the smartest person in the room, but will you listen to my idea?"
3. Writing business e-mail messages and instant messages in the same style used by many adolescents and teenagers in communicating with peers, and by many adults when sending "Tweets" (messages on Twitter).
4. Appearing so immature, unprofessional, and uninterested that you quickly develop a negative reputation with your employer or employers.
5. Admitting that your social network is so limited, you can find no one to help you with problems.
6. Laughing at a coworker's suggestion when he or she is serious.
7. Ignoring another worker while he or she is talking by such means as looking at your watch, talking on a cell phone, or checking your e-mail.
8. Maintaining a deadpan expression when others are laughing.
9. Telling racist, sexist, and ethnic jokes that demean the status of others.

10. Shouting, screaming, and swearing at coworkers and subordinates in order gain control of situations.

11. Frequently talking about your own strengths and accomplishments, yet ignoring the strengths and accomplishments of others.

12. Making immature excuses for being late, such as "My alarm clock broke," "The traffic was the worst I've ever seen," and "My hard drive crashed."

13. Denying rather than apologizing for mistakes that were legitimately your fault.

14. Making up implausible excuses for problems such as: "The customer was ready to close the deal but then he found out that his sister was selling the same product as we do."

15. Displaying outbursts of anger when a work associate disagrees with you.

16. Weeping loudly after having received a worse-than-average performance evaluation.

17. Appearing unenthusiastic, even bored, when others talk about their problems, frustrations, and accomplishments.

Self-Presentation of Work Accomplishments

1. Sticking tightly to working within your job description.

2. Demonstrating no particular area of expertise.

3. When asked a job-related question, your typical reply is, "I don't know. I haven't 'Googled' it yet."

4. When asked to perform a task outside of your job description, refusing with the statement, "That's not my job."

5. Dropping work immediately, even in the middle of responding to a question sent by e-mail, precisely at quitting time.

6. Finding a plausible excuse to abstain when invited to join a task force, project, or committee.

7. Assigning yourself implausible amounts of credit for accomplishments within your organizational unit.

8. Starting off slowly on a new assignment, and making no visible progress after several months.

9. Keeping your boss uninformed about your progress on a project or assignment.

10. Keeping no documentation of your progress on a project or assignment.

11. Expressing resentment when your boss asks for a progress report.

12. Procrastinating about finishing a report or supplying information your manager needs.

13. Multitasking to the extent that you make so many errors others question your intelligence.

Guidelines for Application and Practice

1. An effective way of persuading others is to focus on their needs and interests. Having shown a sincere interest in others paves the way for selling your ideas, and creating a stronger image in the process.

2. Being civil and polite will often create a strong impression because rudeness and incivility are so widely practiced today. The widespread problem of rudeness has created a strong market for training in etiquette.

3. A health newsletter reminds us that constantly expressing anger can alienate others as well as contributing to health problems including headaches, intestinal disorders, and a heart attack. To take control, follow these steps: (1) Count to 10. When something angers you, give your body time to react. (2) Walk it off. Go for a short stroll until you calm down. (3) Distract yourself. Dive into a task to turn negative energy into positive. (4) Keep a log. Monitor hostile thoughts to discover how frequently your temperature rises. (5) Ask for help. If managing outbursts seems impossible, try counseling, meditation, relaxation techniques, or lifestyle changes.[35]

4. A broad job-focused strategy for creating a positive impression is to be a good organizational citizen. Among the components of citizenship behavior would be taking the initiative on problems and doing extra work; conscientiousness, tolerating ordinary nuisances, being courteous, and participating in company affairs and responding quickly to e-mails. All of these specific behaviors would enhance your image and contribute to high performance. However, certain types of organizational citizenship behavior can be more image enhancing than others, such as altruism being important in an organization that values cooperation.

5. Becoming a subject matter expert on a topic of importance to the organization is an effective strategy for creating a good impression as well as gaining influence. A recommended approach is to specialize in a narrow area of expertise of current and potentially future value to the organization.

6. When taking credit for an event, it is better to explain how you played a major role in the success of the event rather than attempting to take too much, or all, of the credit. The reason is that most significant projects in organizations are team or group activities that require the collaboration of many people. To take too much credit can challenge your credibility, therefore detracting from a positive image.

7. Making a quick showing is yet another impression management tactic that is also functional for the organization. The idea is to display job competence in a first or other early assignment.

8. A general approach to positive impression management is to avoid a wide variety of behaviors that would ordinarily create a negative impression. Poor speech is one aspect of behavior that can create a negative impression. A person needs some careful self-reflection to decide which of his or her

behaviors might be creating a negative impression. Feedback from a trusted person can also help you identify areas needing improvement.

Summary

A major thrust of managing your impression is to demonstrate or imply that you possess characteristics and behaviors that make you a person of worth and a contributor to the department, team, division, or organization. These characteristics and behaviors include (1) being persuasive, (2) developing a positive reputation, (3) publicizing personal connections, (4) using appropriate humor, (5) being civil and humble, and (6) managing anger effectively. The six principles of persuasion can be helpful in being persuasive, as follows: liking, reciprocity, social proof, consistency, authority, and scarcity.

Another broad category of impression management is to emphasize those aspects of the self most directly related to work accomplishment. The tactics of self-presentation of work accomplishment include (1) displaying organizational citizenship behavior, (2) becoming a subject matter expert, (3) taking credit for a favorable report, (4) providing timely progress reports, (5) making a quick showing, and (6) demonstrating the ability to multitask—but watch out for rudeness and performance problems.

In its original conception, organizational citizenship behavior has five dimensions: altruism, generalized compliance, sportsmanship, courtesy, and civic virtue. Initiative taking is also important. Organizational citizenship behavior is generally thought to be aimed at helping others, yet it is also possible that the underlying motive is to foster a good impression. The relationship between citizenship behavior and organizational effectiveness is weaker when citizenship behaviors are motivated by impression management concerns. Organizational citizenship behavior can be linked to impression management via five dimensions: type, target, audience, timing, and magnitude.

Organizational citizenship behavior for impression management has two potential downsides. First, the behavior may detract from direct job performance. Second, organizational citizenship behavior may lead to role overload, job stress, and work-family conflict. An overly stressed person might create a poor image.

An important strategy for creating a positive impression is to avoid creating a negative one. If reversed, any tactic described in this chapter or throughout this book could create a negative impression in many situations. In recognition of the fact that the possibilities for creating a negative impression are almost unlimited, Figure 4-5 lists a sampling of behaviors that would most likely create a negative impression in many work-related situations.

The impression management tactics described in this chapter in large part can be translated directly into guidelines for application and practice. One example is that being civil and polite will often create a strong impression because rudeness and incivility are so widely practiced today. Another example is that a broad job-focused strategy for creating a positive impression is to be a good organizational citizen.

Chapter 5

Surface-Level Approaches to Self-Presentation

In everyday understanding, impression management refers to actions that make a person look good (and perhaps well) on the surface, such as dressing in style, looking physically fit, smiling frequently, and giving firm handshakes. Indeed, all of these behaviors are part of impression management, even if they focus more on superficial characteristics, rather than personality and cognitive characteristics. **Surface-level self-presentation tactics** are those aspects of impression management that focus on readily observable behaviors rather than underlying characteristics. Because a change is on the surface, it does not mean that the change is not important. For example, changing the manner of dress or nonverbal language can have an enormous impact on how well a person is received.

We caution that the difference between deeper-level and surface-level presentation characteristics is not always clear cut, and that the categories overlap. One of many possible examples is social etiquette. Not chewing gum while giving a PowerPoint presentation is surface-level behavior, indicating knowledge of social etiquette. Yet having enough social sensitivity to know that such behavior might be offensive to some people reflects emotional intelligence. An example of an overlapping category to be described in this chapter is *personal branding*, whereby you highlight your assets, giving yourself a brand somewhat similar to Dr. Pepper or Lexus. However, it is your deeper-level characteristics that enable you to create the brand.

Another way of stating the same issue is that inner characteristics direct or lead to more superficial characteristics. You might smile to create a good impression, thereby engaging a surface-level, or superficial, behavior. However, your internal characteristic of insight into people prompted you to understand that a smile would be an effective way of creating a good impression in this situation.

The surface-level self-presentation tactics described in this chapter are outlined in Figure 5-1. We present relevant empirical research where possible, yet most of the tactics described here await additional scholarly research or have yet to receive such research. Although the approaches to impression management described in this chapter are a vital part of impression management, they are superficial from a physical standpoint and in terms of their research substantiation. Figure 5-2 lists the three topics described in this chapter that are the most substantiated by empirical research.

Figure 5-1 Surface-Level Self-Presentation Tactics.

Figure 5-2 Aspects of Surface-Level Approaches to Impression Management Most Supported by Empirical Research

1. Emotional reactions to women perceived to be dressed overly sexily
2. Relationship between physical height and workplace success
3. Negative organizational consequences of rudeness and incivility

Clothing, Dress, and Appearance

A person's clothing, dress, and physical appearance, including sexiness as perceived by others, contribute substantially to the image he or she projects. Much of the popular advice about image improvement deals with a person's outer appearance down to such details as hair styling, handbags, carrying case, and jewelry. Here we describe some of the opinion and research evidence about the link between impression management, and clothing, dress, and appearance. *Dress* in this context refers to a particular type of apparel or guise. Appearance includes weight, height, and grooming.

Clothing and Dress

Common knowledge, along with the advice of career advisors and wardrobe consultants, indicates that clothing is used to manage the impression a person creates. The impression management value of clothing helps explain why people engage in such behaviors as purchasing $2,000 suits or $4,500 handbags. A study with a sample of MBA students reinforces the widely held belief that clothing is often used to create a positive impression. The study found that those who valued workplace attire used it to manage the impressions others formed of them. The students also believed that the clothing worn to work has a positive impact on the way they feel about themselves and the workplace outcomes. For example, wearing stylish, well-fitting clothing helped many of the study participants feel more self-confident and poised. They also believed that their supervisors thought more highly of them because of their choice of clothing.

Dressing to impress others appeared to be particularly effective for high self-monitors and for those in managerial and executive positions. Women were found to have a stronger interest in clothing, and worried more about their appearance than did their male counterparts.[1]

Advice, as opposed to empirical research, is plentiful about how to use clothing and dress for impression management. Much of the advice is consistent, making it possible to summarize this vast body of information into seven categories:

1. *What a businessman should wear.* Designer guru Giorgio Armani summed up his many years of styling experience by offering businessmen five tips. (Armani's advice here is aimed at executives.) First, polyester is a fantastic fabric because it is flexible and does not crease. Second, linen is a disaster because it wrinkles so quickly you look like you have been hit by a truck. Third, it is a myth that men only look credible when they wear pinstripes, an oxford shirt, a regimental tie, and English shoes. Fourth, men look good in shirts and jackets that show a few curves, but are also comfortable. The look should be neither sloppy nor stiff. Fifth, sports jackets should not be worn to a board meeting, sports jackets are for weekends.[2]

2. *How managerial and professional women should dress.* Women in higher-level positions should focus on practicality rather than fashion. Michaela Jedinak, a London-based media and entertainment lawyer, says that women need hard-wearing clothing that does not look sloppy and wrinkled by late afternoon. Women should not wear make-up that must be reapplied because it will make them too self-conscious. A style mistake can be career limiting. Yet too much attention paid to one's appearance risks accusations of frivolity, which can also be career limiting.[3] Situational factors are always important in choosing the appropriate degree of femininity to project in clothing. Even in fields as conservative as banking, the guidelines on what appearance is too feminine are changing. In some brokerage firms, for example, colorful dresses, bold handbags, and even tall boots with skirts are acceptable.[4]

3. *Dress to impress year-round.* According to certified image consultant Diane Feldon, the way you dress "is what you say without saying a word. It's about learning what colors, styles, and fabrics look best on you." It is best for men to wear a long-sleeve shirt when wearing a suit. Tailored khakis or slacks with

a shirt and tie and blazer are more casual. If a tie is not required in your office, wear a collared polo shirt. During the summer, use lightweight fabrics, such as tropical wool or micro fiber. Stick with fabrics that stay looking crisp, and avoid linen. Women wearing city shorts, a skirt, or low-cut blouse should check for modesty issues by using a mirror or receiving feedback from a friend.[5]

4. *Avoid the wardrobe gaffe of appearing too seductive.* Dorothy Waldt, a New York executive recruiter, said that even people applying for executive positions do not understand the messages that their clothes send. She notes that women sometimes do not realize how often a tight skirt or low neckline comes across as seductive. People they meet often assume that the sexual innuendo is intentional. It is more difficult for men to goof up, but they often do. For example, they might be sloppy with untucked or wrinkled shirts or wearing beeping sports watches to conservative business events.[6] A related recommendation is that when an executive attends an after-hours business social occasion, such as a dinner meeting, she should avoid highly sexy attire such as a backless dress, and showing décolletage (cleavage). Patty Fox, a stylist and fashion coordinator for the Academy Awards, advises women to not step outside the bounds of their personal style, even for a special occasion.[7]

5. *Size up the environment when choosing clothing.* To complicate matters about what to wear, following the old dress-for-success rules with ties and starched white shirts would create suspicion and awkwardness at the dressed-down headquarters of most information-technology companies. (As mentioned above, situational factors weigh heavily in decisions about effective clothing and dress.) Job candidates may want to telephone the hiring manager's assistant or ask a recruiter about the appropriate look before they show up for the interview. The general principle is to have clothing match the culture of the industry of the potential employer. When in doubt about a jacket, tie, or other accessory, bring one along. You can remove it, but you can't wear it if you do not have it.[8] Another example of a dress factor that requires a situational analysis is the use of perfume or cologne. In some business settings, such as a high-end retailer, perfume and cologne are considered to be in good taste. In many other settings, wearing a fragrance is regarded as an intrusion on the rights of others.

6. *Dress professionally in the workplace.* Even when taking into account situational factors, dressing professionally in the workplace helps create a positive impression. For example, in workplaces where jeans are acceptable office attire, the jeans worn to the office should not be the same jeans used to work in the garden or attend little league soccer matches. The president of retail sales for a high-fashion clothing store advises:

How you project yourself will greatly determine how others will treat, respect and listen to you, especially if they don't know you. Use image to constantly establish how well you work not only with the tasks at hand, but how much more you can accomplish. Looking and feeling your best sends a clear message that you are at your best, too. Always dress for the job that you want and not for the one that you have.[9]

(The last point is standard advice that has attained cliché status, yet it probably applies well in many work situations.)

7. *Watch out for too many electronic devices dangling from your clothing.* It is not unusual for the wired worker to have several electronic gadgets dangling from his or her belt and head, including a personal digital assistant, a cell phone, a miniature laptop computer, a flash drive, and a hands-free microphone and speaker (such as Bluetooth) on the ear. With all this equipment, the person may project the image of a repair technician when he or she wants to project another image. Also, carrying so much electronic equipment increases the temptation to consult a device such as a BlackBerry while speaking to another person.

An experimental point of view about appearance is to see what happens if you change your appearance. For example, if an organizational actor who used grunge as a fashion standard changes to more business-like attire will he or she attain more successful career outcomes? One person who changed his image, and whose success multiplied after the image change, is Alex Bogusky. He also modified the image of his department. Bogusky is now the executive creative director of the highly acclaimed advertising firm Crispin Porter + Bogusky that won the Microsoft account in 2008.

At age 24 Bogusky was striving to become the junior art director at a small advertising agency. He decided to disrupt how people positioned him in their mind mostly by changing his hair from a crew cut to a Mohawk to long hair to a mullet. He also changed his hair color.

At age 42, Bogusky began to change the image of his agency rather than himself, including changing the titles of departments and people. He believes that by making frequent changes the agency will not be evaluated by the same standard as the previous year.[10]

By making changes in his appearance, Bogusky believes that people thought differently about him. He then began making superficial changes in the image of the agency to change its image.

Perceptions of Sexiness Based on Clothing

Clothing and dress contribute to physical appearance, and the type of clothing worn influences the extent to which a person is perceived as sexy. As everyday knowledge suggests, some clothing is considered to be sexy. Furthermore, an impression of sexiness can contribute to a perception of being competent in some positions, and can lower perceptions of competence in other positions.

A study published in the *Psychology of Women Quarterly* hypothesized that women who dress in a sexy (rather than business-like) manner evoke negative emotions and perceptions of lesser competence if employed in high-status jobs.[11] It was also hypothesized that in lower-status jobs sexy dress would not evoke negative emotions and perceptions of lower competence. The experimental design was for male and female undergraduate students to evaluate videos of a female target whose physical attractiveness was held constant. However, the target was (1) dressed in sexy or business-like attire, and (2) labeled as either a manager or a receptionist. Sexy attire was defined in terms of clothing and grooming emphasizing sexuality.

It was found that study participants exhibited more negative affect toward the sexily dressed manager and rated her as less competent than the manager dressed in business attire. The stronger the emotional reaction, the less competent the woman target was perceived to be. In contrast, manipulating the attire had no effect on emotions toward or competence ratings of the receptionist.

The authors concluded that a sexy self-presentation creates a negative impression in high-status jobs, but not in low-status jobs. It was also stated that a backlash exists against women in high-ranking positions who tend toward dressing provocatively. The researchers also observed that more limited clothing choices for men spare them from too-sexy perceptions. (The researchers may have been unaware of some of the newer business clothing choices for men, including pajama-style suits.) The implication for impression management is that managerial and professional women will create a better impression if they dress in business attire, and that women in low-status jobs need not have the same concerns.

Perceptions of Appearance Based on Obesity and Complaints about Health

According to the National Center for Health Statistics, two-thirds of American adults are either overweight or obese. Despite physical heaviness being essentially normative behavior, being perceived as considerably overweight usually contributes to a negative image. Several employers, including CFI Westgate Resorts and Microsoft Corp., offer employees financial incentives for avoiding obesity. Also, a bank in Indiana raised employee health insurance deductibles from $500 to $2,500, but offered $500 credits to employees who passed screenings for cholesterol, body mass index, blood pressure, and tobacco.[12] *Body mass index* is an estimation of body fat based on height and weight.

Obesity status becomes part of impression management when the individual purposely avoids obesity to create a more favorable impression. Or, the obese individual might lose weight in order to create a more favorable impression in the workplace.

Company efforts directed toward curbing employees being overweight are strongly motivated by finances because overweight employees suffer from more physical illnesses such as high blood pressure and diabetes. Nevertheless, the fact that employers value body mass indexes in the acceptable range adds to the negative image created by being considerably overweight.

Making human resource decisions based on obesity status or body mass index can lead to charges of job discrimination. A possible ethical violation might exist also, following the ethical principles of (1) not wanting a loved one to be treated in this manner, and (2) having the action publicized.

A partial contributor to the perceptions of a person's physical appearance is his or her self-statements about physical status. An individual who occasionally mentions feeling energetic or being in top form will improve his or her chances of being perceived as having a positive physical appearance. An executive newsletter recommends that to safeguard your image you should avoid complaints about your health problems, even during casual chats with close network members. Griping about bodily aches or poorly functioning eyeglasses will erode your image of vitality in the eyes of younger workers.[13]

Height as a Contributor to Image Projection

Weight and self-statements about health are somewhat controllable factors for purposes of projecting a desired image. Height is a much less controllable factor contributing to a person's image. A major reason that height contributes to a person's perceived impression is that above-average height has long been associated with positive organizational outcomes. The notion that taller people are more successful in business has been supported by scholarly analysis.

Timothy A. Judge and Daniel M. Cable conducted a meta-analysis of the available research literature on the effect of physical height on workplace success. A major finding was that height has a positive relationship with success in the workplace. Based on 45 independent studies, a positive correlation was found between height and success as measured in terms of pay level and promotions. Height was also significantly related to earnings, controlling for the possible effects of sex, age, and weight. (For example, seniority might contribute to earnings, and being older might also contribute to weight!) A specific finding was that an individual who is 72 inches tall would be predicted to earn almost $166,000 more over a 30-year career than an individual who is 65 inches tall. A study conducted to supplement the meta-analysis revealed that the effect of height is stable over the course of a person's career rather than having an impact early in the career and then dissipating.

The theoretical model developed by Judge and Cable suggests that height affects career success through several mediating, or influencing, processes. First, height affects how individuals perceive themselves, or their self-esteem, and how they are regarded by others, or social esteem. Second, social esteem and self-esteem affect a person's job performance as well as the perception of job performance by immediate managers. In turn, the managerial perceptions of performance affect career success in terms of performance evaluations and recommendations for promotions and other valuable assignments.[14]

Assuming it is true that having above-average height does create a positive impression, organizational actors who are below average in height can take some steps to neutralize the height advantage. In this way they are managing their impression. First, certain clothing designs, such as vertical stripes and higher heels (for both women and men), create the illusion of being taller. Second, the person who is at a height disadvantage can emphasize good posture, which typically enhances the perception of height. Third, the organizational actor who is average or below average in height can invest more effort in other forms of impression management, including enhancing the feelings of well-being of others.

Business Etiquette

People who are polite and courteous, and take into account the needs of others generally create a positive impression in the workplace, as well as personal life. **Business etiquette** is a special code of behavior required in work situations. The term *manners* has an equivalent meaning. Both *manners* and *etiquette* refer to behaving in a refined and acceptable manner. Etiquette is classified here as surface-level behavior only because it involves actions that are typically perceived to be veneer or polish. However, why some people practice good business etiquette, and others are rude and insensitive is based on personality traits and cognitive skills. One example is that it requires some degree of social sensitivity to observe the behavior of others at a business luncheon to decide whether or not to order several alcoholic beverages.

Other examples of internal factors driving etiquette are rudeness and incivility. **Rudeness** is defined as insensitive or disrespectful behavior engaged in by a person who displays a lack of regard for others.[15] What constitutes rudeness depends heavily on the perception of the target. Visualize two people approaching the right side of a double doorway. As they approach the door the two people notice that a man is opening the door at the left side of the doorway so he can enter the building. The two people barge through the door to their left before the man can enter. The man alone is disturbed by what he perceives as rudeness, and confronts the two people about their rudeness. In turn, the two people shrug their shoulders, and one says to the man alone, "You got a problem?" A lack of concern for the rights of others drives the barging through the door. A counter-analysis here is that the man alone entering the door lacks the mental flexibility to redefine what constitutes acceptable behavior in terms of current norms.

As described in Chapter 4, rudeness has negative consequences for the organization in terms of both task performance and others being helpful. Workers subject to rudeness and incivility will often retaliate with rudeness and incivility of their own.[16]

Etiquette expert Letitia Baldrige helps explain why displaying etiquette contributes so heavily to impression management. She contends that the key to success in the workplace is consideration of others and a kind heart.

> Be sensitive to people and they will want to work with you. They will follow you; pull for you, help you get ahead. Success at work depends on people getting along with you. All winners have manners, and the more well-mannered people there are in the workplace, the happier and more profitable they'll be.[17]

Younger workers who practice business etiquette may create a good impression and gain some competitive advantage because they represent a minority. According to business etiquette specialist Amy Joyce, many younger workers have top-notch technical skills but may be lacking in interpersonal and etiquette skills.[18]

The study of business etiquette is a vast topic. Our purposes will be served here by Figure 5-3, which presents key areas of business etiquette with examples of how they relate to impression management. The general point is that the organizational actor who displays good etiquette in the presence of his or her targets will usually enhance his or her self-presentation. An exception is that targets who dislike the display of etiquette might perceive the actor as being pretentious.

Figure 5-3 Aspects of Etiquette and their Potential Links to Impression Management.

Aspects of Etiquette	Potential Links to Impression Management
Work behavior and clothing	Behaviors such as teamwork and completing projects on time create a good impression. Stylish clothing appropriate to the situation makes a strong self-presentation.
Introductions to people	Providing a little information about the person being introduced shows savoir faire, as does mentioning the person of higher rank first.
Relationships between men and women	Business etiquette is based on equal treatment for men and women, yet a little chivalry, such as a man helping a woman shovel snow from under her car, still creates a positive impression.
Relationships between people of different ages	Respect for elders creates a positive impression but not in such ways as holding doors open for them, offering to access their e-mail, or getting coffee for them.
Use of wire and cell telephones	Putting people on hold after a conversation has begun is a low point in rudeness, and therefore creates a negative self-presentation. Making or receiving calls on a cell phone while talking to a manager, colleague, or customer creates a negative impression with many people.
E-mail, instant messaging, and text-by-phone correspondence	The way in which a message is sent says something about the sender. As a result, messages should be sent in a professional manner rather than the casual style used in personal life. Because instant messaging enables you to intrude on coworkers anytime—and them to drop in on you—the opportunities to create a poor impression via rudeness multiply. Using adolescent-style abbreviations in text messaging, such as "CU ltr," creates a poor impression in the workplace.
Use of electronic devices other than telephones	To create a positive impression in using many electronic devices such as the BlackBerry and other personal digital assistants, it is important to size up the culture in terms of their appropriate use. However, consulting a BlackBerry while interacting with a superior or customer usually projects a negative image.

Working in a cubicle	Cubicles represent a major etiquette challenge because a variety of workers and superiors can observe your everyday work behavior. To create a professional image the cubicle inhabitant has to avoid such activities as displaying non-work-related websites, and allowing a loud, musical cell phone incoming message alert to ring.
Cross-cultural relations	A culture must be studied carefully, including asking questions, to understand what constitutes proper etiquette. One example is that in the United Kingdom and India a fork should be used with the left hand, but in the United States, the right hand is preferred. Another example is that business card exchanges are more formal outside the United States. Knowing the preferred method of exchange, such as giving and receiving cards with two hands in China, creates a positive impression.
Interaction with people with disabilities	Being natural and open generally creates a good impression. Two specific suggestions are: (1) Do not assume that a person with a physical disability needs help. If a person is struggling, ask for permission to assist. (2) To get the attention of a deaf person, tap the person's shoulder or wave your hand.

Source: Some of the information is from "Business Etiquette: Teaching Students the Unwritten Rules," *Keying In*, January 1996, pp. 1–8; Jim Rucker and Jean Anna Sellers, "Changes in Business Etiquette," *Business Education Forum*, February 1998, pp. 43–45; Letitia Baldrige, *The Executive Advantage* (Washington, DC: Georgetown Publishing House, 1999), pp. 1–4; "Culture Shock?" *Entrepreneur*, May 1998, p. 46; Ann Perry, "Finer Points of the Meet and Eat," *Toronto Star*, http://www.thestar.com, January 2, 2004; Blanca Torres, "Good Dining Manners Can Help Get a Bigger Slice of the Job Pie," *Baltimore Sun*, April 5, 2005; Erin White, "The Jungle: Focus on Recruitment, Pay and Getting Ahead," *The Wall Street Journal*, November 2, 2004, p. B8; Amy S. Choi, "Etiquette: Business Cards," *Business Week Small Biz*, June/July 2008, p. 28; Andrew J. DuBrin, *Human Relations: Interpersonal Job-Oriented Skills*, 10th ed. (Columbus, OH: Pearson Prentice Hall, 2009), pp. 249–252.

First-Impression Making

First impressions constitute a major force in impression management, as is widely touted by career advisors. The basic memory principle of *primacy* helps explain the importance of first impressions. Primacy refers to the easy recall of items we first perceive on a list.[19] In terms of impression management this means that what we first observe about a person, we tend to remember.

First impressions are based on both overt and subtle cues, depending somewhat on the interests of the target. For example, some people might respond to the actor's hairdo, another target might respond to voice quality and grammar, and another target might respond to the actor's clothing and dress. Among the factors that figure heavily in positive first impressions are the following:[20]

- Comprehensible speech instead of rapid speaking, fusion of words, and a tone inaudible to most people.
- Physical appearance in terms of projecting an image of positive health and energy versus appearing to be in poor health and lacking energy.
- The appropriateness of the dress for the occasion, such as a presenter at an investment seminar wearing formal business attire.
- Personal grooming in terms of such factors as being clean and tidy, being neatly coiffed, and clean teeth.
- Nonverbal cues, including posture, smile, eye contact, and firmness of the handshake. (Nonverbal behavior for impression management will be described later in the chapter.)
- Appearing calm versus displaying indicators of nervousness, including facial tics, frequent touching of the hair or face, and fidgeting.
- Displaying good manners, politeness, attentiveness, alertness, and courteousness.

An important consideration about factors that enter into the creation of a first impression is that some variation within each category is possible. Among these variations are that many different hairdos contribute to a positive first impression, and so do many styles of clothing. Also people can be polite in many ways, including using a person's name, saying thank you, and paying attention. In this way the organizational actor hoping to create a positive impression has some flexibility in conforming to the perceptions of a variety of targets.

Videoconferencing creates new demands on the worker who wants to create a positive impression. Videoconferences are now used for such purposes as informational business meetings, global brainstorming meetings, and job interviews with executive placement firms. Webcasts in which a company transmits audio and video feeds over the Internet or intranet present the same challenges as a videoconference.[21]

All of the factors listed above for face-to-face first impressions apply to videoconferencing. In addition, the opportunities for success or failure are multiplied because a greater number of people will be observing the participants at the videoconference. "The camera magnifies and exaggerates everything," notes Peggy Klaus, a communication coach. You must be on your most impressive behavior from "the moment you put your toe into that room," with the video camera.[22]

Nonverbal Impression Management

As already stated and implied in this chapter, nonverbal behavior contributes heavily to impression management in terms of both first and later impressions. For example, clothing, dress, and appearance can be considered as one category of nonverbal communication. According to Bozeman and Kacmar, evidence from both social psychology and communication theory supports the belief that nonverbal communication is at least as important as verbal communication in determining impressions formed by the audience.[23] One potential reason that nonverbal cues count so heavily in impression management is the perception that people can readily lie with words, but body language is difficult to fake.[24]

Nonverbal communication is a field of study within itself. Here we list each of the better-recognized categories and indicate the behavior that will create a positive—and sometimes negative—impression for the majority of targets.[25]

1. *Environment or setting.* Where the message is sent influences the impression created by the sender, such as talking to a person while in a clean, neat vehicle versus one that is filthy and cluttered.

2. *Distance from the other person.* Although there are cultural differences, a better impression is usually created when you do not stand too close or too far in talking to a work associate. In the United States and Canada, a distance of about 2–3 feet creates a positive impression.[26] Being too close might be perceived as intimidating, and too far as unwilling to form personal contact.

3. *Posture.* Leaning toward another person will often create a positive impression because it suggests you are favorably disposed toward his or her message. Openness of the arms or legs serves as an indicator of caring or liking, and will be perceived as positive. Standing up straight generally indicates self-confidence, thereby facilitating a positive impression.

4. *Hand gestures.* Frequent hand movements generally communicate a positive attitude, thereby creating a positive impression. However, some people wave their hands vigorously while arguing, leading to a negative impression.

5. *Facial expressions and eye contact.* Maintaining eye contact, except for staring, improves communication with another person and creates a positive impression. However, in some Asian and Middle Eastern cultures, maintaining eye contact is perceived to be disrespectful. A positive impression is likely to be created by alternating eye contact with a focus on the chin, mouth, or one side of the message sender's face.[27] In western cultures, moving your head, face, and eyes toward another person makes at least some contribution to a positive impression.

6. *Voice quality.* A forceful voice, which includes a consistent tone without vocalized pauses, connotes power and control and therefore will often create a positive impression. Avoiding an annoying voice quality, such as a high-pitched squeaky voice or a flat monotone, also creates a positive impression.

7. *Personal appearance.* As already described, the external image plays a major role in creating impressions. People pay more respect and grant more attention to people they perceive as being well dressed and attractive. One study showed that people perceived to be physically attractive tend to receive salaries 8–10% higher.[28]

8. *Touching.* Touch is a powerful vehicle for conveying such emotions as warmth, comfort, agreement, approval, reassurance, and physical attraction. Yet touching behavior in the workplace is governed by cultural attitudes and status.[29] Touching among people of approximately the same organizational rank is frequently used to convey agreement and reassurance. Touching

between people of different rank often indicates power and status differences, with the higher-ranking person more likely to initiate the touching. As a result touching can create a positive impression if status differences are followed. If touching is perceived to have a sexual innuendo, the actor will create a negative impression.

9. *Where a person sits during a meeting.* Where a person sits during a business meeting is yet another aspect of nonverbal communication. When the person has a choice, the placement is probably more significant, yet an impression is created with or without the actor having a choice. A few of the impression management possibilities linked to seat chosen at a meeting are as follows: (1) Sitting at the head of the table sends an impression of leadership; (2) the person to the right of the manager agrees with the leader on most issues, thereby creating a positive impression with the meeting leader; (3) the person who sits away from the table sometimes creates the impression of a maintaining a big-picture perspective; (4) the person who sits directly opposite the leader is typically argumentative, thereby creating a negative impression with many others.[30]

The nine categories of nonverbal communication just mentioned are comprehensive but are not intended to include all aspects of nonverbal communication that create an impression on the audience. Any aspect of behavior that sends a message without speaking can be considered nonverbal communication, even the presence or absence of body piercing. An exception is that hand signals, such as a time-out sign, are not words but they are verbal cues because they are direct substitutes for words.

The Alpha Male or Female

A long-standing belief is that an effective way of creating a positive impression on many people is to be bold, brash, assertive, and unrelenting. Many labels and concepts have been proposed to describe behavior of this nature, including the relatively recent **alpha executive**. Such an executive, or manager at another level, is ambitious, self-confident, competitive, and brash. Within limits, this type of behavior can be functional.

Two executive coaches who work with alpha men and women, Kate Ludeman and Eddie Erlandson, contend that three out of four executives and half of all middle managers are alphas. Non-alphas who aspire to the executive suite apparently will not get there without adapting a few alpha traits.[31] Also, when the alpha characteristics are too exaggerated, the result can be an intimidating, forceful executive such as Bob Nardelli, former GE and Home Depot executive, and CEO of Chrysler Corp. Nardelli deserves credit for recognizing that he had overemphasized his alpha characteristics at Home Depot, and therefore became more congenial at Chrysler and Cerberus.

How alpha characteristics are associated with both good and bad impressions can be understood by looking at seven specific attributes along with their associated strengths and weaknesses:[32]

1. *Self-confident and opinionated.* The value to the organization and the positive impression created are that the person acts decisively and has sharp intuition. The possible negative in terms of risk to the organization and the impression created is that the person is closed-minded, domineering, and intimidating.

2. *Highly intelligent.* The positive side is that the person sees beyond the obvious, and has creative ideas. The negative side in terms of productivity and image is that the alpha person dismisses or demeans colleagues who disagree with him or her.

3. *Action oriented.* The positive side is that the middle manager or executive produces results and is therefore impressive. The negative side is that the middle manager or executive is impatient, and resists changes in the business process that might improve results, at the same time creating a negative impression with thoughtful subordinates.

4. *High performance expectations for himself or herself and others.* The functional consequences are setting and achieving difficult goals. The dysfunctional consequences include constant dissatisfaction, failing to appreciate and motivate others—all leading to a negative impression among targets.

5. *Direct communication style.* The major positive result is moving people to action, and creating a good impression because of his or her straight talk. The major negative results are generating fear, and a gossip-filled culture of protecting one's hide, and compliance with demands.

6. *Highly disciplined.* The functional consequence is exceptional productivity while at the same time finding time and energy for a high level of work and physical fitness—all being impressive to others. The dysfunctional consequences are unreasonable expectations of himself or herself and others, and that he or she may ignores signs of burnout. The executive may generate a negative image of over-striving for perfection.

7. *Unemotional.* A positive consequence is being laser focused and objective, therefore projecting the image of a result-oriented executive. The negative consequences include having difficulty connecting with people, and not having the warmth needed to inspire teams.

Chutzpah, or elevated audacity and nerve, is another term that gets at the boldness of alpha people.[33] A manager with *chutzpah* might influence and create an impression on people by making demands that seem unreasonable—and often workers respond positively. When Jack Welch was the CEO at GE he would make such demands as telling suppliers that either they outsourced much of their manufacturing overseas (offshoring) or they would lose GE as a customer. In fear of losing a valued customer, most suppliers complied.

In summary, the alpha personality often creates a positive impression, yet when emphasized too frequently the results can be dysfunctional. When a leader exaggerates his or her alpha characteristics, many subordinates will rebel in such forms as making negative statements about the leader and quitting the organization. Another dysfunction is that the constant alpha person creates work stress for many people.

Personal Branding

A broad surface-level strategy of self-presentation is to build a **personal brand**, the qualities based on an individual's collection of strengths that make him or her unique, thereby distinguishing the person from the competition. The personal brand becomes a person's external identity as perceived by others. According to Peter Montoya, the personal brand is what a person stands for, including the values, abilities, and actions that others associate with the person. At the same time the personal brand is a professional alter ego designed to influence how others perceive the person, and turning that perception into opportunity. The personal brand tells the audience three things: (1) who the person is, (2) what the person does, and (3) what makes the person different, or how he or she creates value for the target market. Montoya also explains that although the term *personal branding* is modern, the phenomenon of people instantly labeling each other based on reputation and behavior has probably always existed.[34]

Although personal branding has not yet been the subject of extensive scholarly research, the concept has some similarities to the **public self**—what the person is communicating about himself or herself, and what others actually perceive about the person. In contrast, the *private self* is the actual person that one may be.[35]

As mentioned at the outset of the chapter, the personal brand is a surface-level self-presentation tactic only because the focus is on the external person. However, a valid personal brand is based on a variety of supporting cognitive and personality skills. Here we describe several aspects of personal branding.

The Personal Brand as a Professional Identity

Another conceptual approach to understanding the personal brand is that it is essentially the *professional self*. Daniel J. Lair, Katie Sullivan, and George Cheney explain that within the personal branding movement, people and their careers are marketed as brands. The features of these brands include promises of performance, specialized designs, and tag lines (or slogans) for success.[36]

Judith Sills explains that your reputation is what people think of you, and your résumé is your self-description in written form. Your personal brand includes these two factors but in total is the professional identity you create in the minds of others. Sills regards a personal brand as an important survival tool in a world where job security within a company or industry is difficult to find. The personal brand is part of the impression an individual creates, yet at the same time makes a person more employable across companies and even industries. Part of the reason that branding contributes to job security is that a person's brand emphasizes his or her expertise. However, the surface-level brand must be supported by valid capabilities.

An example of terms incorporated into a personal brand that would facilitate job security (if the terms appeared valid) is as follows: "Consistency, reliability, brings it in under budget, delivers on time, creative thinker, and problem solver."

Self-descriptions alone do not constitute a brand. Instead, Sills explains that visibility is important for demonstrating a person has the capabilities mentioned in the brand. Visible events for displaying a brand include speaking engagements at professional conferences and working with groups other than one's own to help solve problems.[37]

Coaching Assistance with Branding

Professional assistance in building a personal brand is offered by a variety of practitioners referred to as *business coaches, executive coaches*, or *personal coaches*. Both career beginners and people with more work experience receive assistance in developing their personal brand. Here is an example of a brand identity developed for a 25-year-old college graduate, Rob Borden:

> The branding consultants learned that Borden had opened a landscaping business in college, captained an NCAA-championship lacrosse team and was deeply interested in land development and conservation. They drafted a marketing plan around five qualities: a passion for commercial real estate, strong business experience, leadership abilities, and a sparkling wit when not nervous. In job interviews, Borden hammered away at those key points and, after meeting with about eight companies, landed a job that he loves in commercial real estate.[38]

A personal brand will be more effective if it is authentic in the sense of accurately reflecting the person. A person might add a little drama to his or her strengths, but the strengths should still be true. For example, if Ashley regularly volunteers time to feed homeless people, she might describe herself as having "enduring humanitarian values." Yet it would be a stretch for her to say that she "is committed to ending world hunger."

Another approach to personal brand development offered by career coaches is to help the individual develop an Internet presence. As career coach William Arruda exaggerates, "If you don't show up in Google, you don't exist." He believes that career-minded people need a presence as distinctive as a Nike swoosh. Arruda also believes that what makes people unique makes them successful. His specific advice for helping a person stand out is to writes blogs, give speeches, and improve their style of speech and dress. Creating an effective personal website can also be helpful.[39]

Strong Personal Brands for Businesspersons and Professional Athletes

A handful of entrepreneurs have been successful in linking a strong brand and name to the products of their company. Martha Stewart, founder of Martha Stewart Living

Omnimedia, developed her brand into a highly visble and successful brand. The Martha Stewart brand is found on bedroom sheets, dishes, pots, paints, as well as other household products. Stewart also has her own magazine, television show, and a service for the architectural design of new homes. The brand remained vibrant even after Stewart spent time in prison for lying to prosecuters about a stock sale.

Virgin Group founder Richard Branson is well known and higly admired in the United Kingdom as well as throughout the world. The Virgin label on over 200 businesses is closely associated with Branson's name. Branson portrays himself in his autobiographies and in media presentations as an out-of-the-ordinary pathfinder in business, as well as a daredevil who has escaped death by a sinking ship, gunfire, and a hot-air balloon crash. Branson uses his swashbuckling image to make deals and gain publicity for the broad range of companies the Branson group operates.[40]

Donald J. Trump is another entrepreneur-style person whose name has become a solid brand to the point that his name emblazoned on a commerical or residential building enhances the commerical value of the building. Trump is a developer, reality-TV-show star, casino operator, best-selling author, and also a retailer. His name is on a line of men's clothing, ties, candy bars, and cologne, among other products. In 2006, "The Donald" opened the Trump Exchange in the Trump Taj Mahal Casino & Resort to sell Trump-branded retail items. His line of men's clothing is distributed through other retailers also. The link to personal branding and impression management is that Trump has built such equity in his name that the Trump brand works in many venues. Trump has his critics who believe he is needlessly flamboyant and ego-centric, and less financially successful than he pretends to be. Yet Trump remains perhaps America's best-known businessperson.[41]

Corporate executives who are not entrepreneurs are less likely to profit from personal branding. Gurnek Bains, the head of a corporate-psychology consultancy, notes that a high-profile CEO could be important for a company that is seeking a stronger identity in the financial markets. He cautions, "All our research shows that it's humbler executives with less ego—the ones who stay very connected to their employees and customers—who get the best results for their businesses."[42]

Tom Kuczmarksi, a consultant on business innovation, and a professor at the Kellogg School of Management at Northwestern University, offers a similar analysis: "When you're the rock-star brand at the top, you're conveying to people in the ranks that they're second-class citizens—and you stop thinking about how to develop the next group of people who will run the show."[43]

Personal branding for sports celebrities illustrates how personal brands are built for commerical purposes. A notable example is Alex Rodriguez, the New York Yankee star who is regarded as one of the all-time great offensive (batting) players in baseball history. He signed with the William Morrison agency, a talent-representation company. Similarly to a small number of other athletes, he (or his agent) has attempted to turn himself into an enduring brand name that can attract corporate sponsorships in addition to his lucrative employment contracts. The building of the Rodriguez brand represents the kind of atttention that has been mostly focused on movie and music celebrities rather than athletes.[44]

An outstanding example of a sports person building a brand based on legitimate expertise is LeBron James, who by age 23 had become one of the most famous professional basketball players of all time. By 2007, James perceived himself to be 80% basketball player and 20% businessman. He said, "At this point, it's 80/20. When I first entered the league, it was 100/0 and so in five years, hopefully we'll be at 70/30."

James, a small-forward for the Cleveland Cavaliers, worked with his advisors to become one of the most successful branding stories in sports. He has lucrative endorsement deals with several brands, including Sprite, Powerade, and Microsoft, and a $90 million contract with Nike that includes his athletic shoe line. Much of James' brand development is accomplished by working with LRMR Innovative Marketing & Branding, a sports marketing company he founded with three of his childhood friends.[45] The personna of LeBron James has become so recognizable that he appears in some television commericals without mention of his name. In marketing terms, the personal brand "LeBron James" has exceptional brand equity.

Guidelines for Application and Practice

1. Barbara Pachter, a business etiquette coach, offers this concise advice for wearing clothing that will create a positive image: fit (avoid too-short skirts or too-tight anything); accessories (particularly foot wear); color (when in doubt, go with dark); and style (when in doubt, dress like the boss). The No. 1 mistake is looking too sexy. Pachter says that neither cleavage nor toes are part of the corporate look.[46]

2. Videoconferencing places extra demands on making a good first impression. Keep the following considerations in mind for creating a good first impression at a videoconference: (1) Choose your clothing carefully. Some participants expect the screen to display only their upper torso, and therefore wear business attire above the waist, and perhaps shorts and sports shoes below. Busy patterns do not look good on camera. (2) Speak in crisp, conversational tones, and pay close attention. Maintain eye contact with live participants and remote viewers. Getting up to leave the room looks particularly bad on camera. (3) Never forget the powerful reach of the video camera. Behavior such as falling asleep or rolling the eyes in response to an executive's suggestions is readily seen by associates in the same and other locations. (4) Avoid culturally insensitive gestures. For example, large hand and body motions make many Asians uncomfortable. (5) Decrease nervousness about video interviews by rehearsing. Use a camcorder to see how you appear and sound during a practice interview, engaging the help of a friend. Solicit his or her feedback about your performance.[47]

3. Business etiquette and manners refer to superficial aspects of behavior, yet they can have a significant impact on career advancement, particularly in a

bureaucracy. Although many business executives can be found who are brash, abrasive, and rude, polite and refined behavior is considered important for occupying leadership roles.

4. A helpful way of enhancing the first impression you create is to view yourself in a camcorder, and also invite feedback from people whose judgment you trust. Keep in mind that first impressions are based on much more than clothing. The audience forms an opinion of the actor also based on nonverbal behavior and oral communication skill. Viewing video recordings of yourself and soliciting feedback are equally useful in evaluating the impact of your nonverbal behavior.

5. Developing the alpha-person aspects of your personality and behavior is a worthwhile consideration if you are a manager who wants to advance, or aspire toward a managerial and executive career. A person may not be able to readily develop all the aspects of the alpha male or female, but a few might be tackled for improvement. Two such possibilities are becoming action oriented and developing high-performance expectations for yourself and others.

6. When developing a personal brand, keep certain potential pitfalls in mind, as recommended by Judith Sills. (1) Do not make your niche of expertise too narrow, such as "business processes within accounts receivable." Instead, use "business processes in finance." (2) Speak up to show what you know but be willing to admit what you do not know. Balance the fine line between demonstrating your expertise and being egotistical. (3) Stick close to your strengths and do not claim expertise you have not yet developed.[48]

7. Brand consistency is essential to developing customer loyalty in business, and that rule of thumb is helpful to keep in mind in developing a professionally oriented personal brand with blog content.[49] Photos posted should also show some consistency, for example promoting a consistent professional image, such as a certified personal planner avoiding photos of himself or herself clad in underwear and drinking beer. Nevertheless, the person who wants to build a professionally oriented personal brand might also want have separate blogs and depictions on social networking sites, such as Facebook, to appeal to social friends.[50] The risk, however, is that professional contacts might form a less serious image of the actor.

8. When implementing the various surface-level approaches to impression management, it is helpful to send a similar positive message with each approach. If you create a positive message with one approach, attempt to send the same positive message with other approaches. For example, if you dress in a professional manner, make sure to speak in a professional manner. Similarly, if you dress well yet display poor business etiquette the positive impact of your dress and appearance will be negated.

Summary

Surface-level presentation tactics refer to those aspects of impression management that focus on readily observable behaviors rather than underlying characteristics. Surface-level characteristics can be quite important.

A person's clothing, dress, and physical appearance, including sexiness as perceived by others, contribute substantially to the image he or she projects. Clothing is widely used to manage the impression a person creates. A study with MBA students found that those who valued workplace attire used it to manage the impressions others formed of them. Dressing to impress appeared to be highly effective for high self-monitors and for those in managerial and executive positions.

Seven categories of suggestions for using clothing and dress for impression management are as follows: (1) what a businessman should wear; (2) how managerial and professional women should dress; (3) dressing to impress year-round; (4) avoiding the wardrobe gaffe of appearing too seductive; (5) sizing up the environment when choosing clothing; (6) dressing professionally in the workplace; (7) watching out for too many electronic gadgets dangling from the clothing. Making changes in appearance may lead to changed perceptions of the person.

A study about women and dress found that a sexy self-presentation was viewed negatively in a high-status job, but not in low-status jobs. It was also found that a backlash exists against women in high-ranking jobs who dress provocatively.

Being perceived as considerably overweight usually contributes to a negative image. An individual who occasionally mentions feeling energetic or being in top form will improve his or her chances of being perceived as having a positive physical appearance.

A meta-analysis of available studies found that height has a positive relationship with success in the workplace. A positive correlation was found between height and success in terms of pay level and promotions. Height appears to affect success through the mediators of self-esteem and social esteem. For example, managerial perceptions of performance lead to higher performance evaluations and pay increases. Erect posture is one method of appearing taller.

Business etiquette contributes heavily to impression management. Baldrige contends that the key to success in the workplace is consideration of others and a kind heart. Younger workers who practice good etiquette may have a competitive advantage because interpersonal and etiquette skills are not widespread. In general, the organizational actor who displays good etiquette will usually enhance his or her self-presentation.

First impressions constitute a major force in impression management, somewhat due to the principle of primacy. These impressions are based on both overt and subtle cues, depending somewhat on the interests of the target. Variations in what makes for a good impression in a category of appearance or behavior are possible, including what hairdo will create a good impression. Videoconferencing creates new demands on the worker who wants to create a good impression because the camera can magnify or exaggerate all behavior.

Nonverbal behavior contributes heavily to impression management in terms of first and later impressions. Categories of nonverbal behavior lending themselves to first impressions include (1) environment or setting, (2) distance from the other person, (3) posture, (4) hand gestures, (5) facial expressions and eye contact, (6) voice quality, (7) personal appearance, (8) touching, and (9) where a person sits during a meeting.

Being an alpha person, within limits, can be functional in terms of creating a good impression. Attributes of the alpha person include (1) self-confidence and opinionatedness, (2) high intelligence, (3) action orientation, (4) high performance expectations for self and others, (5) direct communication style, (6) a high level of discipline, and (7) unemotionality. *Chutzpah* gets at the boldness of alpha people.

The personal brand becomes a person's external identity as perceived by others, and is similar to the public self. The personal brand can also be regarded as a professional identity. Many people today receive coaching to enhance their personal brand. A growing trend is for business people as well as professional athletes to develop a personal brand, with the basketball player LeBron James being an outstanding example.

Surface-level approaches to self-presentation lend themselves to many guidelines for application and practice in such areas as wearing appropriate clothing, looking good in a videoconference, displaying the proper etiquette, making a good first impression, becoming an alpha person, and developing a strong personal brand.

Chapter 6

Being Impressive by Making Others Feel Good

As described in Chapter 1, impression management is often considered synonymous with self-presentation. You present a positive image of yourself if you want to create a positive impression, and you create a negative image of yourself if want to create a negative impression. If impression management is framed exclusively as self-presentation, an important fact is ignored. One of the best ways to create a good impression with a given target is to make the other person feel good about his or her appearance, personality, behavior, or performance. Pay a person the right type of compliment, or recognize and praise him in some other way, and you create a good impression. Recognize, however, that the difference between self-presentation and other-enhancement is not always clear cut. If you practice good etiquette, you present yourself in a positive light. At the same time good etiquette might enhance others, such as saying thank you or remembering the other person's name.

In this chapter we focus on ways of managing an impression by enhancing other people in some way. **Enhancement of others** refers to efforts by an actor to increase his or her attractiveness to a target based on the use of favorable evaluations of the target's attributes, behavior, or performance.[1] The bulk of our attention focuses on ingratiation because this topic has received more attention, including empirical research. Figure 6-1 classifies the topics and subtopics related to the enhancement of others based on the amount of empirical support.

Figure 6-1 Topics and Subtopics Related to Enhancing Others According to Basis of Support.

Well Supported by Empirical Research	Supported More by Anecdote and Opinion
Ingratiation	Humor
Balance theory	Political correctness
Political skill and ingratiation	
Flattery for ingratiation	
Opinion conformity	

Ingratiation for Enhancing Others

Ingratiation deals with getting the other person to like you. Ingratiating tactics identified in a pioneering study about influence tactics included the following:

- Made him or her feel important (for example, "Only you have the brains and talent to do this").
- Acted very humbly toward him or her while making my request.
- Praised him or her.
- Asked in a polite way.
- Pretended I was letting him or her decide to do what I wanted (acted in a pseudo-democratic manner).[2]

The quiz presented in Figure 6-2 provides you an opportunity to measure your own ingratiating tendencies and to think through further what ingratiating yourself to your boss means in practice. Remember that being liked helps you get promoted, receive more compensation, and avoid being downsized. However, being dishonest would violate many ethical standards.

Getting somebody else to like you can be considered a mildly manipulative influence tactic—particularly if you do not like the other person. Frank P. Quattrone, the high-tech investment banker, was a master of ingratiation at one point in his career. More than 300 high-tech executives and venture capitalists received shares in hot IPOs (initial public offerings), to facilitate their giving investment-banking business to Quattrone's firm, Crédit Suisse First Boston. Quattrone also invited his high-tech pals to play golf with him at exclusive courses, and he entertained them lavishly in his palatial home.[3]

Leaders who ordinarily are the opposite of ingratiating will sometimes go out of their way to be humble and agreeable to fit an important purpose. A case in point is Bill Gates, who is often sarcastic and cutting. When Gates and Microsoft Corporation were being sued by the U.S. Department of Justice for possible monopolistic practices, Gates went on a goodwill tour, an events-packed trip around San Francisco and Silicon Valley. During his meetings with the public, Gates was modest and at times self-deprecating, even praising the competition. He shook hands, signed autographs, and smiled frequently. Gates was so convincing that a schoolgirl said, "You can tell he's not in it for the money. He wants to make software better."[4] (Today Gates and his wife Melinda Gates are world-leading philanthropists, helping poor children throughout the world, so maybe the schoolgirl was insightful!)

Why Ingratiation Is Important

A basic explanation of why ingratiation is effective as a tactic for enhancing others is that wanting to be liked and appreciated approaches the status of a universal human need, closely related to the need for recognition. Even people with underdeveloped interpersonal skills, and who are rude in their daily interactions, still want to be liked by others.

Figure 6-2 Measure of Ingratiating Behavior in Organizational Settings (MIBOS).

Instructions: Indicate how frequently you use (or would use) the tactics for pleasing your boss listed below. N = never do it; S = seldom do it; Oc = occasionally do it; Of = often do it; A = almost always do it. The N–A categories correspond to a 1–5 scale.

	1 N	2 S	3 Oc	4 Of	5 A
1. Impress upon your supervisor that only he or she can help you in a given situation mainly to make him or her feel good.	☐	☐	☐	☐	☐
2. Show your supervisor that you share enthusiasm about his or her new idea even when you may not actually like it.	☐	☐	☐	☐	☐
3. Try to let your supervisor know that you have a reputation for being liked.	☐	☐	☐	☐	☐
4. Try to make sure that your supervisor is aware of your success.	☐	☐	☐	☐	☐
5. Highlight the achievements made under your supervisor's leadership in a meeting he or she does not attend.	☐	☐	☐	☐	☐
6. Give frequent smiles to express enthusiasm and interest about something your supervisor is interested in even if you do not like it.	☐	☐	☐	☐	☐
7. Express work attitudes that are similar to your supervisor's as a way of letting him or her know that the two of you are alike.	☐	☐	☐	☐	☐
8. Tell your supervisor that you can learn a lot from his or her experience.	☐	☐	☐	☐	☐
9. Exaggerate your supervisor's admirable qualities to convey the impression that you think highly of him or her.	☐	☐	☐	☐	☐
10. Disagree on trivial or unimportant issues but agree on those issues in which he or she expects support from you.	☐	☐	☐	☐	☐
11. Try to imitate such work behaviors of your supervisor as working late or occasionally working on weekends.	☐	☐	☐	☐	☐
12. Look for opportunities to let your supervisor know your virtues and strengths.	☐	☐	☐	☐	☐
13. Ask your supervisor for advice in areas in which he or she thinks he or she is smart to let him or her feel that you admire his or her talent.	☐	☐	☐	☐	☐
14. Try to do things for your supervisor that show your selfless generosity.	☐	☐	☐	☐	☐
15. Look out for opportunities to admire your supervisor.	☐	☐	☐	☐	☐
16. Let your supervisor know the attitudes you share with him or her.	☐	☐	☐	☐	☐
17. Compliment your supervisor on his or her achievement, however it may appeal to you personally.	☐	☐	☐	☐	☐

(Continued)

Figure 6-2 Continued

18. Laugh heartily at your supervisor's jokes even when they are really not funny.

19. Go out of your way to run an errand for your supervisor.

20. Offer to help your supervisor by using your personal contacts.

21. Try to persuasively present your own qualities when attempting to convince your supervisor about your abilities.

22. Volunteer to be of help to your supervisor in matters like locating a good apartment, finding a good insurance agent, etc.

23. Spend time listening to your supervisor's personal problems even if you have no interest in them.

24. Volunteer to help your supervisor in his or her work even if it means extra work for you.

Scoring and Interpretation: The more of these ingratiating behaviors you use frequently or almost always, the more ingratiating you are. A score of 40 or less suggests that you do not put much effort into pleasing your manager, and you may need to be a little more ingratiating to achieve a good relationship with your supervisor. A score between 41 and 99 suggests a moderate degree of ingratiating behavior. A score of 100 or more suggests that you are too ingratiating and might be perceived as being too political or insincere. So some honesty is called for, providing you are tactful.

Skill Development: Leaders or future leaders should remember that a moderate amount of ingratiating behavior is the norm in relationships with superiors. Ingratiating yourself to people who report to you can also be a useful influence tactic.

Source: Adapted from Kamalesh Kumar and Michael Beyerlein, "Construction and Validation of an Instrument for Measuring Ingratiatory Behaviors in Organizational Settings," *Journal of Applied Psychology*, October 1991, p. 623. Copyright © by the American Psychological Association. Adapted with permission.

A more complex explanation of why ingratiation can be effective is provided by balance theory, as proposed by Darren C. Treadway and his team of researchers.[5] According to **balance theory**, a balance of sentiments (or feelings) is the implicit goal of interpersonal interaction. In practice this would mean that if you have a positive attitude toward another person, you would hope that your positive attitude is reciprocated. A manager might provide resources the subordinate needs, such as being recommended to an important project or receiving a salary increase. The subordinate can reciprocate through such means as support for the manager's ideas—a form of enhancing another person.

If a balance of sentiments is not attained in the interaction between two people, two remedies exist for resolving the state of imbalance. The first remedy is a change in sentiment relations or a cognitive reorganization for thinking differently about the relationship. The targets align their views of the actor with sentiments toward the action taken by the actor. A person whose positive feelings were not reciprocated might develop negative attitudes toward the other person. The second remedy involves disassociating the second party from the actions he or she took. For example, the target might decide that the actor was not really responsible for the behavior in question. Perhaps the other party was unfriendly because of a pressing job problem. In this instance, the balanced relationship between the two people is preserved because the unfavorable event is not associated with the actor.

After the target evaluates the appropriateness of the actor's attempt at impression management, the target must decide if the behavior establishes a balance or an imbalance of sentiments toward the actor. An example of behavior in this situation might be an actor telling the target that he or she appears to be walking better than ever after having recovered from a knee injury. If the event or activity is deemed inappropriate, balance theory suggests that the target will rate the actor lower to achieve a negative sentiment balance. In contrast, if the behavior is perceived to be appropriate for the situation, the target should rate the actor higher to achieve a positive sentiment balance. If the target is a supervisor and the actor is a subordinate, the rating could take the form of an employee evaluation as well as merely an attitude toward the person.

Ingratiation is typically perceived to be socially appropriate, and is done for the purpose of eliciting goodwill in the target. As a result, it makes sense that balance theory has been used to explain the positive impact of ingratiation in the workplace. Ingratiation is most likely to be perceived as inappropriate when it takes the form of extreme fawning over the other person, and inappropriate flattery. An example of extreme fawning took place when an outside auditor who was unintentionally bald (he did not shave his head) attended a meeting with company representatives to discuss the audit. A manager present, who was bald himself, said to the auditor, "Around here we love bald guys." The auditor rolled his eyes and shook his head in response to this failed attempt at ingratiation.

Political Skill and Ingratiation

Ingratiation, as with all tactics of impression management and influence, requires political skill to implement well. Without political skill, or finesse, an influence tactic might backfire, such as giving an off-the-wall compliment for purposes of ingratiation. Part of a study with 337 employees in two retail firms investigated how political skill mediated (or influenced) the effectiveness of workers in ingratiating themselves to managers.[6]

Political skill was measured by the Political Skill Inventory. The entire inventory consists of statements requiring a self-evaluation of capabilities. Sample statements include the following:

- I always seem to instinctively know the right things to say and do to influence others.

- I am particularly good at sensing the motivations and hidden agendas of others.

Ingratiation was measured by a subscale within the research instrument, Scale of Upward Influence. Sample statements include the following:

- Acted very humbly to him or her while making my request.
- Made him or her feel good about me before making my request.

Observe that these statements ask the actor to report on what he or she did rather than evaluate a capability. To measure the supervisor's assessment of the subordinate's ingratiation behavior, supervisors rated their perceptions of ingratiation attempts. Sample items include the following:

- Acted very humbly to me while making his or her request.
- Attempted to make me feel good before making his or her request.

A key result of the study was that as subordinates reported using more ingratiation, the supervisors of politically skilled employees reported that these employees used less ingratiation. In other words, subordinates with good political skill used ingratiation in a more subtle way. The employees with high political skill were less likely than those with low political skill to have their ingratiation attempts perceived by targets as a manipulative influence attempt.

A side finding of the study that is useful in understanding impression management is that female subordinates were rated as engaging in more ingratiation than male subordinates. A study to be mentioned later in this chapter (pp. 110–111) found that women tend to have a more positive attitude toward flattery and praise. These gender differences in ingratiation support the stereotype that women emphasize building relationships to a greater extent than do men.

An Executive-Level Study about the Effectiveness of Ingratiation

Two studies with the same population of executives demonstrated that enhancing the right people through ingratiation facilitated becoming a member of the board of directors. James D. Westphal and Ithai Stern examined survey data on ingratiation from 760 directors, including CEOs at Fortune 500 companies. The studies also investigated how ingratiatory behavior can provide an alternative path to the boardroom for managers who lack the social and educational credentials associated with the power elite.[7] (The second study was essentially a further analysis of the same data.) The nine statements, or items, measuring ingratiating behavior are presented in Figure 6-3. The three measures of ingratiation within the items are flattery, agreeing with the CEO's opinion, and doing small favors for him or her. All of these behaviors reflect directly or indirectly enhancing the target.

Figure 6-3 Items Measuring Ingratiating Behavior in a Study of Attaining Board Appointments.

1. In talking to the director, to what extent do you express agreement with the director's viewpoint on a strategic issue, even when you do not completely share his or her opinion?

2. In speaking with the director, to what extent do you point out attitudes and/or opinions you have in common?

3. Over the past 12 months, how many times did you disagree with the director's point of view on a strategic issue? [reverse scored]

4. Over the past 12 months, how often have you complimented the director about his or her insight on a particular strategic issue?

5. In the past 12 months, how often have you expressed to the director that you enjoy working with him or her?

6. Over the past 12 months, how often have you complimented the director regarding his or her contributions to the board?

7. In the past 12 months, have you complimented the director regarding his or her career accomplishments or achievements?

8. In talking to the director over the past 12 months, to what extent have you given him or her advice on a personal career matter, without the director asking for it?

9. Have you done a favor for the director in the past 12 months?

Note: Items are responded to in terms of rating on a 1–5 scale, or responding yes or no.

Source: James D. Westphal and Ithai Stern, "Flattery Will Get You Everywhere (Especially If You Are a Male Caucasian): How Ingratiation, Boardroom Behavior, and Demographic Minority Status Affect Additional Board Appointments at U.S. Companies," *Academy of Management Journal*, April 2007, p. 275. The questions quoted are from a portion of a larger table.

A major finding was that top-level managers who ingratiated themselves with their CEO are more likely to receive board appointments at other firms where their CEO serves as a director. Board appointments are also more likely to firms with which the CEO is indirectly connected through network contacts.

Another way for directors to increase their chances of receiving additional board appointments was to provide more advice and information to CEOs, and engage in more ingratiation with peer directors. The impact of providing advice in terms of receiving a board appointment was less than the positive effects of ingratiation. Directors also increased their chances of gaining a board appointment by engaging in low levels of monitoring and controlling the CEO. The behaviors just mentioned are forms of enhancement of others because (1) giving advice enhances the target's stature, (2) ingratiating is typically other-enhancing, and (3) backing off on monitoring the target's behavior conveys trust in his or her judgment.

A closer look at some of the findings of the study illustrates the powerful effect of enhancement of others. Ingratiation toward a fellow director has a strong, positive effect on the likelihood that the focal director (actor) will receive an appointment to the board where the fellow director serves on the nominating committee or as CEO. The likelihood of receiving a board appointment at a company where that director serves on the nominating committee or as CEO increases by 72 percent when ingratiation or other-enhancement in the following forms increases: (1) complementing the director with respect to his or her contributions to the board, (2) disagreeing with the director's point of view on a strategic issue one less time during the past 12 months, and (3) doing one more personal favor for the director during the past year.

Further results suggested that interpersonal influence behavior in the form of ingratiation substitutes to some extent for an elite background or being a member of a demographic majority group, such as a Caucasian male. The researchers interpreted their findings to mean that people outside of the social elite and majority group status face a subtle and perhaps unexpected form of social discrimination. The logic is that they must engage in a higher level of interpersonal influence behavior in order to have the same chance of obtaining a board appointment. The interpersonal influence behavior can also be framed as using ingratiation for purposes of other-enhancement and therefore creating a better impression.

The two studies just presented make a strong case for ingratiation and other forms of enhancement of others in gaining a valuable outcome such as a recommendation to become a board member. Yet impression management was not a substitute for competence. We can assume that if they had not been competent and hardworking the executives surveyed would not have advanced so far in their careers. Nevertheless, impression management gave them an important competitive advantage in terms of gaining a board appointment.

Flattery as a Method of Ingratiation

Applied psychology professor Ronald J. Deluga writes that flattery is ingratiation in its purest form. The person intent on other-enhancement via flattery will engage in exaggerated admiration, praise, and generally "butter up" the target. The particularly astute flatterer will express high positive regard for attributes about which the actor is insecure such as physical appearance or presentation skills. The actor may encourage the target to talk about personal concerns even when the actor has no interest. Flattery can reach the point whereby nearly everything the actor does or is becomes shrouded in glory.[8] Flattery is an effective form of enhancing others because most people want to receive accolades, even if they contain a little exaggeration.[9] Another reason that flattery works well for enhancing others is that most people want to be appreciated, and flattery can focus on their accomplishments. Also, people tend to like other people who like them partially because most people look upon themselves favorably, and appreciate a reinforcement of this perception of self-worth.[10]

Although Deluga perceives flattery to be insincere, flattery can also be sincere and is likely to be a more effective technique of other-enhancement when the actor is sincere. Nonverbal behavior will often tip off the target that the flattery is insincere, such as the actor having a blank stare while the target talks at length about his or her personal concerns. Research evidence supports the contention that constructive compliments are not overblown. Descriptions of what went right are more effective than evaluative phrases such as "magnificent," or "extraordinary."[11]

Making Other People Feel Important as a Form of Flattery

A foundation approach to flattery is to make other people feel important. One of the basic premises of the enduring book *How to Win Friends and Influence People*, by Dale Carnegie, is to make other people feel important, even by such small initiatives as remembering their names.[12] One approach to making a coworker feel important would be to bring a notable accomplishment of his or hers to the attention of the group. Another way of making targets feel important is to ask questions about their work, such as "How is your work going?" or "How does the company use your output?"

The quiz presented in Figure 6-4 is about making others feel important. The items within the quiz might be interpreted as specific behaviors for creating the impression that the actor thinks his or her targets are important. The items with reverse scoring suggest behaviors that would make targets feel unimportant.

Mixing Mild Criticism to Increase the Effectiveness of Flattery

As suggested by Paul Rosenfeld, Robert A. Giacalone, and Catherine A. Riordan, flattery, including compliments, should be discerning. If a target receives only compliments from the actor, the target might soon think that the target is not thinking critically or that he or she is insincere. To augment the power of flattery it is therefore best to mildly criticize the target in an *acknowledged area of weakness*.[13] The reason is that most people do not mind receiving some criticism in an area in which they perceive themselves to need development. To further avoid creating a negative impression on the target, it is advisable to criticize him or her about a behavior that could also be interpreted as a strength. The actor might point out a behavior that in milder doses might be perceived as a strength. A few examples follow of an actor offering a criticism that could also be interpreted as pointing to an asset:

- During this morning's meeting, I thought you came on a little too strong in terms of demanding greater productivity from everybody in the room.
- You are such a patriot that sometimes you forget that not everybody shares the same love for our country.
- You sometimes forget we do not all have the same strong work ethic that you do.

Flattery will gain in strength if a few criticisms are offered also because the criticisms just listed add credibility to the actor. Unless the target is strongly egotistical, he or she will appreciate mild criticism interspersed with compliments.

Figure 6-4 How Important Do I Make People Feel?

Instructions: Indicate on a 1–5 scale how frequently you act (or would act if the situation presented itself) in the ways indicated below: very infrequently (VI), infrequently (I), sometimes (S), frequently (F), or very frequently (VF). Circle the number underneath the column that best fits your answer.

	VI	I	S	F	VF
1. I do my best to correctly pronounce a coworker's name.	1	2	3	4	5
2. I avoid letting other people's egos get too big.	5	4	3	2	1
3. I brag to others about the accomplishments of my coworkers.	1	2	3	4	5
4. I recognize the birthdays of friends in a tangible way.	1	2	3	4	5
5. It makes me anxious to listen to others brag about their accomplishments.	5	4	3	2	1
6. After hearing that a friend has done something outstanding, I shake his or her hand.	1	2	3	4	5
7. If a friend or coworker recently received a degree or certificate, I would offer my congratulations.	1	2	3	4	5
8. If a friend or coworker finished second in a contest, I would inquire why he or she did not finish first.	5	4	3	2	1
9. If a coworker showed me how to do something, I would compliment that person's skill.	1	2	3	4	5
10. When a coworker starts bragging about a family member's accomplishments, I do not respond.	5	4	3	2	1

Scoring and Interpretation: Total the numbers corresponding to your answers. Scoring 40–50 points suggests that you typically make people feel important; 16–39 points suggest that you have a moderate tendency toward making others feel important; 10–15 points suggest that you need to develop skill in making others feel important. Study this chapter carefully.

Self-Perceived Technical Orientation as a Variable that Influences Flattery

Understanding relevant factors about the target is always important for the effective use of impression management tactics. With respect to flattery, it is helpful to observe if the target likes to be flattered. The writings of Dale Carnegie suggest that virtually everybody thrives on flattery,[14] yet his position might be overstated. A study supported the idea that individuals with a strong people orientation may react more favorably to flattery than those with a strong technical orientation. Highly technical people tend not to relish general praise, like "Great job." Instead, they prefer a laid-back, factual statement of how their output made a contribution.

DuBrin investigated the possibility that the self-perceived technical orientation of workers might influence the effectiveness of praise and flattery. The hypothesis investigated was that self-perceived technical orientation correlates negatively with attitudes toward praise and flattery. The participants were 102 working adults in managerial, professional, sales, technical, administrative support, and entrepreneurial positions. Participants provided self-ratings on a 1–10 scale for the question: "In terms of being technical, I would rate my job as follows . . ." The end-points on the scale were "not technical" and "extremely technical." The participants also rated their attitudes toward flattery and praise.

Analysis of the data indicated that self-perceived technical orientation was negatively correlated with attitude ratings for flattery and praise. Working adults who rated themselves as performing technical work tended to have negative attitudes toward being praised and flattered. In contrast, working adults who perceived themselves to be performing less technical work tended to have more positive attitudes toward being praised and flattered. An implication of the study is that flattery, including praise, might be even more effective if the moderating influence of self-perceived technical orientation is taken into account. The study also indicated that women have more positive attitudes toward praise and flattery than do men.[15]

Opinion Conformity as a Method of Ingratiation

Another major technique of ingratiation is to agree with, or conform to, the opinion of another person. The target feels enhanced because the actor agrees with him or her. The more valued and credible the actor, the more enhanced the target feels. **Opinion conformity** refers to the actor expressing opinions or acting in ways consistent with the target's attitudes, beliefs, and values in order to increase the target's liking of the actor.[16] In short, opinion conformity is practiced to "get in good" with the target, who is often a person's immediate manager.

One reason the target is enhanced by opinion conformity is that he or she feels self-confident. The logic proceeds as follows: "If ____ agrees with me, I must be right, so that makes me feel more confident in what I am thinking." Deluga observes that opinion conformity may take the form of being a yes-man or yes-woman, with the subordinate eagerly nodding his or her head and smiling warmly at the manager's every comment or suggestion. Laughing at the boss's humor is also a form of opinion conformity because the actor agrees that what the target said is funny.[17]

In addition to enhancing the target, opinion conformity often improves the relationship between the two parties. As proposed by Donn Byrne's law of attraction, the greater the proportion of similar attitudes shared by two people, the more they will like each other.[18] The improved relationship, in turn, can lead to enhancement because most people feel better when they add a new compatriot to their network.

Opinion conformity as an ingratiating tactic works best when there is a power differential between the actor and the target. In one of the earliest studies on ingratiation, a team of researchers demonstrated that opinion conformity took place when a supervisor had the formal authority to evaluate a subordinate's performance. (It would be a rare organization in which the supervisor was not responsible for performance evaluations.) The experimental task was for the participants to rank the effectiveness of advertising slogans in increasing sales. Participants later overheard a supervisor express either the value of group cooperation or of independence in accomplishing work assignments. The supervisor was (1) to have the authority to evaluate the performance on the assignment, or (2) not to have such authority. An attitude survey conducted after the participants found out about the authority arrangement indicated that the participants expressed opinion conformity only when the supervisor had the authority to evaluate performance.[19]

The more power an individual holds within an organization, the more likely it is that many people will conform to his or her opinion. For a powerful person, the opinion conformity will be found among direct reports, others in the chain of command, and many people throughout the organization. The more hierarchical the organization, the more we can anticipate opinion conformity. When an organization is less hierarchical, many employees will demonstrate opinion *non-conformity*. For example, in some firms where equality is emphasized, some employees will post blogs disagreeing with top management's position. At one software company, the CEO was openly in support of the program for distributing $100 laptop computers to children in developing countries. An independent-thinking employee posted a blog contending that playing with laptop computers would distract children in third world countries from the really important skills of learning to read and write.

Humor for Ingratiation and Enhancement of Others

In order to be liked in the workplace as well as social life, many people use humor, thereby categorizing humor as another form of ingratiation. An advantage of humor, according to the research synthesis of Cecily D. Cooper, is that it may be perceived as less manipulative than tactics such as doing favors for the audience or complimenting their behavior. The meaning of humor is generally understood, yet the technical definition offered by Cooper helps link humor to ingratiation. She defines humor as "any event shared by an agent (e.g., an employee) with another individual (e.g., a target) that is intended to be amusing to the target and that the target perceives to be as an intentional act."[20] We observe that unintentional humor can also ingratiate an actor with the audience, such as a humorous spelling error in a PowerPoint presentation. Two examples are "Texass" for "Texas" and "pubic" for public.

Humor has the potential to ingratiate the actor expressing the humor with targets who enjoy the humor. Workers who make judicious use of humor can help the organization by improving morale because effective humor can trigger positive emotional contagion.

Humor also enhances others, but indirectly. Two purposes of humor are to make the target laugh, and feel good. When these purposes are attained, the target is enhanced because laughing and feeling good are positive emotional states. Also the humor helps build a better relationship between the actor and the agent; as a result the agent's work life receives at least a modest boost. Another way in which humor enhances the target is that he or she might feel complimented because the actor thinks highly enough of him or her to share humor. Few people share humor with people they perceive to be enemies.

Political Correctness for Enhancing Others

A subtle way of enhancing other people is to respect their uniqueness and dignity rather than insulting them in some way based on a demographic characteristic. **Political correctness** refers to being careful not to offend or slight anyone, and being extra civil and respectful.[21] Being politically correct also contributes to making a good impression because the actor projects the image of being modern rather than traditional or old-fashioned. For example, a person who says "lady CEO" instead of "CEO" would project the image of being sexist and behind the times.

Political correctness enhances the other person because he or she is not singled out based on a demographic or physical characteristic not under his or her control, and that usually has no relationship to job performance. Assume that Jenny, who is 70 years old, is a mortgage specialist at a mortgage broker. Jenny will feel enhanced when the manager introduces a client to her thus: "Jenny, one of our most experienced and capable mortgage specialists. She will take great care of you." Jenny would feel much less enhanced, and perhaps demeaned, if she were introduced to the same client thus: "Jenny is working way beyond her retirement age, but can take great care of you based on her many years of experience." Two more examples of how being politically correct can enhance others, whereas being politically incorrect can diminish others, follow:

- *Scenario A:* The manager has a new opening for a supervisor of data analysis. One of the top performers in the group is Ashok, who was raised in India but is now an American citizen working in the United States. The manager says to Ashok, "We have an opening for a supervisor, but I assume that because of your background you would prefer to work with numbers and data." The manager is being politically incorrect because he assumes that Indians are interested in technical work at the exclusion of work involving considerable interaction with people.

  A more politically correct statement by the manager would have been, "Ashok, we have an opening for a new supervisory position in our department. Let me know if you are interested, and I will consider your credentials along with those of other data analysts interested in a supervisory position." Ashok now feels enhanced because he is perceived to be a technical specialist who might also be interested in a position involving considerable interaction with people.

- *Scenario B:* The manager of a customer-service group within a call center is making the rounds with a visitor from the home office, the vice president of information technology. As the manager walks down the corridor with the vice president he says, "Here is our wonderful customer-service team. As you can see, we have three guys and two girls working here." The men in the group hardly notice the manager's comment, yet the two women ("girls") think something to the effect, "What a put-down. We are *women* or at least *gals*. Jud (the manager) didn't label the guys as *boys*." Jud was therefore using a politically incorrect term, and delivered a slight insult as a result. If Jud had used a phrase that gave equal status to the men and women in his group, the women (or gals) would have been enhanced, or at least not demeaned a little.

Political incorrectness can also take the form of a **microinequity**, a small, semiconscious message sent with a powerful impact on the receiver. A microinequity might also be considered a subtle slight. The inequity might take the form of ignoring another person, a snub, or a sarcastic comment.[22] When the slight appears to be based on race, gender, religion, physical status, or other social identity group, the slight may appear to be political incorrectness. For example, the manager might say, "We are scheduled for outdoor training next month, and every physically capable member of the department will be invited." One of the department members listening to the manager is a wheelchair user, so he feels left out and slighted.

Avoiding microinequities is politically correct, and also enhances others. To be included is to be enhanced to some extent—and to be excluded because of a demographic characteristic is to be demeaned. Getting back to our manager, he or she could have avoided a microinequity and have been politically correct by saying, "We are scheduled for outdoor training next month, and there will be challenging activities for anybody willing to participate."

A caution about political correctness is that if carried to extremes it can be patronizing rather than enhancing. Robin J. Ely, Debra E. Meyerson, and Martin N. Davidson write that they embrace the commitment to equity that underlies political correctness, and then positive changes brought by that commitment.[23] They are troubled, however, by the barriers that political correctness can create to developing constructive, engaged relationships in the workplace.

Assume that Rick, a Native American, shows up at the office inebriated after lunch on two occasions. Sandra, his supervisor, wants to confront Rick about the problem and take the first step of discipline, an oral warning. Yet Sandra is in conflict because of political correctness. She thinks to herself, "The cultural stereotype is that Native Americans have problems with alcohol. If I confront Rick, he might think that I am confronting him about his drinking just because he is Native American. Maybe I should wait a little longer."

Guidelines for Application and Practice

1. Sincere flattery is one of the most effective techniques for enhancing others, thereby creating a positive impression. Guidelines have been developed for the skillful use of flattery, as described next.[24]

    *   Deliver it with credibility, or saying something about the target that is plausible and based on his or her legitimate accomplishment. For example, a credible compliment to a tech support specialist would be: "Thanks for

helping me out of a terrible jam. I can now continue my work." An incredible compliment would be: "It if were not for you, I would have given up using computers for life."

- Individualize your compliments rather than using the same old compliment for everyone. Your work associates will perceive you as insincere if they all hear the same compliments from you.

- Compliment what is of greatest importance to the flattery target. One approach to obtaining this information is to carefully observe what your target talks about with the most enthusiasm, such as his or her children or investments.

- Listening intently to another person is a powerful form of flattery. Just as most people do not receive enough compliments, most people also suffer from not being listened to enough. One of the most effective listening techniques is to paraphrase, or rephrase and summarize concisely what the target is saying. For example, if your target goes on a tirade about the company shipping hundreds of jobs overseas, you might respond, "You are upset about global outsourcing."

- Flatter by quoting the other person. By referring to or quoting (including paraphrasing) your target, you are paying him or her a substantial compliment. Part of the technique in question is to make reference to how your target handled a given situation. You might say, for example, "When Ashley faced a similar crisis, here's how she worked her way out of it."

- Giving positive feedback about the target's statements, actions, and results is a mild form of flattery. This approach to flattery involves giving people a straightforward declaration of what they did right. Feedback of this type is more effective when it is specific, such as: "Your suggestion for using smaller boxes for mailing our orders resulted in a $125,000 savings the first year."

- Remembering the names of people with whom you have infrequent contact flatters them because it suggests that you have paid close attention to them, and that they are important. Perhaps the most effective suggestion for remembering another person's name is upon first meeting to carefully listen to the person's name and then repeat it several times—to the target or to yourself.

2. When your target appears to be strongly people oriented, lavish general praise might be effective. However, when your target is more technically oriented, flattery and praise are more likely to be effective when muted, and pointed toward quite specific accomplishments.

3. Opinion conformity can be a useful form of enhancing another person, yet for best effectiveness should not be done to the point that you agree indiscriminately with your target. Agreement on all issues, including outside-of-work opinions,

might label you as a yes-person, thereby as lacking credibility as an independent thinker.

4. Judicious use of humor is an effective technique for enhancing others. Most targets will feel enhanced if they can appropriately joke and kid with a work associate.

5. Political correctness is useful in enhancing others because it can prevent one from insulting or demeaning others. Yet political correctness can backfire if done to the point of patronizing others by assigning them labels they do not want. For example, some adult female workers prefer to be referred to as "girls" rather than "women," perhaps because the term "girl" connotes a youthful outlook. Also, many black people in the United States prefer to be referred to as "black" rather than "African-American," especially when their country of origin is not the United States.

6. Techniques for enhancing others can give you a competitive edge, providing your job performance is also quite strong. However, excessive and indiscriminate enhancement of others can lead to the negative reputation of being a sycophant.

Summary

Enhancement of others refers to efforts by an actor to increase his or her attractiveness to a target based on the use of favorable evaluations of the target's attributes, behavior, or performance. Ingratiation is the major other-enhancing technique. Wanting to be liked and appreciated approaches the status of a universal human need, closely related to the need for recognition.

Balance theory helps explain the effectiveness of ingratiation. According to balance theory, a balance of sentiments (or feelings) is the implicit goal of interpersonal interaction. In practice this would mean that if you have a positive attitude toward another person, you would hope that your positive attitude is reciprocated.

Ingratiation, as with all tactics of impression management and influence, requires political skill to implement well. Without political skill, or finesse, an influence tactic might backfire, such as giving an off-the-wall compliment for purposes of ingratiation. Two studies with the same population of executives demonstrated that enhancing the right people through ingratiation facilitated becoming a member of the board of directors. Ingratiation toward a fellow director had a strong, positive effect on the likelihood that the focal director (actor) would receive an appointment to the board where the fellow director served on the nominating committee or as CEO.

Flattery is an effective form of enhancing others because most people want to receive accolades, even if they contain a little exaggeration. Another reason that flattery works well for enhancing other people is that most people want to be appreciated, and flattery can focus on their accomplishments. Also, people tend to like other people who like them, partially because most people look upon themselves favorably, and appreciate a reinforcement of this perception of self-worth. Flattery can be sincere and is likely to be a more effective technique of enhancing others when the actor is sincere. Nonverbal behavior will often tip off the target that the flattery is insincere. A foundation approach to flattery is to make other people feel important.

If a target receives only compliments from the actor, the target might soon think that the actor is not thinking critically or that he or she is insincere. To augment the power of flattery it is therefore best to mildly criticize the target in an acknowledged area of weakness. A study supported the idea that individuals with a strong people orientation may react more favorably to flattery than those with a strong technical orientation.

Another major technique of ingratiation is to agree with, or conform to, the opinion of another person. The target feels enhanced because the actor agrees with him or her. The more valued and credible the actor, the more enhanced the target feels. The more power an individual holds within an organization, the more likely it is that many people will conform to his or her opinion.

In order to be liked in the workplace as well as social life, many people use humor, thereby categorizing humor as another form of ingratiation. Humor has the potential to ingratiate the actor expressing the humor with targets who enjoy the humor. Workers who make judicious use of humor major can help the organization by improving morale because effective humor can trigger positive emotional contagion.

Political correctness enhances the other person because he or she is not singled out based on a demographic or physical characteristic not under his or her control, and that usually has no relationship to job performance. Political incorrectness can also take the form of a microinequity, a small, semiconscious message or slight sent with a powerful impact on the receiver.

A major guideline for effective flattery is to deliver it with credibility, or saying something about the target that is plausible and based on his or her legitimate accomplishment. Opinion conformity can be a useful form of other-enhancement, yet for best effectiveness should not be done to the point that you agree indiscriminately with your target. Other-enhancement techniques can give you a competitive edge, providing your job performance is also quite strong.

Chapter 7

Self-Protection Techniques

Most of the techniques of impression management described so far focus on the positive, such as being liked by others, making them laugh, doing favors, and creating a positive physical appearance. Impression management can also focus on attempting to avoid being seen negatively by others, such as covering up for a major mistake. As mentioned in Chapter 2, **self-protection techniques** (or identity protection techniques) are strategies and tactics directed toward the prevention of damage or harm to the actor's social identity in the perception of the target.[1] The actor does not want to be perceived in some negative way, such as being foolish or lacking good judgment, so the person finds a way to change how he or she is perceived by the audience.

For convenience, we place techniques of self-protection into two categories. The first category includes techniques of making excuses in advance just in case your performance is not so good, referred to as *self-handicapping*. The second category relates to patching up mistakes after they have occurred, referred to as *damage control*. Here we refer to damage control at a personal level, yet the same strategy is widely used at an organizational level when a company has committed a mistake such as having widely distributed contaminated food.

Figure 7-1 classifies the topics and subtopics presented in this chapter in terms of the amount of direct empirical support backing up the conclusions. However, several

Figure 7-1 Topics and Subtopics Related to Self-Protection Techniques According to Basis of Support.

Well Supported by Empirical Research	Supported More by Anecdote and Opinion
Effects of status on self-handicapping	Self-esteem protection
Gender differences in self-handicapping (based on older research with young adults)	Procrastination (including perfectionism) and self-handicapping
	Damage control: apologizing, pardon seeking, and making excuses; self-serving bias; error-recovery; and anger control

of the topics supported more by anecdote and opinion are based on systematic observation of extensive behavior samples. An example is the use of self-handicapping for purposes of self-esteem protection.

Self-Handicapping

Most people are familiar with self-handicapping as reflected by such statements as "I may not play at my best today, because my left ankle is still hurting from when I turned it a week ago" and "I might not give a good presentation today because I am still nursing a sore throat, so bear with me." If these people do perform well in their respective tasks, they should be admired because they have overcome a disabling problem. However, if they do not perform well their image will still be protected because they had a legitimate excuse for not performing well.

As defined by Edward R. Hirt, **self-handicapping** is an individual's attempt to reduce a threat to self-esteem by actively seeking or creating factors that prevent poor performance itself being perceived as a cause of failure. A causal explanation is thereby offered for failure that does not focus on the actor. With self-handicapping, the person creates an excuse for any potential failure before having tried to succeed. The goals of self-handicapping are to disregard ability as the cause of a poor performance and to pinpoint ability as the cause of success.[2] Another interpretation of these goals is that they are both designed to help the actor make a good impression. The self-handicapper sometimes creates physical conditions that will impair a future performance just to preempt perceptions of low ability as the cause of failure. A troubleshooter sent to a distant location to take care of an urgent problem might purposely take a late-night/early-morning flight that interferes with sleep. If the troubleshooter does not perform well, he or she has the ready excuse of having taken a "red-eye flight."

Here we look at several aspects of self-handicapping related to impression management, including self-esteem protection, status effects, procrastination, and gender effects.

Self-Esteem Protection

Although it may not appear logical, self-handicapping is a way of dealing with threats to self-esteem. As analyzed by Steven Berglas, self-handicapping behaviors are one of several modes of impression management available to those aiming to sustain a positive self-image.[3] In turn, the protected self-image protects the self-esteem. Self-handicapping behaviors stand alone among self-presentation tactics in their capacity to frame the context within which evaluations of the person take place. Instead of focusing on statements about the self, the actor manipulates the situation. Possible negative feedback is deflected or preempted entirely because the actor has provided an advance excuse for any possible below-par performance. For example, Fred says, "I will do what I can to make a coherent presentation this morning, but I was up all night helping with the flood damage in our office."

The self-handicapper controls the impressions of targets by getting into situations or circumstances that appear quite negative, but paradoxically allow the person to sustain an image of competence, and even sympathy. In the example at hand, "Fred is really wonderful. He made a reasonable presentation this morning despite being fatigued from dealing with flood damage."

Berglas explains that self-handicapping proceeds in one of two ways. One way is to find or create impediments that make successful performance less likely. The other way is to withdraw effort to make failure probable. After either tactic is implemented, future evaluations of performance become invalid. The self-handicapper's true abilities cannot be measured because impediments and low effort have prevented the true abilities from being displayed. The business sales representative might be able to sustain her image of being a top performer in the region despite having been placed third at the end of the quarter. "I had three giant sales lined up when a giant storm canceled my flight into the region to get the contracts signed." (Note that self-handicapping often takes the form of rationalization or excuse making.)

When the individual is victorious despite the presence of multiple plausible roadblocks, the role of ability is judged to be even greater. Assume that the sales representative did get to the customers, and closed the sales. She could then be judged as a super-heroine, after proclaiming, "The airlines were all shut down. So I jumped in the last car rental available and drove though a snow storm all night to make the sale."

To deal with the fear of deflating an inflated self-concept, the self-handicapper exposes himself or herself to damaging circumstances that lessen his or her capacity to succeed again. The failure is *discounted* because external factors appear to have created the problem. Should the person succeed, his or her competency image would be enhanced. Many people use airport delays (a highly frequent problem) for self-handicapping. If they are late for a meeting, or are distracted during the meeting, they blame the delayed flight. If they arrive on time and perform well, they mention the struggle to arrive on time despite the airport delay. (Self-handicapping could be made unnecessary here by flying the night before.)

As just implied, self-handicapping also helps protect self-esteem because it often results in a no-lose situation. The actor is applauded for doing well despite the handicap, and not blamed should he or she fail on the task. Perceptive targets, however, can often see through self-handicapping. I once told a tennis opponent that I was still recovering from a calf muscle injury, so I would not be playing full speed that day. He replied, "So if you lose you'll have an excuse. And if you beat me, I'll feel like I couldn't even beat an opponent who played on one good leg."

Self-handicapping for self-esteem protection can become pathological, particularly when the actor resorts to alcohol and other drugs as handicapping mechanisms. Assume that an entrepreneur has a command performance scheduled for a Monday morning. She is going to make a pitch to potential investors. To handicap herself in case she fails, she gets drunk on Sunday night. If she fails to obtain the funds she needs, she can blame the rejection on not having been in top form. If she does make a successful pitch for funding, she can give herself extra credit for have performed well despite her hangover. Command performances in the future, including meeting with a major customer, are likely to also include alcohol intoxication as a handicapping mechanism.

The Effects of Status on Self-Handicapping

Considering that self-handicapping occurs primarily when self-esteem is threatened, it follows that high-status individuals are more likely to self-handicap than low-status individuals. The logic is that high-status individuals care more about esteem. Status and self-esteem are therefore intertwined. Jeffrey W. Lucas and Michael J. Lovaglia conducted an experiment to investigate the proposition that social status plays a role in the decision to handicap.[4] (The effects of gender and race on self-handicapping were also investigated, with gender results described here later. Race did not receive enough attention in the study to report here.)

The researchers defined **status** as a person's rank in a social hierarchy based on the esteem accorded that person by the self and others. Lucas and Lovaglia reasoned that if self-handicapping serves to reduce a threat to esteem, and if high-status people have more esteem to protect than do those with low status, then high-status individuals would be more likely to self-handicap.

Background Information about Status and Self-Handicapping

It has been found that self-handicapping is more likely when the results of a performance will be publicly known, such as a sales contest, or the posting of productivity data on a company internal website. *Status characteristics theory* proposes that members of a group form expectations about the competence of each other to contribute to group goals based on their status characteristics. For example, Bill may be expected to perform well because he has an MBA from the Kellogg School of Northwestern University. Those persons expected to make a stronger contribution are more highly valued by the group, and held in higher esteem. A **status characteristic** is any feature of an individual for which expectations and beliefs come to be organized.

A *diffuse* status characteristic carries expectations for competence and performance in a wide variety of situations. Two examples are a high level of education, and experience at a prestigious company such as GE or IBM might afford an individual high status in many work situations. A *specific* status characteristic carries high expectations for competence and performance in a narrow range of work situations. Having specific knowledge such as an American worker being fluent in Chinese might give the person high status in a business unit that deals with a Chinese company. Both diffuse and specific status characteristics contribute to establishing a group member's status. The characteristics alter the expectations of competence held by fellow group members of one another, whether or not the characteristics are task relevant.

Status characteristics theory posits that those individuals expected to make competent contributions to group goals are treated in ways that reinforce their competence, and indicate how much esteem they hold. When group members have high status, four positive consequences emerge. First, they are given more opportunities to perform in the group. Second, they in fact perform to a higher extent. Third, their performance is evaluated more highly. Fourth, they have more influence over group decisions.

The esteem accorded to high-status individuals derives from expectations that they will make contributions of value. Those expectations will be reinforced when the individual performs well, and receives high evaluations from the group. Similarly, the expectations will be undermined if the individual performs poorly and receives a negative evaluation. Competence expectations become self-fulfilling because individuals with high status are allowed to perform more, and are more highly evaluated. Getting back to our worker with Chinese-language skills, she might be given the honor of being the host for a visiting executive from China. The woman does a wonderful job as the host, and receives even more status within the group.

A proposition developed by Lucas and Lovaglia, as well as others who research self-handicapping, is that high-status individuals regularly experience non-contingent success. In other words, they succeed without having done anything in particular to merit that success. High-status individuals are amply rewarded in life but they wonder why they deserved the success, and if the rewards (or their lucky streak) might end. High status results in non-contingent success that is conducive to self-handicapping. A primary reason is that when someone receives non-contingent success, he or she wonders, "Was I successful for what I did or for who I was?"[5] The ambiguity seems to encourage self-handicapping.

Research Design and Results of the Study

The researchers predicted that if status has an effect on self-handicapping, European-American participants will self-handicap more than will African-Americans, Asian-Americans, or Hispanic-Americans. (The researchers apparently believed that European-Americans have higher status than the three other demographic groups.) The student participants completed a standard ability test with the expectation that their test performance would be made public in a subsequent group discussion. Prior to taking the test, students were able to select the amount of study time they wanted to use to prepare for the test.

The measure of self-handicapping used in the study in question was the amount of practice time that participants choose before taking a test. The same measure of amount of time invested in study had been used by other experimenters. Choosing more time to study indicates less self-handicapping. (If you do not study much for a test, you cannot blame your cognitive skills as the cause of poor performance.)

European-American men (24 students) selected the lowest amount of study time to prepare for the tests, an average of 8.38 minutes. The study time chosen by non-European-American men was consistently higher than that by European-American men, an average of 11.45 minutes. The results indicated that European-American men self-handicapped more than did non-European-American men. (By putting less time into studying, the European-American men were handicapping themselves more than the men who were not European-American.)

The researchers believed that their study supported the hypothesis that self-handicapping behavior is related to the desire to protect a valued status position. In other words, if you believe that you have high status you are more likely to self-handicap in order to protect that status.

Procrastination as Self-Handicapping

A widely practiced form of self-defeating behavior as well as self-handicapping is to delay taking action when it is needed. **Procrastination** is delaying a task for an invalid or weak reason. Taking the quiz presented in Figure 7-2 provides some

Figure 7-2 A Quiz about Procrastination Tendencies.

Instructions: Circle "Yes" or "No" for each item.

1. I usually do my best work under the pressure of deadlines.   Yes   No

2. Before starting a project, I go through such rituals as sharpening every pencil, straightening up my desk more than once, and reading and responding to all possible e-mails.   Yes   No

3. I crave the excitement of the "last-minute rush," such as researching and writing a paper right before the deadline.   Yes   No

4. I often think that if I delay something, it will go away, or the person who asked for it will forget about it.   Yes   No

5. I extensively research something before taking action, such as obtaining three different estimates before getting the brakes repaired on my car.   Yes   No

6. I have a great deal of difficulty getting started on most projects, even those I enjoy.   Yes   No

7. I keep waiting for the right time to do something, such as getting started on an important report.   Yes   No

8. I often underestimate the time needed to do a project, and say to myself, "I can do this quickly, so I'll wait until next week."   Yes   No

9. It is difficult for me to finish most projects or activities.   Yes   No

10. I have several favorite diversions or distractions that I use to keep me from doing something unpleasant, such as a difficult homework assignment or finding an error in my checkbook.   Yes   No

Total Yes Responses _____

Scoring and Interpretation: The greater the number of "yes" responses, the more likely it is that you have a serious procrastination problem. A score of 8, 9, or 10 strongly suggests that your procrastination is lowering your productivity.

insight into procrastination. The person who delays action for a good reason, such as not purchasing a mutual fund until its value declines, is not procrastinating. He or she is timing a purchase for what appears to be a valid reason—an existing price that is inflated. Two of the factors contributing to procrastination (being overwhelmed and perfectionism) help explain why delaying a task for an invalid or weak reason is linked to self-handicapping. A major reason for procrastinating is that we find a task facing us to be overwhelming.[6]

Max, a small-business owner preparing to pay income taxes, procrastinates. To avoid the overwhelming task of gathering all the data to complete the income tax form, Max floods himself with small, easy-to-do tasks. By getting submerged in all these tasks, Max will not have sufficient time to do a superior job of tax preparation, and will most likely miss the deadline for submitting the tax form. Max can say to himself after the income tax task is finally completed, "I could have done a much better job, and done it on time, if I didn't get tripped up by so many other urgent tasks." A true self-handicapper, he has found a good reason that blocked his true task competence from surfacing. Max has therefore protected himself from projecting a poor image to himself, and perhaps to those close to him.

Perfectionism is a second contributing factor to procrastination that also ties in with self-handicapping. Perfectionists attempt to get a project just right before admitting it is completed. As a result, the person procrastinates not about beginning a project, but letting go. When asked, "Have you finished that project?" the perfectionist replies, "No, I have a few more small details to work out." Another indirect method of self-handicapping has now taken place. The many small, necessary details to the project prevented the true talents of the self-handicapper from being visible. If he or she had the project completed on time, feedback on his or her abilities would be received earlier. However, by getting bogged down in details the self-handicapper believes that he or she has protected himself or herself from creating a negative impression. The quiz contained in Figure 7-3 provides insights into many of the everyday symptoms of perfectionism.

The person who uses perfectionism for self-handicapping seems to ignore two important facts that could damage the impression he or she creates. First, perfectionism is viewed negatively by many targets because perfectionists appear to be obsessed over details, and they are often quite critical of others. Second, not delivering a project on time will be viewed quite negatively by deadline-conscious managers and other workers.

A small-business owner wrote a letter to psychiatrist and columnist Kerry Sulkowicz, asking for help with his procrastination problem. The letter illustrates the self-handicapping element to procrastination, as follows:

> I procrastinate and always have. When I had a corporate job, I would put off work that was challenging, then cram to make the deadline as my stress level soared. Now I own a small business, and the pattern remains. If I'm to give a presentation to potential clients,

Figure 7-3 Tendencies toward Perfectionism.

Instructions: Many perfectionists hold some of the behaviors and attitudes described below. To help you understand your tendencies toward perfectionism, rate how strongly you agree with each of the statements below on a scale of 0–4.

1.	Many people have told me that I am a perfectionist.	0	1	2	3	4
2.	I often correct the speech of others.	0	1	2	3	4
3.	It takes me a long time to write an e-mail because I keep checking and rechecking my writing.	0	1	2	3	4
4.	I often criticize the color combinations my friends are wearing.	0	1	2	3	4
5.	When I purchase food at a supermarket, I usually look at the expiration date so I can purchase the freshest food.	0	1	2	3	4
6.	I can't stand when people use the term "remote" instead of "remote control."	0	1	2	3	4
7.	If a company representative asked me "What is your *social*?" I would reply something like, "Do you mean my *social security number*?"	0	1	2	3	4
8.	I hate to see dust on furniture.	0	1	2	3	4
9.	I like the Martha Stewart idea of having every decoration in the home just right.	0	1	2	3	4
10.	I never put a map back in the glove compartment until it is folded just right.	0	1	2	3	4
11.	Once an eraser on a pencil of mine becomes hard and useless, I throw the pencil away.	0	1	2	3	4
12.	I adjust all my watches and clocks so they show exactly the same time.	0	1	2	3	4
13.	It bothers me that clocks on personal computers are often wrong by a few minutes.	0	1	2	3	4
14.	I clean the keyboard on my computer at least once a week.	0	1	2	3	4
15.	I organize my e-mail messages and computer documents into many different, clearly labeled files.	0	1	2	3	4
16.	You won't find old coffee cups or soft-drink containers on my desk.	0	1	2	3	4
17.	I rarely start a new project or assignment until I have completed my present project or assignment.	0	1	2	3	4
18.	It is very difficult for me to concentrate when my work area is disorganized.	0	1	2	3	4
19.	Cobwebs in chandeliers and other lighting fixtures bug me.	0	1	2	3	4
20.	It takes me a long time to make a purchase such as a digital camera because I keep studying the features on various models.	0	1	2	3	4

(Continued)

Figure 7-3 Continued

21.	When I balance my checkbook, it usually comes out right within a few dollars.	0	1	2	3	4
22.	I carry enough small coins and dollar bills with me so when I shop I can pay the exact amount without requiring change.	0	1	2	3	4
23.	I throw out any underwear or tee-shirts that have even the smallest holes or tears.	0	1	2	3	4
24.	I become upset with myself if I make a mistake.	0	1	2	3	4
25.	When a fingernail of mine is broken or chipped, I fix it as soon as possible.	0	1	2	3	4
26.	I am carefully groomed whenever I leave my home.	0	1	2	3	4
27.	When I notice packaged goods or cans on the floor in a supermarket, I will often place them back on the shelf.	0	1	2	3	4
28.	I think that carrying around anti-bacterial cleaner for the hands is an excellent idea.	0	1	2	3	4
29.	If I am with a friend, and he or she has a loose hair on his or her shoulder, I will remove it without asking.	0	1	2	3	4
30.	I know that I am a perfectionist.	0	1	2	3	4

Scoring

91 or over:	You have strong perfectionist tendencies to the point that it could interfere with your taking quick action when necessary. Also, you may annoy many people with your perfectionism.
61–90:	Moderate degree of perfectionism that could lead you to produce high-quality work and be a dependable person.
31–60:	Mild degree of perfectionism. You might be a perfectionist in some situations quite important to you, but not in others.
0–30:	Not a perfectionist. You might be too casual about getting things done right.

for instance, I prepare only at the last minute, my anxiety mounting as the day approaches and I do nothing. How can I change?[7]

Observe that the last-minute presentation means that the small-business owner probably does not do the best possible job he could. Yet in the owner's eyes, it would be unfair to judge his performance negatively because he did not have much time to prepare.

Gender Differences in Self-Handicapping

According to research and opinion, self-handicapping is more frequent among men than women. The study mentioned above involving self-handicapping by studying for shorter periods of time examined gender differences in addition to status differences. According to the author's argument, based on observations and research prior to 2005, men have generally been granted higher status than women in our society. Men would therefore have a stronger incentive to self-handicap than would women. According to the synthesis of Lucas and Lovaglia, various studies have found that men do indeed self-handicap more consistently than do women, and in a variety of contexts, including school settings and social situations. Several of these studies were conducted with grade-school children during the 1990s.[8]

Gender differences were found with respect to the amount of study time chosen to prepare for an exam. Both European-American women and non-European-American women prepared for the exams more than did their male counterparts. We repeat the operational definition of self-handicapping—the longer the study time the less the self-handicapping. Status differences were also found among women, with European-American women studying less than non-European-American women. The interpretation given by the researchers is that European-American women self-handicapped more than did non-European-American women.

We caution the reader that women have higher status in the workplace today than when the research on gender differences in self-handicapping took place. Also, the time selected to study for an exam is only one manifestation of self-handicapping.

A series of three studies involving several hundred subjects conducted by Edward R. Hirt, Sean M. McCrea, and Hillary I. Boris provides more understanding of gender differences in self-handicapping. The researchers found that women have less tolerance for self-handicapping on test performance whether done by men or women. When men make lame excuses for poor test performance, the women are not convinced. The women routinely made negative evaluations of self-handicapping by participants, even when alternative explanations for withdrawing effort, such as peer pressure, were made known. Women in the study were found to be more suspicious of people who blow things off or withdraw effort. Furthermore, the women had a stronger tendency to think a self-handicapper is lazy, unmotivated, or lacking in self-control.

The researchers believed that their findings reflect a fundamental difference between men and women in what they consider valuable in task performance. Men were shown to be more lenient in their attributions of self-handicapping targets than were women. The men in the study were also less likely to attribute negative motivations to self-handicappers. In contrast, women have little respect for those who fail to expend effort in important performance settings because they have low motivation.

According to Hirt, McCrea, and Boris, gender differences in attitudes toward self-handicapping might reflect broad gender differences in personality.[9] Yet we caution that as women have achieved more equality with men in the workplace in terms of status and position, they may have developed more tolerant attitudes toward self-handicapping.

Damage Control

A buzzword in business and politics relating to self-protective impression management is **damage control**. It refers figuratively to taking positive action to make excuses for or repair the negative consequences of having made a serious mistake, and received unfavorable publicity. A business executive accused of traveling around the world in a corporate jet, often accompanied by his wife, while at the same time masterminding the layoff of several thousand workers might feel compelled to repair his image. An explanation is sent by e-mail to all company employees explaining that the executive's time is so valuable that flying by corporate jet is cost effective. If he were forced to fly on commercial planes he would lose valuable time that could otherwise be invested in company business. As for the wife, she is a bargain to shareholders because she provides a variety of administrative tasks for the executive at no extra cost to the company.

A less grandiose attempt at damage control to protect the image would take place after a manager made an abusive and insulting comment toward a colleague at a meeting. The participants at the meeting suddenly halt their work, and stare in shock at the manager. She replies, "Please excuse me folks. I'm so passionate about what we are doing here today. I got wound up too tight. Please don't judge me based on this one isolated outburst."

Four approaches to damage control covered here are admitting mistakes; apologizing, pardon seeking, making excuses; recovering from a major error on the job; and anger control.

Admitting Mistakes

Many people believe that to create a good impression it is best to cover up for mistakes. In this way you will not appear vulnerable. However, mistakes are often obvious, and attempting a cover-up will create a negative impression. For purposes of protective impression management it is therefore better to admit mistakes, thereby appearing more forthright and trustworthy. The simple statement "I goofed" will often gain you sympathy and support, whereas an attempted cover-up will decrease your social capital and damage your impression.

After having made a mistake, honesty is a recommended plan of action to protect your image. Career coach Rhoda Smackum suggests you say something like: "This is what I thought at the time, this is why I made the decision I did, and now based on current information, I think we should have done X, Y, and Z." Smackum also says that when you lay things out and communicate openly with people, they may become upset when you do change course. However, they at least know that you are going to try to make decisions based on honesty, and your best available information.[10] When using this approach you are taking responsibility for your mistake, and then arriving at a solution for the problem—both of which are effective approaches to protective impression management.

Apologizing, Pardon Seeking, and Making Excuses

Protective impression management frequently involves dealing with the potential negative effects of having made a mistake or done something wrong. The intent is to protect the actor's image after it would have been reasonable for the target or targets to develop a negative evaluation of the actor. Among the tactics for "covering one's hide" are offering apologies, seeking a pardon for the misdeeds, and making excuses.

Apologizing and Pardon Seeking

An antecedent to offering apologies is to admit mistakes, thereby appearing forthright and trustworthy. At the managerial level, a mistake often involves making a major decision that proved to have expensive negative consequences such as a change in organization structure that resulted in poor customer service.

Apologizing can also strengthen the actor's image because a person who admits mistakes may gain in credibility. Conflicts can sometimes be resolved quickly if a manager will admit having made a mistake with a subordinate, and then offer an apology. "I'm sorry" are usually perceived to be powerful words because people in positions of authority are often hesitant to apologize for a mistake.[11] Here is an example of a scenario that would involve a manager apologizing for a mistake that disappointed a subordinate:

> A manager told a contract employee working as a direct-mail specialist that she would be offered full-time employee status as soon as the new budget cycle began. One month after the new budget cycle began the specialist's employment status still had not changed. She sent an e-mail to the boss wondering what happened. The manager immediately telephoned the specialist and said, "I goofed. You were on my to-do list, but I did not follow through. But I will make your change in status retroactive to the first day of the new budget cycle."

Asking for a pardon typically follows the apology because the latter helps gain support and sympathy. Convicted felons who express no remorse for their acts often receive a more severe sentence than if they had apologized or expressed regret. A sales representative asking for a pardon from his or her manager might take this form: "I should never have offered the client a kickback. I just got too caught up in trying to close the deal. Please give me another chance to prove myself."

Excuses and the Self-Serving Bias

For many people, the easiest way to preserve their image is to explain why a negative event was not their fault. According to Tedeschi and Riess, "Excuses are explanations in which one admits that the disruptive act is bad, wrong, or inappropriate but dissociates himself or herself from it."[12] The actor frequently attempts to avoid responsibility for the negative outcome by pointing to a force beyond his or her control that created the outcome. When asked by the board why voluntary turnover among key people is so high, the CEO might reply, "Our turnover is high because we are so successful. Other companies are eager to hire our managers and professionals because of our reputation. The competition will pay outrageous salaries and bonuses to steal our people."

Excuses have also been framed as being a component of *accounts*—an explanation of a predicament-creating event to minimize the negative impact of the predicament. The account will usually involve excuses, defenses of innocence, or justifications. The actor explains why some factor beyond his or her control created the problem in order to preserve a positive impression. For example, a worker explains to the supervisor, "I don't know what happened to the hydraulic press. I've kept up with the maintenance, but it's not working correctly. It must have been defective."[13]

Both comments about excuses made above point to the general principle of the **self-serving bias**.[14] The self-serving bias in attributing causes refers to the almost reflexive tendency of individuals to attribute successful outcomes to themselves and failed outcomes to external factors. In terms of self-protective impression management, blaming the environment or external factors deflects attention from a damaged social identity. Reflect on the familiar scenario after an automobile accident. The person who crashed into another vehicle, or hit a pedestrian, or ran into a building says, "It wasn't my fault. My brakes gave way." Poor brakes, not poor driving, were the cause of the accident, so the driver's image as a good driver is preserved. A deeper look at this scenario would suggest that a *good driver* has the brakes inspected regularly, and does not wait to replace them so long as they squeeze by inspection.

As a workplace example, think of the real estate agent who tells his boss, "I couldn't make my quota this quarter. Nobody is buying real estate. The economy is putrid." The agent's image as an effective real estate agent is preserved—in his or her perception. The manager who does not buy into the self-serving bias might comment, "Real estate sales are down 20% this year in our region. That hardly translates into *nobody is buying*."

Some excuses are more effective than others. Based on a synthesis of relevant research, Rosenfeld, Giacolone, and Riordan have identified three characteristics of effective excuses, particularly as they relate to the workplace.[15] The first characteristic is *perceived adequacy*, or the extent to which the excuse is perceived as logical and reasonable under the circumstances. An adequate excuse conforms to the facts and presents enough detail to be convincing. The CEO of one company eliminated the year-end bonuses for employees one year. At first, most employees were outraged. The CEO then gave a detailed presentation of how a competitor was beating the company on price, therefore making cost-cutting a necessity. To her credit, the CEO also explained in detail how eliminating the bonus for the year in question would save nine jobs.

The second characteristic is *norm conformance*, or how actions should be explained. Certain accounts may be perceived as appropriate to the situations, whereas others may be perceived as inappropriate. A construction delay on the highway might be an acceptable excuse for being late for a Monday morning briefing. However, the same construction delay would not be perceived as an appropriate excuse for being late for a strategy meeting with top-level officials. The late attendee would be seen negatively for not having planned enough extra time to deal with a contingency. In other words, an excuse has to offer an acceptable explanation. For example, "I forgot to back up my file" is no longer an acceptable excuse, but it did work in the past.

The third characteristic is *perceived sincerity*, or truthfulness of the excuse. The CEO mentioned above was perceived as sincere when providing the excuse for not giving employees a year-end bonus. Two factors contributed to the employee perception of sincerity. She had a good track record of credibility, and the management team was also denied a bonus that year.

Recovering from a Major Error on the Job

Self-protective impression management increases in importance in direct relation to the magnitude of the mistake. An eight-step procedure has been developed to recover from a major error in the workplace that incorporates many of the ideas already presented in this chapter. Examples of a major error include missing a delivery date by several months on a major product, hiring an executive who is later discovered to have a criminal record, and allowing a product with a major safety or health problem to be distributed. The error-recovery procedure is as follows:[16]

1. *Take responsibility.* Taking responsibility for blame rather than finger pointing creates a positive impression. Taking responsibility also makes a person appear strong in control, whereas making excuses projects an image of weakness and ineptness.
2. *Analyze the failure.* An essential step for personal growth is to take time to figure out what really went wrong, and devise a plan to prevent the mistake from happening again. Key individuals in the organization can then be informed that the setback is now under control, and will not reoccur.
3. *Avoid beating yourself up.* One big mistake does not mean that a person is incompetent, or that a career is ruined. Negative self-talk will only make the person feel worse and will often project a poor image.
4. *Keep it in perspective.* It is recommended that you try the five test: Ask yourself, "How much will this matter to my company in five days? In five weeks? In five months? In five years?" In this way you avoid thinking of this as a life-or-death situation. Failure on the job is usually a *temporary* situation, particularly if the individual had a positive reputation before the major mistake occurred.

5. *Talk it over with someone you trust.* Talking with a trusted person outside the organization can have a calming effect on the individual. Also, discussing feelings about a setback is a major step in the recovery process.

6. *Give it time.* A person should take sufficient time to recover from and regroup after the negative experience, yet not continue to ruminate on the mistake. In the meantime the person should put on a "game face." Projecting the appearance of the walking wounded will not instill confidence in others and will create a negative image.

7. *Consider training.* If the mistake or failed project is the result of a lack of specific skill or technical expertise, the person should seek out training. For example, lateness on a project can sometimes be attributed to limited skill in forecasting and scheduling.

8. *Get over it.* The mistake should be thought of as a learning experience. After that the person should move on because dwelling on failure is paralyzing and creates a negative image.

Anger Control

Damage control is often necessary after a person has exhibited an outburst of anger. A proactive approach to impression management would therefore be to manage anger before it manifests itself in outward behavior that damages a person's social identity. A health newsletter provides a representative quick guide to anger management. To take control of anger: (1) give yourself time to defuse before reacting by counting to 10; (2) go for a short walk until you calm down; (3) distract yourself by diving into a task to convert negative energy to positive; (4) keep a log of hostile thoughts to understand how frequently your temperature rises; and (5) try professional help if managing outbursts seems impossible on your own.[17]

Guidelines for Application and Practice

1. Self-handicapping is a widely practiced form of protective impression management, yet self-handicapping will frequently lead to negative consequences. Many targets will perceive the self-handicapper as making lame excuses, such as "I was up all night with a sick child so I may not perform well in this morning's meeting." Self-handicapping by such methods as getting drunk the night before a command performance is self-defeating, and could lead to a pattern of such behavior.

2. Limited studying for an exam has been used frequently as a research measure of self-handicapping. A self-handicapping technique of this nature fools only the self-handicapper, not other people. Imagine the negative consequences of failing an important exam in school, or for such purposes as gaining advanced certification in a field (e.g. CPA or nursing license), because the person chose to self-handicap.

3. Self-handicapping in the form of creating excuses in advance for poor performance can conceivably work well once or twice. However, repeated use of self-handicapping will create a negative rather than a positive impression.
4. Procrastination is a strongly negative form of self-handicapping because procrastination is a major type of self-defeating behavior. Procrastinating too frequently creates a poor image, and often leads to impaired performance which intensifies the poor image.
5. Perfectionism contributes to procrastination, yet is less self-defeating than a form of procrastination such as not even getting started on a project. Also, targets may have sympathy for an agent who proclaims, "I am almost ready with my report, but I need to refine a few more details."
6. For purposes of impression management, the bottom line of being wrong is (1) admit the error, (2) request guidance, (3) step up, repair, and (4) learn from it. Requesting guidance is helpful because it conveys the impression that you have humility and that you trust the advice and counsel of others.[18]

Summary

Self-handicapping is an attempt to reduce a threat to self-esteem by actively seeking or creating factors that prevent poor performance itself from being perceived as a cause of failure. With self-handicapping, the person creates an excuse for any potential failure before having tried to succeed.

Self-handicapping is a complicated way of protecting against threats to self-esteem. Self-handicapping behaviors stand alone among self-presentation tactics in their capacity to frame the context within which evaluations of the person take place. Instead of focusing on statements about the self, the actor manipulates the situation. The self-handicapper's true abilities cannot be measured because impediments and low effort have prevented the true abilities from being displayed. The failure is discounted because external factors appear to have created the problem. Self-handicapping also helps protect self-esteem because it often results in a no-lose situation.

High-status individuals are more likely to self-handicap than low-status individuals. Self-handicapping is more likely when the results of a performance will be publicly known. A diffuse status characteristic carries expectations of competence and performance in a wide variety of situations, whereas a specific status characteristic is focused on a narrow range of work situations.

Status characteristics theory posits that those individuals expected to make competent contributions to group goals are treated in ways that reinforce their competence, and indicate how much esteem they hold. The esteem accorded to high-status individuals derives from expectations that they will make contributions of value. High-status individuals regularly experience non-contingent success—succeeding without having done anything in particular to merit that success. Non-contingent success leads to self-handicapping. A study summarized here supported the hypothesis that self-handicapping behavior is related to the desire to protect a valued status position.

Procrastination is a widely practiced form of self-defeating behavior as well as self-handicapping. Two leading contributors to procrastination are the desire to avoid an overwhelming task, and perfectionism, both of which can be used to self-handicap. Both provide excuses for not performing to capacity.

According to research and opinion, self-handicapping is more frequent among men than women. A contributing factor could be that, at least in the past, men have generally been granted higher status than women in our society. It has also been found that women have less tolerance for self-handicapping on test performance by both men and women.

Damage control is a major category of self-protective impression management. For purposes of protective impression management it is better to admit mistakes, thereby appearing more forthright and trustworthy. After having made a mistake, honesty is a recommended plan of action to protect the image.

Protective impression management frequently involves dealing with the potential negative effects of having made a mistake or done something wrong. An antecedent to offering apologies is to admit mistakes, thereby appearing forthright and trustworthy. Apologizing can also strengthen the actor's image because a person who admits mistakes may gain in credibility. Conflicts can sometimes be resolved quickly if a manager will admit having made a mistake with a subordinate, and then offer an apology. Asking for a pardon typically follows the apology because the latter helps gain support and sympathy.

For many people, the easiest way to preserve their image is to explain why a negative event was not their fault (an excuse). Excuses are part of accounts—an explanation of a predicament-creating event to minimize the negative impact of the predicament. The self-serving bias in attributing causes refers to the tendency for people to attribute successful outcomes to themselves and failed outcomes to external factors. Blaming the environment or external factors defects attention from a damaged social identity. Effective excuses have perceived adequacy, conform to norms of acceptable excuses, and perceived sincerity.

An eight-step procedure has been developed to recover from a major workplace mistake: (1) take responsibility, (2) analyze the failure, (3) avoid beating yourself up, (4) keep it in perspective, (5) talk it over with someone you trust, (6) give it time, (7) consider training, and (8) get over it.

Managing anger before it manifests itself in outward behavior that damages a person's social identity is advisable. Among five recommended steps are to go for a short walk until you calm down, and keep a log of hostile thoughts to understand how frequently your temperature rises.

Guidelines for application and skill development in relation to self-protective impression management include: (1) minimize self-handicapping, (2) avoid procrastination, and (3) admit you were wrong.

Chapter 8

Impression Management for Job Search and Performance Evaluation

For many workers and prospective workers, impression management connotes creating a good impression when conducting a job search. To a lesser extent, impression management connotes creating a positive impression on the manager during a performance review or appraisal. In this chapter we review and integrate representative research about impression management for purposes of the job interview, traditional and video résumés, and the performance evaluation. We also present several representative recommendations for using this information to conduct a successful job search. Figure 8-1 organizes the information in this chapter according to the amount of research substantiation.

Impression Management Related to the Job Interview

Impression management is similar to an advertising campaign that individuals conduct on their own behalf with the intent of highlighting their own virtues and minimizing their deficiencies. As Clive Fletcher notes, there can be few situations, if any, that bring such activities into sharper focus than the employment interview.[1] Job candidates are active participants in the interview process, and they consciously attempt to manage their self-presentation and the enhancement of others in order to influence the interviewer.[2] Fletcher observes also that all job candidate behavior in interviews can be framed as impression management, although with varying degrees of conscientiousness, control, and success.[3]

Our approach to understanding the use of impression management related to the job interview encompasses the following: tactics frequently used during the interview; situational influences on the choices of impression management tactics; the role of self-monitoring; the relative contribution of impression management versus job competence behaviors to interviewer judgments; and impressions created after the interview.

Figure 8-1 Topics and Subtopics Related to Impression Management during the Job Interview and Performance Evaluation According to Basis of Support.

Well Supported by Empirical Research	Supported More by Anecdote and Opinion
Impression management tactics frequently used during the interview: assertiveness, ingratiation, entitlements and enhancements, physical appearance and attractiveness	Impression management tactics frequently used during the interview: self-promotion, opinion conformity, excuses, justifications, apologies, nonverbal behavior
Candidate self-monitoring and interview ratings	Situational attributes that influence the choice of impression management tactics (interviewee, interviewer, situation itself)
Impression management versus job competencies in determining interview ratings	Post-interview impression management
Impression management for traditional résumés; frequency of lying on résumés	Impression management for video résumés
Ingratiation to enhance performance evaluations	Variables influencing impression management for performance evaluation
	Performance blips to enhance performance evaluations

Impression Management Tactics Frequently Used during the Job Interview

The job interview is a natural stage for engaging in impression management. As a result, most of the known tactics of impression management have been reported in research studies about job interviews. A list of most of the tactics identified in research studies follows, with a statement of how each one relates to an employment interview.[4]

Assertiveness

To be effective during a job interview, the candidate usually has to be assertive in such areas as volunteering information, asking questions, complimenting the company and the interviewer, and providing opinions when asked. Assertiveness is essential for the candidate to portray himself or herself as a particular type of person with appropriate skills, talent, and experience. Assertiveness is also a personality trait that supports the tactics of impression management that follow.

Self-Promotion

The natural impression management tactic to use during a job interview is to emphasize competence and skills in talking with the interviewer. The newcomer to the job market might emphasize high-class standing, as well as important field projects and internships. The experienced worker might mention objective accomplishments such as the amount of money a project saved the company, attaining a high quality standard, or exceeding a sales quota. Self-promotion is important in virtually all job interviews, yet is even more important when the interviewer has high status, such as being an executive. A key reason is that high-status workers are likely to appreciate others who have accomplished enough to merit high status. This is particularly true when the high-status worker earned his or her position via accomplishments.

Figure 8-2 gives you an opportunity to think through specific self-promotional statements you might use during a job interview.

Ingratiation

The job interview provides a natural setting for attempts to be liked by the other person through such means as complimenting the potential employer and its products and services, the interviewer, the company's treatment of him or her, and how well he or she has been treated. The purpose of ingratiation in this setting is to get the interviewer to like and be attracted to the applicant. A subtle form of ingratiation during the job interview is to express interest in becoming a long-term member of the hiring organization. Ingratiation attempts are such a natural part of being interviewed that the interviewee who does not engage in ingratiation might be perceived as being low in social skill.

Figure 8-2 Self-Promoting Statements for the Job Interview.

When being interviewed for a position you want to obtain, consider choosing some of the statements below to promote yourself—providing the statements reflect the truth. The statements below might also be regarded as a self-analysis of the strengths you might bring to a prospective employer. Prior to choosing among these self-promoting statements, you might want to solicit feedback about your strengths from another person who knows you well. As you read these statements, check those that appear to accurately reflect what you can do now.

Task Focus

1. My productivity is much higher than average. ☐
2. I have received a lot of compliments about my work ethic. ☐
3. You can count on me to meet or beat a deadline. ☐
4. I have been accused of being somewhat of a perfectionist. ☐
5. If I am hired by your company, my key goal will be to add value to your company. ☐
6. I will put in as much time as necessary to get the job done. ☐
7. If I do not meet or surpass your expectations, I hope that you would fire me. ☐

8. Troubleshooting is one of my best skills. ☐
9. My IT skills are exceptional even in comparison to Generation Y people. ☐
10. I am at my best under the pressure of a tough task. ☐
11. You will never find me surfing the Internet in company time. ☐
12. The joy of accomplishment is more important to me than the joy of a paycheck. ☐
13. I will never pretend I know the answer when I don't. Instead, I will go find the answer. ☐
14. I'm a winner, and I will help my team win. ☐
15. If you need something done right away, please call on me. ☐

Interpersonal Focus

1. I am considered to be an outstanding team player. ☐
2. I have had a lot of success in resolving conflict between people. ☐
3. I may be old-fashioned, but I think that dressing to impress is still very important. ☐
4. I am able to smile at customers even if I am having a bad day. ☐
5. Several people have told me that I am a good listener. ☐
6. I get along well with people from different generations. ☐
7. Working well with people from different cultures is a real strength of mine. ☐
8. I regard being criticized as a valuable learning experience. ☐
9. My network is loaded with dedicated and talented people. ☐
10. You will find many different types of people in my network. ☐
11. I think that I can fit in with most organizational cultures. ☐
12. I can work with a difficult customer or coworker by showing him or her compassion and understanding. ☐
13. I feel natural and relaxed socializing with coworkers after hours. ☐
14. If I am angry with somebody, I channel my anger into constructive criticism. ☐
15. Many people have said that I am likeable. ☐

Source: The concept underlying this checklist of statements stems from Cynthia Kay Stevens, and Amy L. Kristof, "Making the Right Impression: A Field Study of Applicant Impression Management during Job Interviews," *Journal of Applied Psychology*, October 1995, pp. 587–606.

Ingratiation also takes the form of enhancing the person by making positive comments about his or her appearance or accomplishments to bolster the interviewer's self-esteem. A frequent form of enhancement is to make a comment about the interviewer's physical fitness, such as "You look to be in very good shape. Do you work out a lot?" A comment about the interviewer's accomplishments often takes careful observation because the interviewer does not typically discuss his or her accomplishments with the applicant. Yet the applicant might look around the interviewer's work area for a tip-off to an accomplishment. An example: "I notice from your coffee mug that you are probably a Notre Dame grad. That's quite an accomplishment."

Self-promotion and ingratiation are widely used approaches to impression management during job interviews. A study by Cynthia Kay Stevens and Amy Kristof conducted at a college placement service found that self-promotion was used more frequently than ingratiation by recruits. We use the term *recruits* because many students who interview with company recruiters are exploring job possibilities rather than truly applying for a job. Frequency of using the tactics was measured by coders of audiotapes, the employment interviewers, and self-reports by the recruits. An example of these differences is that, according to coder data, self-promotion had 32.50 utterances per interview, whereas opinion conformity had 1.58 utterances, and making the other person feel good 0.83 utterances.

The most frequent self-promoting themes were (1) hardworking and energetic, (2) successful, confident, and competent, (3) interpersonally skilled, (4) growth oriented or flexible, (5) goal or results oriented, and (6) effective leaders.[5]

Entitlements and Enhancements

During the interview the applicant claims responsibility for positive events or outcomes although personal credit for such outcomes is not deserved or is greatly exaggerated. A firefighter applying for a new position said, "Last week we dealt with a four-alarm fire, and thanks to my superior physical abilities, we managed to get everyone out of the building without injury." A frequent form of entitlements among applicants for an executive position is to take too much credit for revenue growth of the company during a given time frame. For example, an applicant for a top-level marketing position might say, "Since I was the brand manager for cosmetics especially for women of color, sales of that line have quadrupled." (In reality, the competition experienced similar sales growth for the same product line, so the applicant might be taking too much credit for the results at his or her company.)

Basking in Reflected Glory

The idea of enhancing one's image by claiming association with prestige figures or institutions has gained cachet during employment interviews because of today's heavy emphasis on being connected. A modern approach to basking in reflected glory is to slip into the conversation mention of high-status persons in one's social network. For example, the applicant might say, "Five of my connections in Linkedin are small-business owners, and they have all mentioned that your industry is the place to be."

A positive consequence of basking in reflected glory is that the interviewer might think that individual has high competence, otherwise he or she would not have been chosen as an associate of the prestigious person or institution mentioned. The sensible tactic of mentioning being a member of a key company or community task force is therefore an effective way of creating a positive impression.

Opinion Conformity

Using this tactic, the applicant expresses opinions, beliefs, or values that are presumably held by the interviewer. If the interviewer makes a statement about how the organization believes that work-life balance is important, the interviewee would then describe how hard he or she has strived to attain such a balance. (The applicant is not necessarily distorting the truth, but emphasizing a value that he or she holds to some extent.) Another approach to opinion conformity is to describe experiences that are probably similar to those of the interviewer. Returning to the Notre Dame mug, the applicant might say, "I have a very fond memory of Notre Dame. A few years ago, I took a weekend ethics seminar at Notre Dame, and I was so impressed with the faculty and students I met."

A subtle form of opinion conformity during the employment interview is for the candidate to imply that his or her values are a good fit for the organization. Because most employers seek to hire workers who fit their organizational culture, this technique has merit. An example of such an attempt at opinion conformity would be: "I have seen on your website that you are a customer-centric company. I would like to work for such a company because I think the purpose of any business firm is to provide solutions to customers."

Excuses

A straightforward impression management technique of self-protection is for the job candidate to make an excuse in the form of claiming no responsibility for a negative outcome or behavior. Excuse making is likely to occur when the candidate's present or former employer was involved in negative behavior that received considerable publicity. An interviewer remarked to an interviewee that her employer, an investment bank, lost $5 billion in a recent quarter. The applicant replied, "I agree that the loss was a terrible turn of events. However, I work in the retail division, which actually performed quite well. All the losses are associated with mortgage-backed derivatives."

A similar form of excuse making is to deny having been involved in a widespread problem. For example, an automobile manufacturer was found guilty, and fined, for the widespread occurrence of sexual harassment in the workplace. A plant manager applying for a position with another company said, "I admit our company was guilty, but our plant did not have one charge of sexual harassment against us."

Justifications

A variation of excuse making is to justify an unfavorable development when the interviewer is probably aware of the situation. Using this tactic, the person accepts responsibility for a negative outcome or event, yet explains that the event was not as bad as it seems. At times, justification is used to convince the interviewer that he or she would have acted in the same way placed in the same situation. Justification is typically used to explain or justify an action or event that appears quite harsh on the surface. Two examples follow:

- A former CEO involved in downsizing a company, applying for another CEO position might say, "It really tore my heart out to have to lay off one-third of our workforce, and to subcontract as much work as we could to Mexico and Eastern Europe. But we had no choice. I wanted to see if I could save the jobs of the other two-thirds of our workforce. We did stay in business for another year, before we sold what was left of the company to a private equity firm. Most of our workers were able to keep their jobs, so we salvaged something."
- A civil engineer who worked for a city government when a viaduct collapsed might say, "That viaduct collapsing was a tragedy. I had inspected the bridge a few months earlier, and submitted a report saying that the structural weaknesses needed to be taken care of soon. The city officials filed the report, and said that they would consider it carefully. If I had more power I would have demanded that the viaduct be repaired immediately. But in our city, a civil engineer does not have enough clout to make such a demand. Fortunately, when the viaduct collapsed nobody was killed or seriously injured."

Apologies

Another self-protective technique of impression management that might be required during an employment interview is apologizing. The candidate accepts responsibility for a negative outcome or event and at the same time admits to the negative implications of such responsibility. Apologies are most likely to be offered when the candidate is confronted with a negative event or behavior uncovered through a reference check or background investigation, including an Internet search. A candidate who had crashed into a store front and been found guilty of driving while impaired, made this apology:

> I was fatigued from overwork, and I made the mistake of having a few drinks before driving home. Being fatigued, the drinks got to me quickly. I did smash into the store by accident. The next day I worked hard with the business owner to help clean up the damage. I made good the portion of his repair bill not covered by insurance. I promise you that I will never again be involved in an incident of this type.

You will observe that the candidate combined excuse making (being fatigued from overwork) with offering an apology. This illustrates the general point that impression management tactics in job interviews and elsewhere are often used in combination.

Falsification and Information Filtering

A widespread form of impression management in job interviews, as well as other aspects of job search, is to lie about one's accomplishments or deliberately omit negative information about oneself. Both self-promotion and ingratiation behaviors may involve an element of distortion, yet they do not represent deliberate lying. For example, the person who said he thoroughly enjoyed his experience at Notre Dame might be slightly exaggerating his feelings. A lie related to bringing up Notre Dame for the purposes of ingratiation would be never to have really attended the weekend seminar, but to claim he did knowing that Notre Dame had offered weekend ethics seminars. A candidate who claimed to have graduated from a particular school but did not would be using a naïve form of impression management because facts about schools attended are readily verified.

A common form of lying to create a favorable impression is to cover gaps in employment by stretching the dates of starting and stopping employment. A person who started a position in March 2008 and left the position in March 2009 might list that employment as 2008–2009, thereby omitting 11 months of unemployment. Another form of lying is to cover gaps in employment by claiming to have been a freelance consultant, even though the person did not have even one client assignment.

Lying to a job interviewer may not be illegal, but it does represent an ethical violation. For example, one of the questions in the ethical screen presented in Chapter 1 the lying job candidate would fail would be as follows: "Would you be comfortable if the details of your decision or actions were made public in the media or through e-mail (or on a website)?"

Information filtering amounts to avoiding mention of information that is likely to be perceived unfavorably by the interviewer without outright lying. So long as the interviewer does not ask directly about the negative behavior or event, in the interests of creating a positive impression, the interviewee does not provide the information. For example, the candidate might be asked about a patent he or she received. The candidate provides ample details about the patent, but does not mention that the previous ten patent applications were rejected.

Nonverbal Behavior

Nonverbal behavior contributes heavily to the impression a person creates during the job interview. Among the standard nonverbal ways of creating a positive impression would be smiling, a firm handshake, dressing well, exhibiting good posture, appearing relaxed and confident, and not displaying too many nervous mechanisms. In the past, some employment interviewers would leave an empty ashtray in close reach of the candidate. After the interview was completed, the interviewer would count the number of cigarette butts to gauge the tension level of the candidate. However, imprecise this method, it still had currency among some employment interviewers. This chapter's section "Guidelines for Application and Practice" (pp. 154–156) provides specific suggestions about the application of nonverbal behavior for creating a positive impression during a job interview.

Physical Appearance and Attractiveness

Physical appearance and attractiveness is a category of nonverbal behavior that merits separate attention as an approach to impression management during the job interview. A survey of MBA students indicated that those who valued workplace attire made use of it to help manage their impressions. The students believed that their mode of dress positively impacted the way they felt about themselves as well as workplace outcomes, including being favorably viewed by, and receiving job offers from interviewers.[6]

Although the importance of dressing appropriately for job interviews is common knowledge, some job seekers do not make good use of the information. The director of an MBA program received several complaints from prospective employers that two different students for the program appeared for the interview in business suits, yet wore athletic shoes.

A synthesis of many studies suggests the existence of a stereotype labeled "what is beautiful is good." Two meta-analyses demonstrated that physical attractiveness has three major effects: (1) a strong effect on perceptions of social competence, social skills, and sexual warmth; (2) a moderate effect on perceptions of intellectual competency, general effectiveness, dominance, and general mental health; and (3) a weak effect on perceptions of integrity and concern for others. Because of this stereotype, physical attractiveness is related to being perceived positively by employment interviewers.

Another meta-analysis indicated that 31 different studies demonstrated a positive relationship between being perceived as physically attractive and being hired. The synthesis of studies also found that professionals were as susceptible to the attraction bias as were college students, and attractiveness was as important for men as women. Another conclusion was that the biasing effect of physical attractiveness has decreased in recent years.[7]

Physical attractiveness can be manipulated in such ways as a careful choice of clothing, hairstyle, and grooming. Getting a makeover is the professional approach to modifying a person's appearance through hairstyle. In addition, many job candidates who want to appear more youthful and vibrant resort to Botox treatment and facial plastic surgery to give them an edge.

The tactics of impression management mentioned so far illustrate the range of possibilities for job candidates who want to create a positive impression. The extent to which the person does use impression management tactics depends on several factors, to be described in the following section.

Situational Attributes that Influence the Choice of Impression Management Tactics

A synthesis of relevant research by Clive Fletcher reveals that three sets of factors influence the use of strategic self-presentation during employment interviews. These factors are (1) attributes of the interviewee, (2) the real and perceived attributes of the interviewers, and (3) the attributes of the situation. Here we highlight some of Fletcher's findings, and also present a few additional observations.[8]

Attributes of the Interviewee

Individual differences exert a strong influence on which tactics of impression management will be utilized during a selection interview. A starting point might be the candidate's ethical posture. An entirely honest person would strive to portray a highly accurate image. In contrast, a less ethical person would feel comfortable in projecting an image designed to get the job whether or not the image was accurate. Interviewees also vary in their propensity toward self-disclosure, with research suggesting that females are more willing to be open in the way they present themselves in interviews. The implication could be that women would make less use of defensive self-presentation tactics such as falsification, information filleting, and excuses.

As described in Chapter 3, personality factors might mediate the choice of impression management tactics. Extraverts would feel more natural in projecting themselves in a positive way, and talking about their accomplishments. The right amount of anxiety might propel a job candidate to make an effective self-presentation, whereas too much anxiety might prevent the individual from performing well. The candidate's tendency toward self-monitoring might influence his or her willingness to enhance the interviewer, as will be described separately later in the chapter (see p. 147).

The attributes of courteousness and politeness can also influence impression management. People who are naturally polite will find it easy to enhance the interviewer by such gestures as expressing thanks, greeting the interviewer in a friendly manner, and saying goodbye. People who are naturally rude might engage in such negative impression management tactics as interrupting the interviewer and yawning.

Experience as an interviewee could lower anxiety about the situation and also boost a person's self-confidence, assisting the candidate in performing well. An experienced and knowledgeable interviewee will also know that he or she should listen as well as talk, and ask a few sensible questions.

Cultural factors can also influence impression management during the interview. The most frequently observed example is that many Asians prefer not to brag about their accomplishments, and therefore are less likely to engage in heavy forms of self-promotion. In contrast, many Americans and Europeans would feel more comfortable in engaging in self-promotion. Another key cultural dimension that could influence self-presentation would be formality versus informality. A person from a more formal culture, such as India, is less likely to treat the interviewer as having equal status to him or her. A typical American job candidate might behave more informally toward the interviewer, perhaps even making a statement such as "How do you guys like working here?"[9]

Attributes of the Interviewer

The personality characteristics and style of the interviewer will sometimes influence which tactics of impression the perceptive candidate will choose. A starting point is that if the interviewer appeared relaxed and informal, the interviewee would be more likely to use joking, kidding, and laughter to ingratiate himself or herself to the interviewer. If the interviewer appeared to be more formal and conservative, the candidate might emphasize such behavior to create a positive impression.

Closely related to the personality of the interviewer is his or her nonverbal behavior. Being relaxed and informal is reflected in such mannerisms as smiling and leaning toward the candidate. Under these circumstances, the candidate might feel more comfortable in making positive self-statements, and exhibiting positive nonverbal gestures such as smiling and projecting facial expressions of enthusiasm.

More experienced and competent interviewers might be more adept at encouraging interviewee behavior that dealt with direct job qualifications, and discourage heavy emphasis on self-promotion. For example, the experienced interviewer is more likely to reinforce desired interviewee behavior through nods and smiles. The experienced interviewer would also discourage undesired impression management tactics such as excessive bragging or excessive complimenting the interviewer through such means as ignoring the tactics.

Attributes of the Situation

A major situational factor is the importance of the job to the candidate. When few desirable positions are available for a given candidate, the candidate is more likely to work hard at creating a good impression. Similarly, the more the candidate wants the position in question, even if other job opportunities might exist, the greater the possibility of intense effort directed toward self-presentation.

The organizational culture and the industry will also influence which techniques of impression management are chosen. Candidates for positions in investment banking and the fashion industry will pay much more attention to dress and appearance than candidates for positions in the fast-food and information-technology industries. (Again, we are drawing broad stereotypes.) A culture that emphasizes technical accomplishment, such as the cultures of Microsoft and Google, is likely to see candidates attempt to focus on describing their talents more than their personality characteristics. Ingratiation by the candidate is likely to take the form of attempting to be liked by focusing on technical accomplishments and discussing technical issues rather than flattering the interviewer.

Another situational variable is whether the interviewer is the hiring manager, or another person who will be working directly with the candidate. Candidates who assume they will be working with the interviewer will often soften their self-assessments because they are concerned about later being perceived as having deceived the interviewer. As Fletcher observes, the need to maintain consistency between what was promised during the job interview and subsequent job performance may reduce the amount of self-promotion.[10]

Candidate Self-Monitoring and Interview Ratings

The personality trait of self-monitoring facilitates a person making a good impression by enhancing others. If during a job interview the self-monitor tells the interviewer what he or she wants to hear, the interviewee should be better received by the interviewer. Esther Dedrick Long and Gregory H. Dobbins conducted a study testing this proposition. The study participants were 233 job candidates interviewing for positions at a college placement center, along with 30 college recruiters. The sample of job candidates was composed of 147 men and 86 women.

The students completed a self-monitoring scale similar to the one presented in Figure 3-2. The interviewers were given a packet which included several rating scales about the interviewees' capabilities and potential for hire. Each recruiter was requested to describe the position for which he or she was interviewing, along with the qualifications of the ideal candidate. The researchers and the placement center director classified each position as being primarily people oriented or primarily technically oriented. A position was categorized as people oriented if (1) the interviewer indicated that a job candidate would not be successful without strong interpersonal skills, and (2) the job required the incumbent to spend the majority of time working with people. Engineering positions, computer science, and accounting positions were classified as technically oriented. The majority of people-oriented positions consisted of sales, management trainee, and distribution management (logistics) positions.

The objective job qualifications were taken into account or controlled for in analyzing interview ratings. Control measures were used to test the true effect of self-monitoring, rather than the effect of work experience or grade point average (GPA). The researchers wanted to determine whether two students with equal job qualifications, yet different tendencies toward self-monitoring, would receive different interview ratings.

A major finding of the study was that candidates' self-monitoring scores were more strongly related to interviewer ratings when the position is people oriented than when it is technically oriented. Another finding was that high self-monitoring candidates were more effective at verbal impression management. It appeared that the high self-monitors may have received higher interviewer ratings based partially on their impression management skills.[11] It could be argued therefore that impression management skills are a potential asset for people-oriented jobs.

Impression Management versus Job Competencies in Determining Interview Ratings

An important issue in understanding the contribution of impression management tactics to the job search is how much job interviewers are influenced by factors directly related to job competence versus skill in impression management. The study just cited partially answered this question because it appears that for people-oriented positions skill in impression management *is* a criterion for effective performance.

David C. Gilmore and Gerald R. Ferris conducted a study to explore the effects of applicant impression management tactics on interviewer judgments.[12] A field experiment was conducted with 62 employment interviewers from a large public utility. The experiment was conducted as part of an interviewer training and development program. Applicant credentials were manipulated by using one of two different résumés that made the applicant appear highly qualified or poorly qualified for a customer-service representative position. Utility officials listed the most important job credentials to be school major, grade point average, and prior work experience. Impression management behaviors were manipulated by developing two videotaped interview segments in which the applicant engaged in high or low levels of impression management. The two segments included the same woman applicant dressed identically, and being interviewed in the same office setting.

For the high impression management segment, the applicant smiled frequently, and complimented the interviewer for asking good questions. She also flattered the interviewer by stating that she would like to report to a good manager like the interviewer, and she also emphasized her positive traits. For the low impression management segment, the applicant simply answered the interviewer's questions, rarely smiled, but still maintained eye contact.

According to the design of the study each applicant was (1) high or low on relevant job qualifications, and (2) high or low on impression management behaviors. After reading the job description and résumé as well as viewing the videotaped interview segment, interviewers completed a questionnaire about such factors as the likelihood of hiring, recommended starting salary, and performance in the interview.

A major finding of the study was that when the applicant used impression management tactics in the interview she was perceived as performing better than when she did not use these techniques. Interviewers were slightly more positive in their hiring recommendations for the candidates who used impression management tactics. Another finding was that impression management techniques influenced interviewer judgments more than did objective job qualifications. A cynical interpretation of the findings proposed by Gilmore and Ferris is that interviewers are impressed not by objective qualifications but by self-presentation and other enhancement. Yet, similar to the study cited above, having good impression management skills might have been perceived by the interviewers as being essential for the position of customer-service representative.

A more recent study about the relative impact of impression management tactics versus objective job qualifications found less support for the heavy weight given to impression management. Filip Lievens and Helga Peeters studied two samples of interviewers (55 master industrial/organizational psychology students and 18 professional interviewers) who observed and evaluated videotaped interviewees who were instructed to make a positive impression. Videotapes were made of 88 students, equally divided between men and women who were screened for a training program in communication skills and group processes. The screening was implemented to provide an assessment of the students' standing on training-related competencies. The competencies rated in this study were interpersonal skills, adaptability, and perseverance.

The results of the study showed that the importance of verbal and nonverbal impression management tactics was relatively small in comparison to the importance attached to job-related competencies. *Importance* refers to the contribution to overall rating of the candidate in terms of suitability for employment. The relative weights the interviewers gave to the impression management cues were significantly lower than the relative weights for the relevant competencies. For example, on a seven-point scale interpersonal skills were rated 4.81; perseverance, 4.40; other-focused impression management, .90; and self-focused impression management, 1.39.

The researchers note that the results do not mean that the impact of impression management is negligible. Instead, the results suggest that the impact of impression management is relatively small *compared* to more relevant cues.[13] An area of possible confusion in the study was that interpersonal skill was rated as a job competency, yet impression management is part of interpersonal skills.

Another perspective on the effects of impression management versus qualifications on job interview results is that moderating variables should be considered. A study conducted in Taiwan, involving 151 job applicants in 25 firms, examined the moderating roles of three factors on the extent to which impression management tactics influence interviewer evaluations. The three moderating variables were interview structure, customer-contact requirements, and interview length. Interview structure refers to such factors as asking the exact same question of all applicants. Impression management statements included:

- I smiled a lot during the interview.
- I always maintained eye contact with the interviewer.

Customer-contact requirement was measured through a type of job analysis. A stopwatch was used to measure interview length. On average, the interview length was 33.97 minutes. With respect to structure, when the interviewer asks the same questions of each interviewee, and the questions are closely related to the job description, there might be less room for the interviewer to be swayed by tactics of impression management. The results indicated that a higher level of interview structure reduced the influence of applicant nonverbal impression management tactics on the evaluation of interviewers. However, self-focused impression management tactics did influence interviewer evaluations. The explanation offered by the researchers is that a structured interview focuses the interviewer's attention on answers to questions, whereas nonverbal behavior receives less attention.

Consistent with the results of studies already reported in this chapter, when customer contact required for a job was relatively low, the influence of applicant self-focused tactics on interview evaluations was minimized. Expressed in positive terms, impression management was more important in interviews for jobs requiring customer contact. The results also showed that when the interview was longer, the effects of applicant self-focused impression management were minimized. It is likely that the longer the interview lasts, the easier it is for the interviewer to obtain job-relevant information about the applicant.[14]

Post-Interview Impression Management

Impression management surrounding the job interview continues past the job interview in terms of a follow-up letter, e-mail, text message, or phone call. A follow-up letter or other correspondence relates to impression management because it reflects good manners, and also suggests that the interviewee wants the job. Sending a positive follow-up letter is anticipated, so the fact that the letter is sent will not count heavily as a positive impression. However, not sending follow-up correspondence could create a negative impression. Also, sending unpolished or remarkably poor follow-up correspondence will often create a negative impression depending on the attitudes of the receiver.

According to a *Wall Street Journal* report many young job candidates are creating a negative impression on hiring managers because they use an overly casual form of *textspeak* when sending follow-up correspondence to a job interview. Among these errors are words such as "hiya" and "thanx," along with multiple exclamation points and a smiley-face emoticon. Hiring managers questioned say that an increasing number of job seekers are too casual with respect to communicating about career opportunities in cyberspace and on mobile devices. Many e-mails contain shorthand language and decorative symbols, while some job seekers are sending hasty and poorly reasoned messages to and from mobile devices. Recruiters say that such faux pas can be instant candidacy killers because they create the impression of immaturity and questionable judgment.[15]

Impression Management for Traditional and Video Résumés

Submitting a job résumé is a natural part of the job search process for creating an impression—good, neutral, or poor. Here we look briefly at some of the impression management aspects of traditional résumés, as well as those submitted by video.

Traditional Résumés

Almost unlimited advice can be found for submitting a paper or electronic résumé that is likely to create a positive impression. Suggestions for résumé construction are even included in standard software such as Microsoft Word. Most readers are probably familiar with admonitions such as a section for skills and accomplishments, including a job qualifications summary, avoiding errors in spelling and grammar, and providing accurate contact information.

A major purpose of submitting a job résumé is to be invited for a face-to-face job interview, or at least a telephone interview. A study conducted with 64 business professionals provides some useful information about which résumé characteristics are perceived positively enough to invite a job candidate for an interview. The business professionals reviewed résumés for new business graduates. The following résumé characteristics were more likely to lead to first choices for an interview: one page in contrast to two pages, a specific objective statement in comparison to a general objective statement, relevant coursework better than no coursework listed, GPAs of 3.0 in contrast to no GPA listed, GPAs of 3.50 in contrast to GPAs of 2.75, and accomplishment statements in contrast to no accomplishment statement.[16] These findings therefore provide some empirical evidence for which résumé characteristics create a positive impression. In support of these findings, a résumé that does not list the candidate's skills and accomplishments is considered insufficient today.

A robust approach to creating a negative impression with a résumé is to present false information, followed by the employer detecting the lie or misinformation. Lying on the résumé has derailed career beginners as well as top-level executives. InfoLink Screening Systems, a company specializing in background checks, estimates that approximately 14% of job applicants in the USA lie about their education on résumés. A frequent lie is for men to claim they were members of the college football team. ResumeDoctor.com, a firm that assists with résumé construction, found that of 1,000 résumés it vetted over a six-month period, 43% contained one or more significant inaccuracies.

Lying on the résumé can be framed as impression management in the form of an extension of the human impulse to want to be perceived more favorably by others. Roland Kidwell, who has researched distortions in résumés, says that lies are a way to "resolve the discrepancy between the average applicant you think you are and the ideal applicant you think they seek."[17] Although such lying might provide a short-term benefit to the applicant, if the lies are discovered he or she is likely to be immediately rejected from consideration for the position. If he or she is hired and the lying is detected later, the employee is subject to immediate dismissal.

Video Résumés

A current approach to résumé construction is the online video type. Turning the camcorder or webcam on himself or herself, the job seeker presents much of the basic information that would be found on a written résumé. The video technique is good for capturing a person's appearance, personality, and oral communication skills, thereby multiplying the opportunity for impression management—positive, neutral, or negative. Some job seekers place their video on their website or on YouTube, or simply add it as an attachment.

For purposes of creating a positive impression, unless a person is highly skilled at video presentation it is best to get professional help in constructing a video résumé. Careful editing might be needed to eliminate vocalized pauses and inadvertent distracting expressions that can contribute to a negative image. In speaking about her work as a video presentation trainer, Karen Friedman provides an analysis of how a video résumé helps a job candidate evaluate the impression he or she creates, as follows:

> People will tell you that they're perceived as dynamic, engaging, and interesting, with full command of the material. And then they see themselves on videotape or DVD and it's a rude awakening, because they see how other people really see them. You can pick up odd mannerisms you're not aware of. You may have the words down and the verbal techniques, but your body language might give away that you're nervous or unsure of yourself.[18]

A caution about the video résumé is that some employers are concerned about possible job discrimination charges from selecting or rejecting certain candidates. Many recruiters will not accept CVs with photos attached for fear of lawsuits, with videos accentuating these concerns. The recruiters are worried that video résumés will encourage lawsuits by candidates who could claim bias based on demographic factors such as race, sex, or age—all not obvious on paper but readily detectable on video.[19]

Impression Management during Performance Evaluation

Another natural arena in which to make a positive impression is during performance evaluation (or appraisal). Almost every strategy or tactic of impression management has relevance to the performance evaluation. Take, for example, supplication, or asking for help. When the subordinate asks the manager for help during the performance evaluation, the manager is likely to sympathize with the subordinate and evaluate him or her more leniently. Consider also personal appearance. The organizational actor who dresses better than usual for the evaluation session might be viewed favorably by the superior. Part of the reason is that the better-than-average dress implies that the subordinate perceives the evaluation to be a highly important occasion. Here we look at several of the variables affecting the relationship between impression management and performance evaluations. We also look at two specific impression management tactics that appear to influence performance evaluations.

Variables Influencing Impression Management for Performance Evaluation

A starting point in influencing the extent to which organizational actors engage in impression management during performance evaluation is the predisposing individual and organizational factors described in Chapter 3. Among the individual factors would be a predisposition toward self-monitoring, and Machiavellianism. Organizational factors would include a culture emphasizing high performance and competitiveness.

The ambiguity of performance standards is a major factor moderating whether impression management takes place during the evaluation.[20] When the actor's performance can be readily judged, such as in production data, impression management tactics will be less effective. When subordinate performance has to be judged more subjectively, such as in the work of a public relations and communication specialist, attempts at impression management are likely to be more prevalent.

A manager who has the reputation of being an easy target for flattery will likely experience more ingratiation during performance evaluation. Similarly, a manager who is known to welcome flirting is likely to be flirted with during the evaluation session. The sexual orientation of the target will strongly influence whether or not the actor who flirts is of the opposite sex.

The evaluator's propensity for giving negative feedback is another factor that can moderate the use of impression tactics by the person receiving the evaluation. If the manager does not feel comfortable giving negative feedback and engaging in confrontation he or she is an "easy mark" for impression management. The subordinate recognizes that the manager might be looking for an excuse to not give a negative evaluation. Impression management, such as ingratiation, gives the manager a good excuse—perhaps pre-consciously—to avoid a negative evaluation.

Performance Blips and Ingratiation to Enhance Performance Evaluations

A task-oriented approach to impression management surrounding the performance evaluation is for the subordinate to perform extra well in a short period of time preceding the performance review. The **performance evaluation blip** is a surge in performance quantity or quality right before the performance review.[21] The blip helps answer the implicit question asked by reviewers: "What have you done for me lately?" One reason a late performance surge may elevate the performance evaluation is based on the principle of *recency*, the fact that we tend to readily remember recent events. The blip approach to impression management is less likely to be effective with managers who document performance over time, and therefore carefully base their evaluations on performance over the entire review period.

The fact that ingratiation by subordinates leads to more favorable judgments of performance is supported by observations as well as empirical evidence. A study of interactions between bank employees and their supervisors showed that purposely trying to create a positive impression on the supervisor led to better performance ratings. Among the ingratiating tactics reported in this study were (1) "Take an immediate interest in your supervisor's personal life," and (2) "Agree with your supervisor's major ideas."[22]

A later study with 111 supervisor-subordinate dyads (pairs) supported a model proposing that impression management by subordinates influences performance evaluations in a positive direction. The underlying process was that the supervisors liked the ingratiating subordinates and perceived themselves to be similar to the subordinates.[23]

Although the two studies just cited link ingratiation to performance evaluation results, the studies did not deal with the issue of ingratiation *during* the evaluation session. We assume, however, that ingratiation during the performance review can enhance performance ratings as long as the evaluator has not already decided on the ratings prior to the review session. Two examples of ingratiation behaviors that are probably effective during the review session are (1) thanking the supervisor for his or her coaching in recent months and (2) complimenting the superior on his or her dress and appearance.

Our focus in this section has been on the person being evaluated. Impression management by the rater can also influence performance evaluations. A major consideration is that some managers and supervisors will give generous evaluations for several reasons. One reason is that when subordinates receive high evaluations it suggests that the manager is doing a superior job of managing his or her organizational unit. As an effective coach, the manager or supervisor has been able to guide and motivate group members toward high performance. Another reason that high evaluations serve the interests of the manager is that having people labeled high performers implies that the manager has done an excellent job of selecting workers for his or her unit.

Guidelines for Application and Practice

1. Considerable opinion exists that the first 30 seconds count heavily in terms of a how a job candidate is perceived, so the interviewee should be prepared to manage the first half-minute effectively. To capitalize on the first 30 seconds, the candidate should choose business-appropriate attire for the interview. He or she should stay focused and eliminate any electronic distractions such as a BlackBerry or cell phone that could throw him or her off track. Introductory comments and greetings should be rehearsed, as well as body language. A firm handshake, good posture, and a confident stride are contributors to making a positive first impression.[24]

2. Job interviewers typically expect job candidates to manage their impression in terms of putting their best foot forward. A candidate who made no attempt at creating a positive impression might be regarded negatively. However, an overly strong approach to impression management, such as excessive boasting or overdressing, might also result in a negative perception from the interviewer.

The recommendation here is to manage your impression during a job interview, but do not overdo or under-do the impression.[25]

3. According to Nina Jamal and Judith Lindenberger, employer representatives are strongly irritated by inappropriate dress, mumbling, and poor handshakes by job candidates during interviews. The authors present a statement from a senior recruiter to support their conclusion, as follows: "Especially in the financial industry, which tends to be a more conservative environment, what a lot of the younger people don't understand is that we are looking for someone to represent the company. So your appearance is not just representative of you; you will also be representing the company the way we want it to be represented."[26]

4. Creating a favorable impression during the job interview should include favorably impressing other people who might be associated with the interviewer, particularly the receptionist, who sees the job candidate first. Many employers believe that the manner in which a job candidate treats a receptionist reflects how the candidate will deal with coworkers and direct reports. Whether or not this belief is valid, the candidate must deal with the perception. Greg Gostanian, a managing partner at an executive and career coaching and outplacement firm, offers the following suggestions for creating a favorable impression on receptionists:

    •   Be friendly but formal. Take the time to learn the receptionist's name because such attentiveness usually leaves a positive impression.

    •   Treat the receptionist with respect rather than as an underling. If offered a beverage, keep it simple and don't expect the receptionist to go out of the way to serve you.

    •   Anticipate that everything you say to the receptionist will get back to the interviewer so use good judgment in what you say. Avoid making cell phone conversations that could cast you in an unfavorable light, such as saying loudly to the person at the other end of the phone, "This place would be my last choice, but I'm getting desperate."

    •   Remember to thank and say goodbye to the receptionist after completing the interview because last impressions are likely to be remembered.[27]

5. Cathy Chin, a hiring manager at a marketing firm, says that there is no excuse for using shorthand in messages to recruiters. "A thank-you note—even if it's on Facebook or email—should be written like a proper letter. If I'm going to give you a job, do I really want you communicating to our clients in this fashion? No."[28]

6. Job candidates should be aware that some of the more overtly manipulative tactics of strategic self-presentation are likely to rebound on them. The negative impact is more likely to occur when the interviewer dislikes exaggerated self-presentation such as giving oneself too much credit for a business company's success while working for the company. Less manipulative, and less exaggerated self-presentations are more likely to have a positive impact on interviewer judgments.[29]

7. The results of performance evaluation often have a major impact on a person's career, such as amount of salary increase, promotion, assignment to key projects, and being retained during a company downsizing. It is therefore strongly recommended that the person being evaluated make judicious use of impression management during the review session, including offering the manager appropriate compliments and thanking him or her for coaching and guidance received since the last review session.

Summary

The employment interview brings impression management tactics into sharp focus. Impression management tactics include the following: (1) assertiveness, (2) self-promotion, (3) ingratiation, (4) entitlements and enhancements, (5) basking in reflected glory, (6) opinion conformity, (7) excuses, (8) justifications, (9) apologies, (10) falsification and information filtering, (11) nonverbal behavior, and (12) physical appearance and attractiveness.

Factors related to the interview that influence the choice of impression management tactics include the following: (1) attributes of the interviewee such as ethical posture, personality factors, and cultural background; (2) attributes of the interviewer such as formality, nonverbal behavior, and skill in focusing the interview on job qualifications; (3) attributes related to the situation such as the importance of the job, the organizational culture, and whether the candidate will be working for the interviewer if hired.

A study with college students showed that self-monitoring scores were more strongly related to job interview ratings when the position is people oriented than when it is technically oriented. It was also found that high self-monitoring candidates were more effective at verbal impression management.

A study based on a videotaped interviewee for a customer-service position showed that when she used impression management tactics in the interview she was perceived as performing better than when she did not use these techniques. A more recent study of interviewees showed less weight given to impression management by interviewers in comparison to job-related competencies. Three moderating variables studied in relation to the importance of impression management tactics during the job interview are interview structure, customer-contact requirements, and interview length. Impression management was found to be more important for customer-contact positions, less effective in a structured interview, or a long interview.

Impression management surrounding the job interview continues into the follow-up letter, e-mail, text message, or phone call. A report noted that many young candidates create a negative impression by using casual *textspeak* when sending follow-up correspondence.

The job résumé creates another opportunity for impression management, both positive and negative. Presenting an accomplishments section is one way of creating a positive impression. Presenting false information and lying creates a strongly negative impression. The video résumé is good for capturing a person's appearance, personality, and oral communication skills, thereby multiplying the opportunity for a range of impressions. Professional help is recommended to create a positive impression via a video résumé.

Another natural arena for creating a positive impression is during performance evaluation, with almost any technique of impression management being potentially useful. Variables influencing impression management for performance appraisal include: (1) predisposing individual and organizational factors, (2) ambiguity of performance standards, (3) the manager's receptivity to flattery, and (4) the evaluator's propensity for giving negative feedback.

The performance evaluation blip (a surge in performance close in time to the performance review) can be considered a form of impression management. Ingratiation over a period of time enhances performance evaluation ratings, and may also be applicable during the performance review.

Among the guidelines for application and practice covering the information above is (1) to remember the importance of the first impression, (2) not to overly manage the impression in the job interview, (3) to be mindful of appearance, (4) to impress all people in the employment situation, (5) to avoid shorthand messages to interviewers, (6) to be mindful that overtly manipulative tactics are likely to rebound, and (7) to use impression management during the performance review.

Chapter 9

Impression Management
for Leaders

To be effective as a leader, a person needs a wide variety of personal attributes, including the right personality traits and cognitive skills. The leader also needs to work in a setting appropriate to these attributes. At the same time, the leader's combination of attributes must impress constituents that he or she is competent enough to carry out the role of a leader. As leadership researcher and theorist Bernard M. Bass notes, it is the leader's *perceived* competence that determines if he or she will be able to influence followers. For example, the leader must convince the group that he or she has the appropriate experience to help with the group task for his or her ideas to be accepted.[1] This is why self-confidence has long been associated with leadership effectiveness—the leader has to look the part of a person capable of being in charge.[2] Convincing others of one's skills and capabilities is one of the essential purposes of impression management.

The observation that creating a good impression is part of leadership does not mean that effective leadership consists mostly of creating a good impression. The effective leader has to be a good problem solver, think strategically, and implement plans, among many other attributes and skills.

In this chapter we describe two major topics intertwined with each other: how leaders project a leadership image, and how impression management contributes to charismatic leadership. The reader should recognize, however, that all other information about impression management presented in this book can also work in the service of being an effective leader. Unless you are able to impress people in the right way, you will not be able to lead them. Impression management must then be supported by many other leadership traits and competencies. Figure 9-1 organizes some of the major themes in this chapter based on amount of empirical support.

Projecting a Leadership Image

Projecting the image of a leader could be a subject without limits, depending on how *image* is interpreted. For example, developing a personal brand helps project a leadership image, as does demonstrating cognitive skills, displaying extraversion, and being well

Figure 9-1 Topics and Subtopics Related to Impression Management for Leadership According to Basis of Support.

Well Supported by Empirical Research	Supported More by Anecdote and Opinion
Implicit leadership theories and image projection	Acting skills required for winning over an audience: connecting; listening empathetically; improvising; radiating confidence; projecting discipline and toughness; and honesty
Being a servant leader	Influence tactics for projecting a leadership image
Impression management to create and maintain a charismatic identity (dramaturgy)	High self-esteem and high self-monitoring to project a leadership image
	Impression management behaviors of framing, scripting, staging, and performing

groomed. Therefore any discussion of impression management for leaders by projecting a leadership image can at best be illustrative. As outlined in Figure 9-2, here we concentrate on four approaches to projecting a leadership image that have been the subject of careful observation and research.

Acting Skills Required for Winning over an Audience

Political science professor Thomas E. Cronin argues that political leaders, in common with talented actors, develop skills to win over audiences. He notes that modern-day leaders must hone their self-promotion, likeability, and leadership attributes. At the same time they must not project the appearance of being pretenders or dissemblers. Most leaders need well-honed acting skills, yet being a skilled performer is only a means to effective leadership, not an end in itself.[3] Here we report on Cronin's observations but apply them to organizational leaders rather than those in the world of politics.

Connecting with the Audience

An essential aspect of projecting the image of a leader is to connect with the audience, which translates into emotional rapport with group members. Based on the premise that wanting to connect is a basic human need, the actor intent on projecting a leadership image develops a phrase that facilitates this connection. A vision can be useful in creating the connection, as in "Everything we do will help provide better nutrition to the world." The connection will often be stronger when the leader focuses on specific benefits to the employees, as with the statement "Our best days of high profits and bonuses are ahead of us."

Figure 9-2 Projecting a Leadership Image.

A wide variety of behaviors and attitudes help a person project the image of being an effective leader, with those outlined in this figure having major significance.

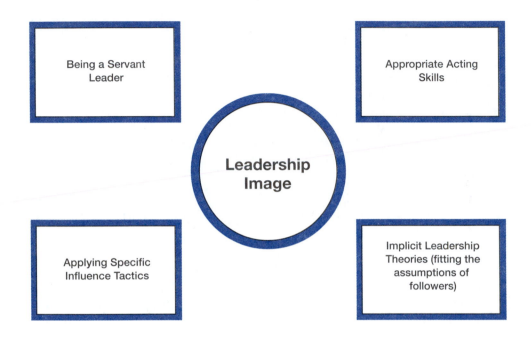

Understanding and Exploiting Symbols

Political leaders in particular make references to symbols that are part of the culture, such as the Declaration of Independence, the Constitution, Franklin Delano Roosevelt, and Martin Luther King, Jr. Making references to these symbols is considered bipartisan rather than partisan because the symbols just presented are associated with *good* rather than *evil* by the vast majority of constituents. Organizational leaders have to search to find symbols related to their business considered positive by most of their employees. A heroic founder of the business will sometimes suffice. Wal-Mart managers can make reference to founder Sam Walton because the story (not necessarily false) widely circulates about the humanitarian values of Walton. A manager at UPS (United Parcel Services) can make reference to how the company has delivered valuable medical documents that saved lives.

An analysis prepared by Jeffrey Pfeffer further explains how the leader makes use of symbols to create a positive impression among constituents. He reasons that symbolic management operates fundamentally on the principle of illusion. By using *political language, ceremonies,* and *settings*, the leader effectively elicits powerful emotions in people, and these emotions interfere with rational analysis.[4] Keep in mind, however, that the leader might use symbols not to override rational analysis, but to create a positive impression so followers will take appropriate action. For example, a CEO might answer her own e-mails and drive a compact car to work to symbolize frugality—not to circumvent rational analysis by employees. An explanation of Pfeffer's three components of symbolic management is as follows:

- *Political language*. The intent of political language is to soften the impact of the more accurate term. By using political language, the leader can create a positive impression by not appearing harsh. Instead of referring to laying off thousands of people, the leader talks about "rightsizing the organization." Instead of referring to getting rid of costly American workers, the leader talks about the "importance of global outsourcing to remain competitive in the global marketplace."
- *Ceremonies*. The leader uses ceremonies as occasions to help organizational members feel better about doing what needs to be done. Among these ceremonies or ceremonial events are annual meetings, regional meetings, sales meetings, training sessions, offsite (or outdoor) training, award ceremonies, video conferences, and web seminars. Being the head or host of a ceremony is regarded as part of a leader's role, so conducting a ceremony well creates a positive impression among constituents.
- *Settings*. Physical space can be used as a tool for the exercise of power and influence. Simultaneously, physical space can be used to create an impression. To create the symbol of being a hands-on leader, some executives place their office among workers of lower rank. One example is Sergio Marchionne, the head of the combined Chrysler and Fiat companies. He placed his office in a manufacturing setting in Auburn Hills, Michigan to demonstrate his desire to be close to operations.

Another link between impression management and symbols is that mention of certain organizational symbols gives the leader an aura of being emotionally connected to the company and therefore worth following. For example, a Wal-Mart store manager might mention Sam Walton as a symbol of treating customers well, and being frugal.

Listening Empathetically

Listening to subordinates not only creates a good impression; the process is one of the major tactics of effective leadership. "Followers have a say in what they are being led to. A leader who neglects that soon finds himself (or herself) without followers," writes Gary Willis. "To sound a certain trumpet does not mean just trumpeting one's own certitudes. It means sounding a specific call to specific people capable of response."[5] A specific way in which listening creates a good impression is that the leader demonstrates a willingness to collaborate with group members by processing their input.

A standard approach for a newly appointed high-level organizational leader is to take a listening tour by such means as having interviews with a variety of people throughout the organization, often in a variety of locations. The listening tour creates a good impression for several reasons. First, it demonstrates that the new leader wants input from a variety of organizational members before taking action. Second, the tour demonstrates that the new leader respects the opinion of experienced workers.

Kim Simon was appointed as the first patient-advocacy director for Alexion Pharmaceuticals, a small biotechnology company. Simon met face to face with approximately one dozen colleagues in his first two weeks, picking up much information about politics at the company. Without the insights from his listening tour, he believes, "I might have been at a disadvantage on some projects." He also walked down the corridors at least twice a day to brainstorm and bond with the headquarters team.[6] Part of the success Simon has had in his position can be attributed to the positive impression he created by listening to colleagues and later involving them in his patient-advocacy initiatives.

Another mechanism for creating a good impression by listening is for the leader to make the rounds, sometimes referred to as *rounding* or *management by walking around*. During the rounds the leader can make a personal connection by asking about a key event in a subordinate's life, such as the health of a newborn. Describing follow-up action on an issue raised in a previous rounding creates a favorable impression. Giving workers a commitment to fixing problems they bring up during the rounds is another technique for the leader to create a good impression.[7] During her rounds a middle manager heard complaints from several employees about a heating and cooling system that often created conditions that were too warm during cold weather, and too cool during warm weather. After the manager worked diligently with the facilities department to resolve the problem her stature as a leader increased considerably.

Improvising

To project an impression of authenticity it is important for the leader not to appear fully scripted, meaning not to react to all problems with a response that appears rehearsed. By improvising responses, questions and problems, the leader gives the impression of wanting to really find answers and solutions. To appear stiff, wooden, or uncomfortable during interaction with constituents detracts from the leader's effectiveness.

A leader will appear rehearsed when he or she explains losing money with a declaration of the nature "A weakening economy combined with low consumer demand created pressures for us." The same statement could be made to explain away all poor business results. A response that might create a better impression is: "We faced the same poor economy as everybody else. What we did particularly wrong was not to have the products that people would buy even during a poor economy. We will be working hard to fix that problem."

Radiating Confidence

As mentioned at the outset of the chapter, projecting confidence is an essential leadership characteristic. Even during bad times, followers want the leader to be optimistic and radiate confidence. United States presidents are sometimes given the label "the nation's First Optimist." A leader who projects pessimism is likely to lose credibility with his or her constituents. During an emergency planning session, an executive at Ford Motor Company told the group, "Ford is doing well in many areas. We have attractive new models coming down the pike. Our cost structure is in place, and we have a first-rate workforce. All we need is more sales." The comment provoked laughter, but also helped the executive gain currency. Should consumer demand increase, Ford would capitalize on the situation. Also, the automotive executive in question projected the image of a person with hope for the company and its employees.

Projecting Discipline and Toughness

A high-level leader will often create the impression of being effective by taking stern action when necessary to attain an important goal. A football coach who suspends a key player just before a big game for "having violated team rules" gains in credibility. Political leaders might call for war, or a one-time strike against another country, yet business leaders have to display discipline, toughness and sternness in other ways. Unfortunately for many employees and the economy as well, this toughness often takes the form of laying off thousands of employees to attain the goal of company survival. Mark Hurd of Hewlett-Packard (HP) is but one of many executives in recent years who have been responsible for the firing of over 30,000 employees to improve organizational efficiency. Yet he retains the image of being a capable executive who is a whiz at operations and cost effectiveness.

Another way in which a CEO can demonstrate toughness is to exit a business long associated with the company. An extreme example was CEO Jeffrey R. Immelt at General Electric (GE) stating several years ago that he was considering getting the company out of the lightbulb and appliance businesses. Doing so reinforced Immelt's image as a bold executive whether or not GE does sell the lightbulb and appliance businesses.

Honesty

Few people expect political leaders to tell the truth all the time, yet the expectations for business leaders are high despite all the publicity about financial scandals. One such scandal several years ago involved leaders at a major investment bank authorizing the short selling of the same mortgage-backed securities they were simultaneously selling to clients as sound investments. By planning to sell short, the leaders were predicting that the price of the shares in these investments would decline substantially. These scandals aside, the leader who projects the image of honesty and trustworthiness is more likely to endure.

Martin Chemers writes that the primary goal of image management is to establish a legitimate basis for the leader's influence attempts. Competence and trustworthiness (or honesty) are key criteria for the leader's legitimacy. Other research has also found that the two most frequently cited characteristics of an outstanding leader are task competency and honesty. The leader who is competent and honest therefore projects the image of (and *is*) an effective leader.[8]

A concluding observation based on Cronin's analysis is that projecting the image of leadership is positive rather than manipulative and deceitful. Unless a leader gives the impression of being a leader, he or she cannot accomplish good deeds. Visualize a manager attempting to re-start a restaurant destroyed by a hurricane and a flood. Unless he or she projects the image of being composed and being able to build a path out of the crisis, the employees will most likely disband because they have no hope of the restaurant being restored.

Implicit Leadership Theories and the Projection of a Leadership Image

A personality-based perspective on how people create the impression of being a leader is that they do so by meeting the expectations people have of leaders. **Implicit leadership theories** are personal assumptions about the traits and abilities that characterize an ideal organizational leader. These assumptions, both stated and unstated, develop through socialization and past experiences with leaders. The assumptions are stored in memory and activated when group members interact with a person in a leadership position. Our assumptions about leaders help us make sense of what takes place on the job, and what kind of behavior we expect from a leader. Assume that Brett was raised in a household and neighborhood in which business leaders are highly respected and thought to be dedicated and intelligent. When Brett later works in a full-time professional job, he is most likely to be influenced by a supervisor he perceives to be dedicated and intelligent because this person fits Brett's preconceived notion of how a leader should behave. When a leader behaves in this manner, he or she impresses Brett.

According to implicit leadership theory, as part of making assumptions and expectations of leader traits and behaviors, people develop leadership prototypes and antiprototypes. *Prototypes* are positive characterizations of a leader, whereas *antiprototypes* are traits and behaviors people do not want to see in a leader. People have different expectations of what they want in a leader, yet research conducted with 939 subordinates in two different samples in British business organizations shows there is some consistency in implicit leadership theories. The study showed that these theories are consistent across different employee groups and are also stable trait-based stereotypes of leadership.[9] Another study in England showed that if the leader matches employee assumptions about having the right traits, the leader–member exchange (LMX) will be more positive. In turn, the group member will be more readily impressed and influenced by the leader.[10]

Figure 9-3 lists the six traits group members want to see in a leader (prototypes), as well as the two traits they do not want to see in a leader (antiprototypes). Leaders

Figure 9-3 Implicit Leadership Theory Dimensions.

Leadership Prototype	Leadership Antiprototype
1. Sensitivity (compassion, sensitive)	1. Tyranny (dominant, selfish, manipulative)
2. Intelligence (intelligent, clever)	2. Masculinity (male, masculine)
3. Dedication (dedicated, motivated)	
4. Charisma (charismatic, dynamic)	
5. Strength (strong, bold)	
6. Attractiveness (well dressed, classy)	

Source: Gathered from information in Olga Epitropaki and Robin Martin, "Implicit Leadership Theories in Applied Settings: Factor Structure, Generalizability, and Stability over Time," *Journal of Applied Psychology*, April 2004, pp. 297–299.

who fit the prototypes are perceived to be effective leaders. The antiprototype of *masculinity* suggests that followers prefer a compassionate and relationship-oriented leader to a command-and-control leader. An implication of these data is that a leader who fits group members' prototypes is more likely to impress them than a leader who fits their antiprototype.

Specific Influence Tactics for Projecting a Leadership Image

Influencing others is incorporated into most definitions of leadership, so when a leader makes effective use of influence tactics he or she will project the image of being an effective leader. The purpose of influence tactics is to facilitate subordinates attaining important goals. However, in the process of exerting influence, the leader's image is likely to be enhanced. Here we describe briefly six influence tactics that are likely to be perceived by group members as indicative of effective leadership: leading by example and respect; exchanging favors and bargaining; making an inspirational appeal; consultation with others; being a team player; and practicing hands-on leadership.

Leading by Example and Respect

A simple but effective way of influencing group members and projecting a positive leadership image is by **leading by example**, or acting as a positive role model. The ideal approach is to be a "do as I say and do" manager—that is, one whose actions and words are consistent. Actions and words confirm, support, and often clarify each other. Being respected facilitates leading by example because group members are more likely to follow the example of leaders they respect.

Leading by example is often interpreted to mean that the leader works long and hard, and expects others to do the same, with this type of behavior being prevalent among entrepreneurs who hire a staff. This approach to leading by example is more likely to project the image of a workaholic than an effective leader who coordinates the work of others.

Exchanging Favors and Bargaining

Offering to exchange favors if another person will help the leader achieve a work goal is another standard influence tactic. By making an exchange, the leader strikes a bargain with the other party and therefore projects the image of being fair. The exchange often translates into being willing to reciprocate at a later date. It might also be promising a share of the benefits if the other person helps the leader accomplish a task. For example, the leader might promise to place a person's name on a report to top management if that person will help him or her analyze the data and prepare the tables.

Making an Inspirational Appeal

A leader is supposed to inspire others, so it follows that making an inspirational appeal is an important influence tactic, as well as a way of creating a positive impression. As Pfeffer notes, "Executives and others seeking to exercise influence in organizations often develop skill in displaying, or not displaying, their feelings in a strategic fashion."[11] An inspirational appeal usually involves displaying emotion and appealing to group members' emotions. A moderating variable in the effectiveness of an inspirational appeal or emotional display is the influence agent's **personal magnetism**, or the quality of being captivating, charming, and charismatic. Possessing personal magnetism makes it easier for the leader to inspire people while at the same time projecting the image of what many constituents expect from an effective leader.

For an emotional appeal to be effective, the influence agent must understand the values, motives, and goals of the target. Often this means that the leader must explain how the group efforts will have an impact outside the company. A study concluded: "Business leaders tend to think in terms of bottom-line goals, like boosting revenues or profits. But they need to speak about their goals in terms of how they will make a positive difference in the world. If you can see a goal—if you can touch, feel, and smell it—it seems more doable."[12] Having established such a goal, the leader creates the image of an effective leader.

Consultation with Others

A large number of group members want to collaborate with the leader in making decisions. As a result, consulting with group members enhances a leader's image. The influence target becomes more motivated to follow the agent's request because the target is involved in the decision-making process. Consultation is most effective as an influence tactic when the objectives of the person being influenced are consistent with those of the leader.[13] An example would be a business leader consulting with group members on how to reduce costs in order to increase both profits and year-end bonuses. In this situation the leader creates a good impression by consulting with group members about a goal important to them as well as the company.

Being a Team Player

To influence others by being a good team player is an important strategy for getting work accomplished. Also, at any level in the organization, the leader who pitches in creates a positive impression. An example would be an information technology team leader working through the night with team members to combat a virus attack on the company's computer network. Being a team player is a more effective influence tactic in an organizational culture that emphasizes collaboration than in one in which being tough-minded and decisive is more in vogue.

A study of CEO leadership profiles among buyout firms found that teamwork was less associated with success than traits such as persistence and efficiency. Leaders in buyout firms are strongly financially oriented and are much more concerned with making deals than building relationships.[14] In such firms, investing effort in building teamwork may not strongly enhance the leader's image.

Practicing Hands-On Leadership

A **hands-on leader** is one who gets directly involved in the details and processes of operations. Such a leader has expertise, is task oriented, leads by example, and will usually be considered a good team player. By getting directly involved in the group's work activities, the leader influences subordinates to hold certain beliefs and to follow certain procedures and processes. For example, the manager who gets directly involved in fixing customer problems demonstrates to other workers how he or she thinks such problems should be resolved, and therefore projects a positive image.

Hands-on leadership is usually expected at levels below the executive suite, yet many high-level executives are also hands-on leaders. An example is Steve Jobs, the legendary head of Apple Corp. and Pixar Animation Studios. The downside of being a hands-on leader is that if it is done to excess the leader becomes a micromanager, thereby detracting from his or her image as an effective leader.

Being a Servant Leader

When group members believe that a leader's major role is to help them attain their goals, the leader will create a strong impression by focusing his or her efforts on providing such assistance.

A **servant leader** emphasizes integrity and serves constituents by working on their behalf to help them achieve their goals, not the leader's own goals. The idea behind servant leadership, as formulated by Robert K. Greenleaf, is that leadership derives naturally from a commitment to service.[15] Serving others, including employees, customers, and community, is the primary motivation for the servant leader. And true leadership emerges from a deep desire to help others. A servant leader is therefore a moral leader. Servant leadership has been accomplished when group members become wiser, healthier, and more autonomous. Should a leader accomplish these ends, he or she would create a well-deserved positive impression. The following are key aspects of servant leadership:[16]

1. *Place service before self-interest.* A servant leader is more concerned with helping others than with acquiring power, prestige, financial reward, and status. The servant leader seeks to do what is morally right, even if it is not financially rewarding. He or she is conscious of the needs of others and is driven by a desire to satisfy them. Another aspect of service before self-interest is the leader focusing on helping subordinates grow and succeed through such means as making constructive suggestions for professional growth.

2. *Listen first to express confidence in others.* The servant leader makes a deep commitment to listening in order to get to know the concerns, requirements, and problems of group members. (As stated above, listening projects a positive image.) Instead of attempting to impose his or her will on others, the servant leader listens carefully to understand what course of action will help others accomplish their goals. After understanding others, the best course of action can be chosen. Through listening, for example, a servant leader might learn that the group is more concerned about team spirit and harmony than striving for company-wide recognition. The leader would then concentrate more on building teamwork than searching for ways to increase the visibility of the team.

3. *Inspire trust by being trustworthy.* Being trustworthy and ethical is a foundation behavior of the servant leader. He or she is scrupulously honest with others, gives up control, and focuses on the well-being of others. Usually such leaders do not have to work hard at being trustworthy because they are already quite moral. In support of this principle, a survey found that most employees want a boss who is a trusted leader, not a pal.[17]

4. *Focus on what it is feasible to accomplish.* Even though the servant leader is idealistic, he or she recognizes that one individual cannot accomplish everything. So the leader listens carefully to the array of problems facing group members and then concentrates on a few. The servant leader thus systematically neglects certain problems. A leader might carefully listen to all the concerns and complaints of the constituents and then proceed to work on the most pressing issue. A good impression is created by accomplishing something tangible on the road to major improvements.

5. *Lend a hand.* A servant leader looks for opportunities to play the Good Samaritan. As a supermarket manager, he or she might help out by bagging groceries during a busy period. Or a servant leader might help dig up mud in the company lobby after a hurricane.

6. *Emotional healing.* A servant leader shows sensitivity to the personal concerns of group members, such as a worker being worried about taking care of a disabled parent. Showing sensitivity to the personal concerns of group members generates a strong impression because most people place heavy emphasis on wanting their own needs satisfied.

Carrying out the role of a servant leader would result in projecting a positive leadership impression for group members who expect the leader to be helpful. An example is college professors wanting the department head to take care of administrative work so they can concentrate on teaching, advising, and research. In contrast, being a servant leader might create a poor impression when the group members expected a leader to invest most of his or her time in external affairs such as making deals and landing customers.

Impression Management and Charismatic Leadership

Many of the strategies and tactics already described in the chapter contribute to creating the impression of a charismatic leader. Scholarly analysis, as well as observations in the media, indicates strongly that part of being charismatic is to generate the impression of a dynamic, magnetic person who can accomplish important goals for constituents as well as potential constituents. The effective charismatic leader creates a good impression, yet at the same time accomplishes much beyond creating an impression. Among the accomplishments of an effective charismatic leader would be to inspire subordinates to high performance, and to contribute to their job satisfaction by being warm and caring.

Our approach to understanding how impression management is an integral part of charismatic leadership is divided into two parts: definitions of charisma that include an element of impression management, and a model of how organizational actors use impression management to create and maintain a charismatic identity.

Definitions of Charismatic Leadership that Include an Element of Impression Management

Over the years, charisma has been defined in various ways. Nevertheless, there is enough consistency among these definitions to make charisma a useful concept in understanding and practicing leadership. The various definitions also help us to understand that impression management is an important part of projecting charisma. To begin, *charisma* is a Greek word meaning divinely inspired gift. In the study of leadership, **charisma** is a special quality of leaders whose purposes, powers, and extraordinary determination differentiate them from others.[18]

Part of these powers can be attributed to the compelling impression the leader makes on constituents. This is true because charisma is a positive and compelling quality of a person that makes many others want to be led by him or her. The term *many others* is carefully chosen because the charismatic leader does not create the same positive impression on all constituents. A case in point is Steve Jobs of Apple Corp. and Pixar, who inspires thousands with his technical acumen and visionary perspective about consumer electronics. In contrast, he is regarded as overbearing and conceited by some constituents and many business journalists.

The following definitions of charisma indicate directly or indirectly the impression management component of charisma and charismatic leadership:[19]

1. A certain quality of an individual personality by virtue of which he or she is set apart from ordinary people and treated as endowed with supernatural, superhuman, or at least specifically exceptional powers or qualities. (Observe that being treated as being endowed with exceptional powers or qualities suggests that the leader creates a strong impression.)
2. The process of influencing major changes in the attitudes and assumptions of organization members, and building commitment for the organization's objectives. (To exert influence, a leader would typically need to create a strong impression.)
3. Leadership that has a magnetic effect on people. (A magnetic effect is a function of the impression created.)
4. A charismatic leader is a mystical, narcissistic, and personally magnetic savior with extraordinary capabilities and a doctrine to promote. (Being mystical and personally magnetic is based on the impression the leader creates.)
5. Charismatic leaders are those who exert various effects and influences on their followers. These include trust in the leader's beliefs, obedience and acceptance of the leader, identification of the leader, and emotional involvement with the leader's mission. (All of these ends depend on the leader creating a strong, positive impression on group members.)
6. A charismatic person exudes confidence, dominance, a sense of purpose, and the ability to articulate goals that the followers are predisposed to accept. (*Exuding* implies creating an impression.)
7. Inspirational leadership characterized by the charismatic having a call from God for his or her mission. (It takes a strong impression to inspire others, especially when the inspiration appears to be divine.)
8. Charismatic leadership takes place when there is confidence building, shared vision, and the creation of valued opportunities. (Confidence building is based on creating a strong impression.)

The basic reason that these definitions imply that the charismatic leader engages in self-presentation is that charisma is based on perceptions, and perceptions of others are based on the impressions they create.

Impression Management in the Service of Creating and Maintaining a Charismatic Identity

Image building has long been recognized as an important part of charismatic leadership. Impression management techniques bolster the image of the leader's competence, which helps build subordinate compliance and faith in them. Jay Conger and Rabindra N. Kanungo reason that charismatic leaders can be distinguished from other leaders partly because they use oral communication skills and impression management to inspire followers in pursuit of the vision.[20]

According to a model developed by William L. Gardner and Bruce J. Avolio, social (or organizational) actors rely on impression management behaviors to create and maintain identities as charismatic leaders. From this perspective, to be perceived as a charismatic leader depends on projecting the right impression. The Gardner and Avolio model is a comprehensive examination of the relationship between charismatic leaders and their followers. Here we focus on the links between impression management and charisma.[21]

Charismatic leaders use impression management to deliberately cultivate a certain relationship with group members. In other words, they take steps to create a favorable, successful impression, recognizing that the perceptions of constituents determine whether they function as charismatic leaders. Impression management could imply that these leaders are skillful actors in presenting a charismatic face to the world. But the behaviors and attitudes of truly charismatic leaders go well beyond superficial aspects of impression management, such as wearing fashionable clothing or speaking well. For example, a truly charismatic leader will work hard to create positive visions for group members.

The model Gardner and Avolio construct is based on **dramaturgy**, in which actors engage in performances in various settings for particular audiences in order to shape their definitions of the situation. Consistent with this perspective, the actor (leader) and audience (followers) play key roles in the charismatic performance. For example, unless the subordinates are looking to identify with and be impressed by a leader, charismatic influence will not occur. A charismatic relationship will most likely emerge during two conditions. First, the environment must be seen as turbulent; and, second, the organizational context is supportive of change. This proposition helps explain why earlier conceptions of charisma proposed that followers are most in need of a charismatic leader during a crisis.

The Role of High Self-Esteem and High Self-Monitoring

Charismatic leaders typically have high levels of self-esteem. As a result these leaders persist in portraying a confident image in public even when discouraged by repeated failures. The high self-esteem portrayed by the leader often triggers followers to elevate their own self-esteem. A relevant example is that the head of multilevel sales programs are often charismatic figures who engage the cooperation of many people with limited self-confidence to participate in selling their products. The "down-line distributors" feel better about themselves by identifying with the heroic figure at the top of the sales pyramid.

Charismatic leaders are also high self-monitors, which plays a useful role in understanding the type of image followers want to perceive. For example, if the charismatic leader detects that the group members are concerned about job security, the leader will frame messages pointing toward stability of employment. Similarly, the high self-monitoring tendencies of charismatic leaders help them respond to the values of group members. Messages can then be shaped to fit the dominant values. Assume that a chief operating officer of a food company detects that a large proportion of the workforce has developed green (environmentally friendly) values. To gain influence and leadership status with the group, the chief operating officer begins to frame many messages in terms of how the company is contributing to a healthy external environment.

Self-monitoring includes the ability to understand the goals and dreams of subordinates. As a result the charismatic leader can shape visions that group members can identify with. The vision, in turn, is part of the impression the charismatic leader creates. John Chambers, the CEO and Chairman of Cisco Systems, has established a vision of Cisco becoming a highly recognizable brand. The vision Chambers has established for Cisco appears to be based in part on the rampant pride he detects among his employees.

Desired Identity Images

The identity images of trustworthy, esteemed, and powerful are highly valued by charismatic leaders because being perceived as charismatic is dependent on these images. As a result, the charismatic leader works hard at projecting these images. In some circumstances, highly unethical and criminal charismatic people work at establishing an image of trustworthiness to gain the confidence of their targets. Of note is the fact that many wealthy people who have been swindled by financial consultants were so surprised to learn that a person they perceived to be honest and caring proved to be a criminal.

Many charismatic leaders present themselves as being morally worthy, making many references to values and purposes in order to convince their constituents. So long as their self-presentations are true, these leaders retain their charismatic status. Another identity image favored by charismatic leaders is to be perceived as innovative, entrepreneurial, unconventional, and as leaders who have a vision for radical change. As a result, the charismatic leader will sprinkle his or her messages with references to such matters as changing the organizational culture and rewarding entrepreneurial thinking by employees. A. G. Lafley, the esteemed former CEO of Procter & Gamble, made frequent reference to encouraging entrepreneurial thinking among employees. As a result, many employees contributed ideas that have made their way into new products.

Specific Impression Management Behaviors

So far this section has described identity images and general approaches to impression management. Gardner and Avolio have also identified four specific impression management behaviors charismatic leaders employ to secure and obtain their identity images:

1. *Framing.* Charismatic leaders frame their visions to present the organization's (or organizational unit's) purpose in a manner that energizes followers. In

other words, the vision creates a useful impression. An example is the vision formulated by top management at Google: "To make nearly all information accessible to everyone all the time."

2. *Scripting*. Framing provides general ideas, whereas scripts provide the details of the action to take place. Charismatic leaders provide a cast for the script when they define roles for themselves and others. One role for subordinates might be to help stave off a competitor, such as a product developer at Nikon continually improving its high-end digital cameras to the point that lower-priced competitors are at a disadvantage. Another part of scripting is to develop a dialogue that can be invoked frequently to capture the imagination of constituents. Jeffrey R. Immelt, the CEO of GE, relentlessly delivers a message about the importance of growth in revenue, profits, and market share. In recent years GE has slipped from time to time, but the message still drives thousands of managers.

   Charismatic leaders also emphasize nonverbal behavior to deliver the messages in their scripts. Leaders perceived to be charismatic project a powerful, confident, and dynamic presence by way of their body posture, speaking rate, gestures, smiles, eye contact, and non-sexual touching. Andrea Jung, the CEO and chairwoman of Avon, captivates her audience with her careful speech, stylish presence, and warm gestures, among other nonverbal cues. All of these behaviors may be easy for charismatic leaders to accomplish, yet they are also intended to strengthen the impression they create.

3. *Staging*. As in theater and selling a home, staging for the charismatic leader involves creating an appropriate scene and appearance. Charismatic leaders often manipulate their appearance for symbolic purposes, such as an executive at an investment banking firm wearing French cuffs or a luxury handbag to appear wealthy. Staging might also include a business leader taking part in television commercials to promote favorable corporate images, such as George A. Zimmer of Men's Warehouse. His warm, reassuring, and natural voice add to his credibility and charisma. Even when an executive is not particularly telegenic, appearing in a television commercial suggests his or her personal involvement in the business.

4. *Performing*. In the dramaturgical framework, *performing* refers to the enactment of scripted behaviors and relationships. Two specific impression management techniques for creating charismatic images are exemplification and self-promotion. Exemplification is the impression management strategy most closely linked to charisma. The attributions triggered by exemplification are associated with the desired identity images of trustworthiness and morality. As exemplifiers, charismatic leaders engage in self-sacrificing and high-risk behaviors that dramatically illustrate their commitment to the cause they espouse. An example here would include the turnaround manager who agrees to work for a first-year salary of $1 plus stock in the company. The leader's

intent is to demonstrate that his or her compensation will be dependent on the success of the turnaround.

Self-promotion helps the leader appear credible, innovative, esteemed, and powerful. The successful charismatic leader will often self-promote in a subtle fashion, because blatant self-promotion can damage one's credibility. A subtle form of self-promotion might be for the business leader to let it be known that he or she has been appointed to a federal government position. In this way a second party has endorsed the leader's importance. A more typical form of self-promotion is for the leaders to take on challenges they know they can achieve. For example, a CEO might spearhead acquiring another company that is financially troubled and is looking for a suitor.

We reinforce the idea again that almost any strategy or tactic of impression management can be functional in terms of projecting charisma. The tactics of framing, scripting, staging, and performing provide a useful conceptual framework for understanding how charismatic leaders apply impression management.

Guidelines for Application and Practice

1. One of the most effective ways of projecting a leadership image is to satisfy assumptions followers make of how a leader should behave, as described in implicit leadership theory. The personality traits involved, if not already present in a leader, would take a long time to develop. However, most people are capable of making some progress in developing the following attributes: sensitivity, intelligence, dedication, charisma, strength, and attractiveness. A person might not be able to quickly elevate his or her intelligence, but people can learn to improve their intellect through disciplining themselves to think more carefully, and to acquire additional job-relevant information.

2. A recommended approach to asking for a favor is to give the other person as much time as feasible to accomplish the task, such as by saying, "Could you find ten minutes between now and the end of the month to help me?" Not pressing for immediate assistance will tend to lower resistance to the request. Giving a menu of options for different levels of assistance also helps lower resistance. For example, you might ask another manager if you can borrow a technician for a one-month assignment; then, as a second option, you might ask if the technician could work ten hours per week on the project.[22] To ensure that the request is perceived as an exchange, you might explain what reciprocity you have in mind: that you will mention your coworker's helpfulness to his or her manager.

3. Impression management tactics can be helpful in projecting the image of charisma, and therefore being perceived as charismatic. Conversely, behaving charismatically will project a positive impression in many situations.

Following are several suggestions that will both enhance a person's charisma, as well as creating a positive impression:

- *Create visions for others.* Being able to create visions for others will be a major factor in being perceived as charismatic. A vision uplifts and attracts others, as well as projecting the impression of a strong leader.
- *Be enthusiastic, optimistic, and energetic.* A major behavior pattern of charismatic people is their combination of enthusiasm, optimism, and high energy. Without a great amount of all three characteristics, a person is unlikely to be perceived as charismatic by many people.
- *Remember names of people.* Charismatic leaders, as well as other successful people, can usually remember the names of people they have seen just once or several times. Caring about people helps you remember their names, as does concentrating on the name when first introduced and then repeating the name.
- *Develop synchrony with others.* People tend to regard those in synchrony with them as charismatic. A practical method of being in sync with another person is to adjust your posture to conform to his or her posture. When the other person stands up straight, you do; when he or she slouches, you do also.[23]

Summary

Projecting the image of a leader could be a subject without limits, depending on how *image* is interpreted. Four approaches to projecting a leadership image described here are as follows: (1) using appropriate acting skills; (2) displaying the traits found in implicit leadership theories; (3) applying specific influence tactics such as leading by example and respect, and making an inspirational appeal; and (4) being a servant leader.

Impression management is an important part of projecting charisma. Various definitions of charisma point toward its link with impression management. One such definition is that charisma is a certain quality of an individual personality by which he or she is set apart from ordinary people and treated as endowed with supernatural, superhuman, or at least specifically exceptional powers or qualities.

Impression management helps create and maintain a charismatic identity. To be perceived as a charismatic leader depends on projecting the right impression. Charismatic leaders use impression management to deliberately cultivate a certain relationship with group members. A model presented here is based on dramaturgy, in which actors engage in performances in various settings for particular audiences in order to shape their definitions of the situation.

Charismatic leaders typically have high levels of self-esteem, and therefore persist in portraying a confident image in public even when discouraged by repeated failures. The high self-esteem portrayed by the leader often triggers followers into elevating their own self-esteem. Charismatic leaders are also high self-monitors, which facilitates understanding the type of image followers want to perceive.

The identity images of trustworthy, esteemed, and powerful are highly valued by charismatic leaders because being perceived as charismatic is dependent on these images. Also, many charismatic leaders present themselves as being morally worthy, making many references to values and purposes in order to convince their constituents.

Four specific impression management behaviors charismatic leaders employ to secure and obtain their identity images are (1) framing, (2) scripting, (3) staging, and (4) performing. Exemplification and self-promotion are two important techniques for performing.

Guidelines for application and practice presented here include: (1) a leadership image can be projected by satisfying assumptions made about how leaders should behave; (2) it is best to ask for a favor by giving the other person as much time as feasible to accomplish the task; (3) impression management tactics can help project charisma, and behaving charismatically will project a positive impression.

Chapter 10

Impression Management by Organizations

Organizations, as well as individuals, often take deliberate steps to create a positive impression, such as a company that makes a sports drink emphasizing how much it cares about the health and competitiveness of its customers. In this chapter we focus on how organizations engage in impression management. The topic is quite important because if an organization does not create a positive impression, it could be at a competitive disadvantage. Also, understanding how organizations engage in self-presentation could help you manage your own image, such as working hard to develop a positive reputation.

If an organization can truly manage its impression, the organization must have a nervous system along with cognitive skills and a personality. In reality, impression management by an organization is the collective work of people, including managers and professional-level workers, as well as outside public relations and communication specialists. Customers and clients also contribute to the impression an organization makes. For example, some malls have a difficult time attracting visitors because they have developed the reputation as a gathering place for many hostile and aggressive people with criminal tendencies.

Our approach to understanding impression management at the organizational level centers on three related topics: corporate image and reputation; placing a positive spin on negatively toned events; and corporate social responsibility and impression management. Figure 10-1 provides an overview of these relationships. For example, if an organization is socially responsible it will tend to have a positive image and reputation.

Corporate Image and Reputation

Organizations are frequently judged by the image they project, or their reputation. Corporate image, or reputation, is now a business firm, its activities, and its products or services are perceived by outsiders.[1] When managers and other workers are able to project a positive corporate image, or a good reputation, the company is at a distinct competitive advantage. Despite its critics, Wal-Mart's positive reputation for low prices and goods of reasonable quality for the price helped the company prosper during the

Figure 10-1 Key Factors Related to Impression Management by Organizations.

The two-directional arrow between image and reputation, and spin suggests that image and reputation may make spin seem necessary. Also, spin may succeed in enhancing the image and reputation. The arrow in the lower left of the figure suggests that corporate social responsibility will often influence the image and reputation of an organization. The dashed line in the lower-right corner of the figure suggests that organizations might employ spin when they have not performed well with respect to social responsibility.

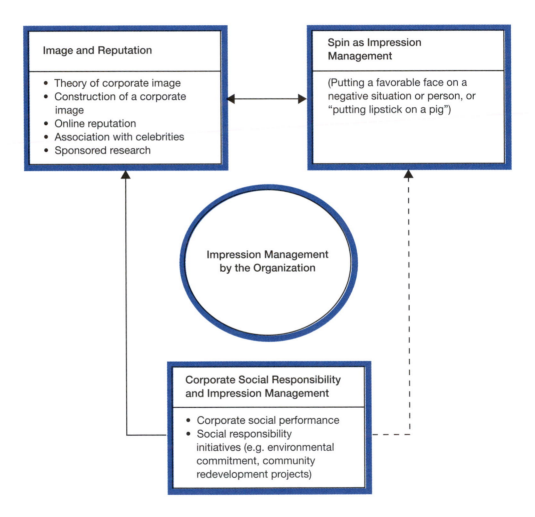

retailing recession of several years ago. Here we describe several major aspects of corporate image and reputation, as follows: the theory of corporate image; the construction of a corporate image; corporate image and online reputation; association with celebrities; and sponsored research to enhance a company reputation.

The Theory of Corporate Image

According to the theory of corporate image, five factors are essential in managing the corporate image: corporate identity, organizational structure, corporate reputation, corporate communication, and feedback.[2] The goal of managing the corporate image is to communicate the company's identity to those stakeholders important to the firm, in such a way that these people develop and maintain a favorable view of the company. Word of mouth is probably the most influential medium for shaping the corporate image, but advertising and public relations (or business communication) can also be influential.

Corporate identity is the reality and uniqueness of the organization that itself is composed of corporate strategy, corporate culture, organizational structure, and operations. The *strategy* is the overall plan, such as positioning Tiffany & Co. as being associated with luxury goods. The culture can help shape the identity of the firm through such means as having high concern for the welfare of employees and customers. IBM has maintained this aspect of culture despite having abandoned decades ago the policy of lifetime employment for adequate performers.

Organizational structure can shape the corporate identity in such ways as being geographically centralized or decentralized. A geographically decentralized firm such as Allstate projects the image of being more personal to many consumers than a more centralized firm such as Microsoft Corp. *Operations* is the totality of activities the firm engages in to implement the strategy, including the manufacture of high-quality goods itself or having the manufacture of products carried out by other companies. A company that simply attaches its nameplate to goods manufactured by others might develop a weak corporate identity.

Corporate reputation refers to the image or reputation among the relevant audiences or stakeholders. The principal stakeholders are typically customers, employees, distributors and retailers, financial institutions and their analysts, shareholders, government regulatory agencies, and labor unions. The company is likely to prosper to the extent that management can create a positive impression among these stakeholders. Every stakeholder counts. For example, creating a positive impression with Wall Street financial analysts can help the company attract more investors to the company. The positive impression Google has created across various stakeholders has helped the company prosper in such ways as attracting advertisers (who are the principal customers), job candidates, and investors.

One way in which corporate reputations have been formalized is the annual *Fortune* list of America's most admired companies. Reputation is based on rankings by executives, directors, and analysts on eight criteria from investment value to social responsibility. (A company has to create a good impression to receive high rankings.) GE had reached the No. 1 rank during the first 25 years of the annual ranking, putting the company in a tie with the pharmaceutical company Merck for the all-time record of first-place rankings. Six other companies with high reputations include Apple, BMW, Southwest Airlines, Target, and United Parcel Service.[3]

Corporate communication is the link between the corporate identity and corporate reputation. Communication can include many corporate activities, including how telephones are answered, the voice-mail system, press releases about the company, company blogs, advertising, and annual reports. What other people write about the company on the Internet is shaped by corporate communications but is not generated by management of the company.

Feedback has been emphasized in the cybernetic model of impression management presented in Chapter 2, and is also quite relevant for the corporate image. Business owners and managers need accurate information about how the company is perceived by stakeholders if they are to make sound decisions. Feedback should be continuous, although periodic surveys about the corporate image are also helpful. Workers who interact directly with customers can be a vital source of information about how the company is perceived. For example, retail store cashiers might inform management that many customers perceive store management as not caring about customers because it takes too long to check out of the store.

The Construction of a Corporate Image

The theory of corporate image provides some clues as to how a corporate image and reputation are constructed. A starting point would be the corporate strategy, which if successfully implemented would lead to the desired image and reputation, such as the Tiffany & Co. strategy of product differentiation through offering luxury products and appealing to status. In many situations the corporate image and reputation stem naturally from having successfully carried out the company's master plan. Other parts of the theory of corporate image are also relevant, such as having a system of communication that effectively delivers the message about the company's image.

Here we illustrate how a corporate image can be built by following the approach used by Ikea, a widely recognized brand. The company strategy is to sell a lifestyle that signifies hip (cool) design, thrift, and simplicity. For the global middle class with aspirations of upward mobility, purchasing Ikea products is a symbol of success. Building the cult brand involves the following steps:[4]

1. *Create the story.* The Swedish retailer is a master at creating buzz, or informal communication, which establishes evangelists for its brand who then communicate the story by telephone, word of mouth, and blogs throughout the world. In one promotion, essay contest winners were given the opportunity to camp out in a store before it opened. Promotions like these excite shoppers and generate substantial publicity.
2. *Inspire the staff.* Employees are not highly paid in terms of industry standards, yet they enjoy autonomy, a minimum of hierarchy, and a family-friendly culture. As a result, the staff internalizes the company philosophy of frugality and style that is a major part of corporate strategy.

3. *Seduce the shopper.* The customer-centric strategy is so intense that even senior management is required to work at the cashiers and in the warehouse for brief stints annually. The stores are designed to promote a fun experience. One approach to fun is the presence of restaurants and play centers that encourage shoppers to spend the day at the store. Simple touches, including free pencils and measuring tapes, make shopping easier.

4. *Surprise on value.* Ikea management mandates price cuts every year. At the same time product designers deliver on appearance and quality. Every year designers must attain demanding goals such as designing a bedroom set for under $200.

The Ikea approach to building a brand, and therefore a corporate image, illustrates that impressing the public is likely to involve systematic rather than random actions. Other companies might take a different approach to brand building and corporate image formation, yet they too are most likely to proceed systematically.

Corporate Image and Online Reputation

A company's online reputation is an aspect of corporate reputation that merits separate attention here because of its surging importance during the last decade. Blogs, forums, and other online chatter can make or break a company's reputation. Positive comments about the company enhance its reputation, and negative comments can drive sales down rapidly. One method of enhancing a company's reputation is to have a high ranking on major search engines such as Google and Yahoo. To create a positive impression through this type of high ranking some companies purchase a software service labeled search engine optimization (SEO). Some observers regard this technology as being web-savvy, whereas others regard it as search result manipulation (or a false impression). Another reputation management service will eradicate negative comments and even write positive blogs on behalf of a client.

Many business executives have come to recognize mentions on the Internet as an early-warning system for when the company reputation is at risk because of a product defect, or a disgruntled customer making exaggerated complaints. Several software companies specialize in monitoring social media, such as Facebook and Twitter, to analyze online computer chatter about their client companies. Among the typical small-business clients are a pet store targeted by animal rights activities or a stockbroker linked to Securities & Exchange Commission violations from many years back. Part of the reputation management service might be to place negative content about the company further down on the list of search results to keep the company reputation more favorable. A key tactic is to keep damaging commentary off the first page of search results.[5]

A more self-enhancing approach to impression management than reputation management is to repair the problem causing the negative comments, and engage in activities that lead to positive comments on the Internet. An extreme example would be a cell phone manufacturer receiving thousands of negative comments on the Internet because a handful of its phones contained batteries that exploded during normal use of the phones. Offering a public apology, along with changing the supplier of the defective batteries, would help repair the company image.

Association with Celebrities

Organizations—or more specifically their managers and public relations advisors—as well as individuals use the impression management tactic of basking in reflected glory. Many firms hope to build their reputation by associating themselves with a celebrity who enjoys a strong, positive reputation. A frequent example would be a general advertising campaign for a product featuring a well-known professional athlete. A less well-known example is that the large business consulting firm Accenture ran advertisements in business magazines and newspapers featuring the illustrious golfer Tiger Woods before public reports of his alleged scandalous behavior. Two of the taglines were "Go ahead, be a Tiger" and "We know what it takes to be a Tiger."

The technique of association with celebrities via advertising is also used to change a company image. For many years Avon Products perpetuated its homey image by featuring unknown women in its ads. To bring about a glamour makeover, Avon turned to ads featuring Hollywood and television celebrities. The global brand president of the company reasoned that Avon was meeting women's needs in quality, variety, and innovation but was falling short in brand image. The image-improvement campaign included hiring the popular actress Reese Witherspoon as the Avon Foundation's first global ambassador and honorary chairwoman.[6]

A variation of basking in reflected glory by featuring ads with celebrities, or employing a celebrity ambassador, is to enhance a corporate image by employing celebrities to engage in the major activities of the firm. An exceptional example is the private equity firm the Carlyle Group that owns over 200 companies. The Carlyle ranks have included former presidents of the United States, and former British prime minister John Major. The collective relationships of the partners helped build a business practice buying, transforming, and selling companies with a specialty in defense companies that sold to governments. Over the years, Carlyle bought more non-defense companies. To help change its focus, Carlyle added Louis V. Gerstner, Jr., the former IBM chairman and CEO, and Norman Pearlstine, the formed Time Inc. editor-in-chief. At one point, top management at Carlyle decided they no longer wanted President George H. W. Bush and Prime Minister John Major as senior advisors because they hurt the firm's image.[7]

Sponsored Research to Enhance a Company Reputation

Another way for a company to manage its impression and reputation is to have a second party conduct research that provides empirical evidence about the value of the company's product or services. In this way the company can point to "scientific proof" that its goods or services are beneficial. Research of this nature is often sponsored or paid for by the company seeking evidence to validate its offering. In the early days of the tobacco industry being challenged for selling a product that could cause cancer, several of the companies sponsored research demonstrating that no definitive evidence could be found linking cigarette smoking with cancer.

A representative provider of sponsored research is the Aberdeen Group that specializes in providing evidence about the contribution of information technology. Aberdeen's approach is to arrive at a research topic, typically involving a new information technology trend, and then approach tech companies selling products associated with the trend. For a fee, a company approached can become a report sponsor. Aberdeen then sends questionnaires to tech users inquiring about their current or future use of the area in question.

The Aberdeen reports often discover that best-in-class companies use, or are thinking about using, whatever technology the report happens to be describing. For example, an executive summary of a report on compensation management technology funded by companies selling such technology concluded: "The research reveals that Best-in-Class companies have implemented organizational processes which support compensation-technology adoption."[8]

The reports are explicit about which companies sponsored the research, yet still appear to enhance the reputation of the company products. Sponsors are able to distribute a news release announcing the report, thereby giving themselves favorable publicity. A criticism of this approach to impression management is that the results of sponsored research are usually flattering, otherwise it would not be sponsored. Entirely objective research might not always be so flattering. Aberdeen management notes that some of its research findings are critical of its sponsors.[9]

Sponsored research to enhance both product and corporate reputation takes place in industries outside information technology, with the pharmaceutical industry as a prominent example. A representative example is that Johnson & Johnson spent a minimum of $700,000 to sponsor the Johnson & Johnson Center for Pediatric Psychopathology at Massachusetts General Hospital. The purpose of the center according to court documents was to generate and disseminate data supporting the use of the antipsychotic drug Risperdal for treating children and adolescents. The center is run by an influential child psychiatrist.[10]

A positive comment about the various approaches to corporate image enhancement is that these efforts often boost the price of company stock. Many executives are finding that the way in which the outside world expects a company to behave can be its most important asset. A specific research finding is that a company's reputation for being able to deliver growth, attract a talented workforce, and avoid ethical problems can account for much of the market capitalization above its book value. This means that the total value of all the company shares exceeds the minimum value of the stock as indicated by book value.

A caution about the link between reputation and stock price is that a company's message must be grounded in reality, and its reputation built over the years. Good financial performance is still a major contributor to a company's reputation. If a company has developed a poor reputation, a public relations (impression management) campaign alone will not change its image. It is necessary to first fix the underlying problems.[11]

Spin as Impression Management

An impression tactic aimed at hundreds, or even thousands, of people at the same time is **spin**, or putting a favorable face on a negative situation or person. The spinner is not necessarily lying, but emphasizing a plausible positive aspect of a negative event. The spin usually has a kernel of truth, with a puffed message spun around the kernel. Spin is part of public relations, except that public relations is also used to bring attention to favorable events, such as a company undergoing a major expansion or making a large contribution to charity. The term spin appears to have been derived from sports in which the player imparts a spin on the ball to gain advantage, such as a spin serve in tennis jumping high or spin on a bowling ball helping it glide into the right position between two pins.

A representative example of spin took place at Microsoft Corp. in 2008 when Chief Executive Steve Ballmer tried to put a good face on the software developer's failed attempt to buy Yahoo Inc. At Microsoft's annual meeting, Ballmer said that Microsoft wanted to avoid buying Yahoo "at the wrong price." He noted that the inability to reach an agreement in the spring prohibited a regulatory review of any deal before a new U.S. president was inaugurated. Ballmer also said that purchasing Yahoo would have created enormous integration expenses to merge the two companies. Furthermore, without Yahoo in the fold, Microsoft would have more flexibility to try to compete against Google Inc., with new technologies and Internet search.[12] So after having hotly pursued Yahoo, Ballmer gave a nice spin on why the purchase falling through was really good for Microsoft. Spin in this situation resembles giving an *account* or excuse.

Spin is sometimes used to overcome negative publicity, thereby protecting a corporate image and creating an improved impression. In November 2005, Paul English established www.gethuman.com, which helps callers bypass automated phone systems. English soon appeared on network news channels, and provided suggestions for consumers. The website quickly became a public relations liability for the interactive voice response (IVR) industry. However, Michael Zirngibl, the founder of IVR provider Angel.com retaliated with spin. Zirngibl and his team used the backlash to their advantage because they wanted to explain how their technology is an asset for business firms and their customers. For example, with IVR the customer listens to a clear, rehearsed voice with a consistent message. Within days the Angel.com team developed a Google advertising program with keywords including "Paul English" and "gethuman.com." After six months had passed, Angel.com's campaign had received in excess of 10,000 clicks, and company revenues increased 140%. Telling the positive side of interactive voice response was spin.[13] At the same time, Zirngibl was smart enough to figure out how to turn an attack against his company into an asset.

Here are a few representative examples of spin whose intent is to influence stakeholders—including employees, customers, and investors—to have a more favorable impression of the company.

- A company sells off a profitable unit to raise cash it desperately needs to pay down debt or pay other bills. The spin is that "by selling this non-core part of our business the management team can get rid of a distraction that is diverting attention from the core business."
- A company enters into Chapter 11 bankruptcy, and offers this spin: "Declaring Chapter 11 is simply a balance sheet adjustment that will not adversely affect our operations. We will emerge as a stronger company soon with a great balance sheet."
- A giant retailer starts a new division of 75 stores to capture a larger market share in a specific segment of the market. The stores lose an enormous amount of money and are all closed within 18 months. The spin offered is that "we are glad we took this risk. A company that does not take risks with innovation will ultimately die."

Creating spin can be regarded as self-protective impression management because the organization attempts to present the positive side of something the organization might have done wrong. However, if the spin is too exaggerated, top-level management at the company might be displaying poor ethics. Assume that an American recycling company has outsourced the disassembly of personal computers and other electronic devices to a third world country. It now faces the problem that disassembling the devices exposes the workers in that country to more toxic substances than U.S. law would allow. When reports of workers being poisoned leaks out, the American firm receives considerable negative publicity. The American firm then engages in spin to explain that it did not violate safety laws in the third world country. Another aspect of the spin is that the disassembling operation created jobs for poor people. The ethical issue is that spin was used to gloss over human suffering.

Consistent with the example just presented, many scholars and consumers regard spin as a negative and unethical tactic of impression management. Nevertheless, spin is widely practiced even by generally ethical organizations.

Corporate Social Responsibility and Impression Management

A major contributor to a company image is its level of social responsibility. For example, with respect to environmental concerns, Pratima Bansal and Iain Clelland contend that organizational managers can actively shape the way in which stakeholders perceive the firm. Organizational actors frequently use shareholder meetings, press releases, annual reports, and other forms of business communication to influence stakeholder perceptions of their firms. Among the impression management tactics used to influence stakeholder perceptions are excuses, justifications, concessions, apologies, denials, and attacks. The social responsibility initiatives described later in this section might be interpreted as tactics of impression management. For example, Bansal and Clelland classify a commitment to the environment as an impression management tactic.[14]

Top-level management often does good deeds based on an altruistic spirit and wanting to be good citizens, rather than an interest in fostering a good impression. Whether or not the intent of being socially responsible is to create a positive impression among stakeholders, socially responsible actions by top management enhance a corporation's impression. One example is that a company perceived to be *green* (environmentally friendly) is likely to attract more customers and earn higher profits. Specific information about the consequences of social responsibility is presented in Chapter 11 of this book. In contrast to socially responsible acts, socially irresponsible acts will often create a negative impression. Here we look at several aspects of social responsibility linked to impression management.

The Meaning of Corporate Social Responsibility

Many people believe that firms have an obligation to be concerned about outside groups affected by an organization. **Corporate social responsibility** is the idea that firms have obligations to society beyond their economic obligations to owners or stockholders and also beyond those prescribed by law or contract. The corporation thereby has an economic and social responsibility to the whole community, and creates a positive impression by meeting this responsibility.

Despite the definition offered here, corporate social responsibility is viewed in several ways, and has recently been perceived as an umbrella term for a variety of business-society relations. Corporate social responsibility relates to an organization's impact on society, beyond doing what is ethical.[15] To behave in a socially responsible way, managers must be aware of how their actions influence stakeholders, including the impressions formed by the actions of management.

A continuing debate concerns what obligations companies have to be socially responsible. The position advanced by a growing number of nongovernmental organizations is business firms should take action on issues ranging from pollution and global warming to AIDS, illiteracy, and poverty. The other position is that many investors want companies in which they invest to focus on the bottom line so they can maximize their returns.[16] In reality, these positions can be mutually supportive. Many socially responsible actions are the by-products of sensible business decisions. For instance, it is both socially responsible and profitable for a company to improve the language and math skills of entry-level workers, and invest in local schooling.

Literate and numerate entry-level workers for some jobs may be in short supply, and employees who cannot follow written instructions and do basic math may be unproductive. Also, a business firm that is environmentally friendly might attract the type of workers who are talented enough to help the firm become more profitable. The talented workers are impressed by the firm that is environmentally friendly, and therefore want to become members.

A problem in practicing corporate social responsibility is that not all interested parties agree on what constitutes responsible behavior. Target stores might have many customers who believe that citizens have a constitutional right to defend themselves with handguns against intruders to their home. To this group of customers, a retailer with corporate social responsibility would sell handguns to the public. The presence of guns for sale at Target would create a good impression with these stakeholders. Another customer group might believe strongly in tight gun controls. For this group, Target not selling handguns to the public would reflect corporate social responsibility, and would create a favorable impression.

Corporate Social Performance

Corporate social performance is the extent to which a firm responds to the demands of its stakeholders for it to behave in a socially responsible manner. After stakeholders have been satisfied with the reporting of financial information, they may turn their attention to the behavior of the corporation as a good citizen in the community. For this group of stakeholders, strong financial performance is not enough to create a positive impression. One way of measuring social performance is to analyze the company's annual report in search of relevant statistical information. For example, you might look for data about contributions to charities, arts, education, and pollution measures.

Another approach to measuring corporate social performance is to observe how a company responds to social issues by examining programs in greater detail. The next section describes corporate activities in relation to a variety of social issues.

Social Responsibility Initiatives

Here we describe positive corporate responses to important social issues. A firm that introduces initiatives in these areas can be considered socially responsible and will therefore impress many stakeholders. An important reason that corporate social responsibility initiatives are linked to corporate image and reputation is that myriad organizations rank companies on their social performance, and these rankings attract considerable publicity. For example, fast-food and packaged-food companies are sometimes held responsible for obesity and poor nutrition.[17]

The five social responsibility initiatives described here are: expressing an environmental commitment, work-life programs, community redevelopment projects, acceptance of whistle blowers, and compassionate downsizing.

Expressing an Environmental Commitment

Many companies take the initiative to preserve the natural environment in a way that pleases environmental groups (e.g. Greenpeace). As a result, the company works in partnership with a group intent on such purposes as reducing carbon dioxide emissions, preserving forests, or protecting a species of fish or animal. Environmental protection is at present a major social responsibility initiative, with business enterprises large and small investing money in preserving the environment. Another key aspect of environmental protection is to prevent pollution rather than control wastes after they have surfaced. For example, a company might eliminate the use of mercury in electrical switches and instead substitute a metal such as copper that is less toxic to the environment. The concern is that when the switch is discarded the highly poisonous mercury could eventually work its way into the ground. Recycling also helps prevent pollution because recycled products are resources in use rather than resources decaying in dumps or landfill. A sampling of social responsibility initiatives centering on protecting the environment is presented next.[18]

- Virgin Group founder Richard Branson plans to invest an estimated $3 billion over a ten-year period in renewable energy projects and technologies that help reduce global warming. The money will be managed through an investment company called Virgin Fuels. (Observe that this initiative could be controversial because many people think that the concern about global warming has no scientific basis.)
- The computer industry in general is introducing a giant initiative to slow down energy consumption when using computers. CPUs are being designed to run cooler; LCD display screens use less than half as much power as the CRTs they replace. Also, modern operating systems interact with hardware to turn off disk drives or slow down microprocessors not in use at a given time. The power supply part of the computer is now designed to meet the federal Energy Star standard by being more efficient.
- Computershare Ltd., an Australian shareholder services company, has launched a campaign backed by one dozen U.S. companies to persuade more shareholders to switch to electronic versions of shareholder-related communications. As an incentive, shareholders are informed that a tree will be planted for everyone who goes the paperless route. The program is called eTree. McDonald's has found that so far more than 6% of its 270,000 registered shareholders have switched to electronic reports. (Observe here that the "paperless" route often translates into people printing the information they need, so the savings in paper are not really so substantial.)

In addition to top-level management taking the initiative to protect the environment, company action often causes employees to think about environmental protection in ways such as carpooling, being a good recycler, not littering.

A caution about environmentally friendly initiatives is that, although they generate favorable publicity and create a good impression on many stakeholders, they do not always accomplish their goal. A case in point is that the World Wildlife Fund praised three large corporations as "climate savers." According to the Fund, Sony, Nike, and Lafarge, the French cement maker, had demonstrated that business can make reasonable and meaningful changes to reduce global warming. Despite the accolades, the companies' own environmental reports reached a different conclusion. During the time period in question, carbon emissions from all three companies had been rising: Sony by 17% in one year; Nike by 50% in nine years; and Lafarge by 11% over two years.[19]

Work-Life Programs

Organizations introduce a major social responsibility initiative when they establish programs that help employees balance the demands of work and personal life. The intent of a work-life program is to help employees lead a more balanced life, and be more satisfied and productive on the job. The most popular of these programs remains flexible work schedules. Flextime has grown in popularity because evidence suggests that it reduces turnover, improves morale, and helps recruit talent. Work-life programs create a strong, positive impression on potential job candidates because the company is perceived as understanding the challenges many family people face.

Community Redevelopment Projects

As a large-scale social responsibility initiative, business firms invest resources in helping rebuild distressed communities. Investing in a community is but one aspect of philanthropy, or charitable giving. Investment could mean constructing offices or factories in an impoverished section of town, or offering job training for residents from these areas. A specific goal of some community redevelopment projects is to replace a crime-ridden development with new housing that is associated with less crime and more community pride.

A notable example of community redevelopment is the Prudential Foundation established by Prudential Financial. The Foundation provides support to innovative direct-service programs that address the needs of the community in three areas: Ready to Learn, Ready to Work, and Ready to Live. Community housing development is included in the Ready to Work initiative that helps rebuild inner cities by investing money in ventures such as grocery stores, housing, and entertainment. The New Jersey Performing Arts Center is one of their investment projects. The Ready to Work program concentrates on initiatives that increase employment opportunities by strengthening job skills and opportunities, and promoting neighborhood development activities. Encouraging entrepreneurship is also emphasized. The program also aims to create decent, affordable housing by working in partnership with Community Housing Development Corporations and community development financial institutions.[20]

Despite the contribution of community redevelopment, this social responsibility initiative does have its drawbacks. Tenants may be forced out of their homes to make way for new development which cannot accommodate all previous tenants. When news of such an unfortunate development spreads, the community development effort may create a negative impression.

Acceptance of Whistle Blowers

A **whistle blower** is an employee who discloses organizational wrongdoing to parties who can take action. It was a whistle blower who began the process of exposing the scandalous financial practices at Enron Corp., such as hiding losses. Sherron Watkins, a vice president, wrote a one-page anonymous letter exposing unsound, if not dishonest, financial reporting. Enron had booked profits for two entities that had no assets. She dropped the letter off at company headquarters the next day. Also, the CEO had announced to employees that Enron's financial liquidity had never been stronger, while exercising his own $1.5 billion in stock options, just ahead of the company's announcement of a $618 million quarterly loss.[21] Watkins later became a public heroine and celebrity because of her role in exposing the Enron scandal.

A whistle blower has to be patient because it usually takes years to resolve a claim, including an agonizing court procedure. Another problem is that whistle blowers are often ostracized and humiliated by the companies they hope to improve, by such means as no further promotions or poor performance evaluations. More than half the time, the pleas of whistle blowers are ignored. So it is important for leaders at all levels to create a comfortable climate for legitimate whistle blowing. The manager needs the insight to sort out the difference between a troublemaker and a true whistle blower. Careful investigation is required. Only an organization with a strong social conscience would embrace employees who inform the public about its misdeeds. Yet some companies are becoming more tolerant of employees who help keep the firm socially responsible by exposing actions that could harm society.

Compassionate Downsizing

To remain competitive and provide shareholders with a suitable return on investment, about 80% of large organizations have undergone downsizing. **Downsizing** is the slimming down of operations to focus resources and boost profits or decrease expenses. Downsizings occur regularly worldwide among companies of all sizes, yet the number of layoffs is more substantial during business downturns. Laid-off employees obviously suffer from downsizing when they cannot readily find comparable employment or are forced to leave their communities. The community can also suffer substantially from mammoth downsizings. For example, the aftermath of the many cutbacks in the Michigan-based automotive industry has been substantial collateral damage. Retailers, restaurants, the housing market, charitable organizations, and community tax bases were all hurt as the state lost an estimated 158,000 manufacturing jobs between 2003 and 2008, according to a University of Michigan study.[22]

To enhance social responsibility and minimize creating a negative impression, a company can take several steps. To begin, a company might challenge the need for downsizing. An ideal goal is to look to expand sales rather than downsize. Quite often a company sees no way out of financial trouble other than downsizing. In these circumstances, compassionate downsizing would include the following considerations:

- *Redeploy as many workers as possible* by placing them in full-time or temporary jobs throughout the organization, where their skills and personality fit. Several companies have turned surplus workers into sales workers to generate new business for the firm. During one downturn in international sales at Lincoln Electric, 54 factory workers were redeployed as salespeople and they grossed $10 million in sales the first year. Workers are guaranteed a job, but as a trade-off get neither paid sick days nor holidays and pay their own health insurance.[23]
- *Provide outplacement services to laid-off employees*, thereby giving them professional assistance in finding a new position or redirecting their careers. (The vast majority of employers do provide outplacement services to laid-off workers.)
- *Provide financial and emotional support to the downsized worker.* Included here is treating employees with respect and dignity rather than escorting them out the door immediately after the downsizing announcement. Many companies already provide severance pay and extended health benefits to the laid-off workers. Financial assistance with retraining is also helpful.
- *Reduce the pay of managers and workers throughout the company*, thereby saving enough money to eliminate the need for downsizing. A similar approach is to place workers on unpaid furloughs to reduce expenses enough to avoid downsizing.

A company that downsizes faces substantial impression management and corporate image challenges. To save face, the CEO will often explain to the public that by downsizing the company will be able to remain competitive and be able to preserve jobs for the rest of the employees.

Guidelines for Application and Practice

1. Developing a positive corporate image or reputation encompasses far more than a one-time effort or a brief public relations campaign. The various stakeholders are likely to be impressed by long-term good deeds such as providing high-quality products and services as well as not receiving negative publicity. It is possible, however, for a small business to experience immediate popularity by filling a niche with a new concept, such as a restaurant or online service. By filling the niche in a sterling manner, a positive impression is created that spreads quickly. A restaurant example is the Cheesecake Factory; an online service example is Facebook.

2. Although *corporate image* is an abstract concept, much like a personal brand, it is possible to plan the construction of a corporate image, such as the Ikea example described in the chapter. Although the corporate image is essentially based on an external perception, the satisfaction of employees is an important part of the image. One reason is that the employees—especially those in entry-level positions—interface with the public, helping to shape the image.

3. A two-pronged approach to managing a company's online reputation has been developed. First, the company should implement a program to deal with customer complaints and modify products and services based on customer feedback. Second, the company should launch a strong offense by ensuring that the company has more positive than negative entries on the Internet. Rob Russo, the president of Defend My Name, a web service provider, says: "No matter what size your company is or what you sell, it all starts with an authentic, quality product or service and the mission to make the customer happy above all else. Customer satisfaction is the key ingredient to weathering any crisis, any negative press, or spurious blog postings."[24]

4. Sponsored research can contribute positively to a corporate image because it may create the impression of giving the firm's product or service scientific validity. However, sponsored research can also backfire as a corporate impression management tactic because the evidence in support of the product or service might appear contrived and subjective.

5. Placing a positive spin on negative events is more likely to be effective as a tactic of corporate impression management if the company spokesperson admits that a problem exists, but that a bright side also exists. For example, the company that purchases another company one year, and two years later sells the company at a loss, might make the following statement: "We made a mistake in purchasing the company that we did, and then having to sell it at a major loss. However, we have cut our losses and we will now proceed in a positive direction and stop losing money on the deal."

6. Corporate social responsibility can be a strategy for corporate impression management, and has also become an inescapable priority for business leaders. In the words of business strategists Michael E. Porter and Mark R. Kramer, corporate social responsibility efforts are counterproductive for two reasons: "First, they pit business against society, when in reality the two are interdependent. Second, they pressure companies to think of corporate social responsibility in generic terms instead of in the way most appropriate to their individual strategies."[25]

Summary

Organizations are frequently judged by the image they project, or their reputation. A positive corporate image, or good reputation, gives a company a distinct competitive advantage. According to the theory of corporate image, four factors are essential in managing the corporate image: corporate identity, corporate communication, corporate reputation, and feedback. The corporate identity is composed of corporate strategy, corporate culture, organizational structure, and operations.

The Swedish company Ikea illustrates an approach to constructing a corporate image, as follows: (1) create the story, (2) inspire the staff, (3) seduce the shopper, and (4) surprise on value. A company's online reputation is an aspect of corporate reputation. Blogs, forums, and other online chatter can make or break a company's reputation. A high ranking on major search engines can enhance the company's reputation. Search engine optimization (SEO) helps elevate the ranking. Another reputation management service will eradicate negative comments and even write positive blogs on behalf of a client. A more self-enhancing approach to impression management than reputation management is to repair the problem causing the negative comments, and engage in activities that lead to positive comments on the Internet.

Many firms hope to build their reputations by associating themselves with a celebrity who enjoys a strong, positive reputation. A frequent example would be an advertising campaign for a product featuring a well-known professional athlete. Association with celebrities via advertising is also used to change a company image. A variation of basking in reflected glory by featuring ads with celebrities, or using a celebrity ambassador, is to employ celebrities to engage in the major activities of the firm.

Another way for a company to manage its impression is to have a second party conduct research that provides empirical evidence about the value of the company's product or service. Research of this nature is often sponsored or paid for by the company seeking evidence to validate its offerings. A criticism of this approach to impression management is that the results of sponsored research are usually flattering, otherwise the research would not be sponsored.

Corporate image enhancement often boosts the company stock price. However, a company's message must be grounded in reality, and its reputation built over the years. Good financial performance is still a major contributor to a company's reputation.

An impression management tactic aimed at many people at the same time is spin, or putting a favorable face on a negative situation or person. The spinner is not necessarily lying, but emphasizing a plausible positive aspect of a negative event. Spin is sometimes used to overcome negative publicity, thereby creating an improved impression. Spin is regarded by some as a negative and unethical tactic of impression management.

Social responsibility initiatives can be interpreted as tactics of impression management. Whether or not the intent of being socially responsible is to create a positive impression among stakeholders, socially responsible actions by top management enhance a corporation's impression. The corporation has an economic and social responsibility to the whole community, and creates a positive impression by meeting this responsibility. Corporate social responsibility relates to an organization's impact on society, beyond doing what is ethical. Many socially responsible actions are the by-products of sensible business decisions, such as investing in local schooling. A problem in practicing corporate social responsibility is that not all interested parties agree on what constitutes responsible behavior.

Corporate social performance is the extent to which a firm responds to the demands of its stakeholders and responds in a socially responsible manner. Socially responsible initiatives include the following: (1) expressing an environmental commitment, (2) work-life programs, (3) community redevelopment projects, (4) acceptance of whistle blowers, and (5) compassionate downsizing.

Guidelines for application and practice in relation to organizational-level impression management include: (1) developing a positive corporate image is a long-term process, (2) a corporate image can be constructed, (3) making the customer happy builds a positive online presence, (4) sponsored research works sometimes but can backfire based on low credibility, (5) spin works better when the problem is admitted, and (6) corporate social responsibility can be a strategy for corporate impression management.

Chapter 11

Functional and Dysfunctional Consequences of Impression Management

As stated and implied throughout this book, impression management is much more than an abstract concept without real-world implications. Depending on how broadly one interprets impression management, it is a personal process, an organizational process, and an industry. In terms of being an industry, people invest money in managing their impression through such means as clothing, hairstyling, working out in gyms, as well as hiring the services of personal trainers, personal brand coaches, and plastic surgeons. Our study of impression management concludes with an overview of its major functional and dysfunctional consequences. However, we emphasize outcomes based on the ethical and appropriate use of impression management leading to positive consequences for individuals and organizations. Figure 11-1 provides an overview of the amount of empirical support for the major conclusions and findings presented in the chapter.

Functional Consequences of Impression Management

The appropriate use of impression management strategies and tactics can benefit the individual and organization in many ways. A basic example is that workers who do their best to create an authentic favorable impression on others will have more harmonious relationships with superiors, subordinates, coworkers, and customers. Here we examine research and opinion about the functional consequences of impression management, as outlined in Figure 11-2.

Successful Outcomes of the Employment Interview

Much of the positive evidence for the effectiveness of impression management techniques was first accumulated in the context of the employment interview.[1] A study already described in Chapter 8 found that customer-service position applicants who used impression management tactics were perceived by interviewers as performing

Figure 11-1 Topics Related to the Consequences of Impression Management According to Basis of Support.

Well Supported by Empirical Research	Supported More by Anecdote and Opinion
Successful outcomes are achieved in the employment interview	False impressions are used to conduct crimes against people
Performance evaluations are improved, including more effective use of organizational politics	Yes-person behavior creates an unethical image and can lead to bad decisions by superiors
Ingratiation is used as a method of career advancement	Too much impression management diverts attention from work
Humor leads to more organizational rewards	Performance suffers among workers who resent flatterers getting rewarded
Impression management facilitates more cooperative behavior and satisfaction within teams	Workers who engage in too much impression management are distrusted
Positive corporate reputation is associated with higher stock price	Too much focus on looking good can result in choking under pressure
Enhancement of corporate image by good environmental performance is associated with higher stock price	
Emotional labor and stress result from being forced to create a false impression	

Figure 11-2 Functional Consequences of Impression Management.

1. Successful outcomes of the employment interview
2. Improved performance evaluation results and supervisory ratings
3. Career advancement
4. Improved relationships with work associates
5. Cooperative behavior and satisfaction within teams
6. Enhanced sales and stock price for the organization

better than candidates who did not use these tactics. Of more significance, the interviewers were more likely to hire the applicants who used impression management tactics. The researchers also concluded that impression management techniques were more important than formal credentials in terms of influencing judgments by interviewers. One explanation for these findings is that skill in impression management is quite important for working as a customer-service representative.[2]

Chad A. Higgins and Timothy A. Judge conducted a study about the effects of ingratiation and self-promotion on recruiter perceptions of fit between the candidate and the job. The group studied was college students who participated in initial employment interviews at the campus placement office. Results of the study suggested that ingratiation had a positive effect on perceived fit for the job as well as hiring recommendations. Self-promotion was not as effective in influencing the recruiters.[3]

Cynthia Kay Stevens and Amy L. Kristof conducted a study with 106 applicants and 78 interviewers who used university placement services during a 16-month period. Some of the interviews were audiotaped to later measure impression management tactics. A major result of the study was that gender, GPA, and job type had little relationship in terms of perceived suitability for the position or the likelihood that the hiring firm would pursue the candidate. In contrast, self-promotion by applicants did predict the extent to which they were judged as suitable and pursuit by the organization (as measured by site-visit invitations). The researchers therefore concluded that impression management tactics are related to interview outcomes.[4]

Improved Performance Evaluation and Supervisory Ratings

Another major setting in which impression management might affect outcomes is the performance evaluation. Ratings by supervisors are usually part of performance evaluations, but employees might also be rated even when this is not part of a performance evaluation. For example, the company might want to rate employees for such purposes as analyzing its workforce capabilities, or perhaps provide ratings as part of a research study.

Sandy J. Wayne and Robert C. Liden conducted a pioneering study on how impression management influences performance ratings. Ingratiation was the impression management tactic chosen, as measured by the subordinate getting the supervisor to like him or her through such means as doing small favors for and agreeing with the supervisor. Performance ratings were noted six months after supervisor-subordinate pairs were formed. A major result of the study was that impression management behavior in the form of ingratiation had a major *indirect* impact on the ratings attained during a performance appraisal. The researchers concluded that impression management by subordinates influenced performance ratings based on (1) how much the supervisor likes the subordinate, and (2) his or her perceived similarity with the subordinate.[5]

Two other studies demonstrate that the relationship between impression management and performance evaluation ratings can be indirect and complex. A study of 112 white-collar employees and theft supervisors explored how organizational politics and impression management interacted to affect supervisory ratings. (An interaction in this sense is a combined influence of two factors.) A major finding of the study was that employees who are making extensive use of impression management are less likely to receive negative performance evaluations when they engage in organizational politics. Employees who make limited use of impression management are more likely receive a negative evaluation from their superior when they (the subordinates) engage in organizational politics.[6] Another interpretation of these findings is that because impression management is part of organizational politics, those workers who are really skilled at organizational politics will not be negatively rated when they engage in political behavior.

A later study conducted in Taiwan also investigated how impression management and organizational politics interact to influence performance evaluations. The study collected data from 290 full-time employees to examine the moderating effect of impression management on the relationship between perceptions of organizational politics and performance ratings. The two types of impression management behaviors observed were supervisor focused and job focused. Job-focused tactics exerted a moderating effect on the relationship between perceptions of organizational politics and performance.

A key finding was that employees engaging in impression management reduced the negative relationship between perceptions of organizational politics and job performance ratings. Specifically, when employees perceived low levels of organizational politics to exist, impression management had an influence on ratings. When perceptions of political behavior were low, employees who engaged in high levels of job-focused impression management tactics were more likely to receive higher ratings than those who made less use of these tactics. As in the study cited above, more extensive use of impression management has some effect on performance ratings.[7] In the study conducted in Taiwan, however, the focus was on perceptions of politics existing in the workplace rather than on the politics engaged in by the employees whose performance was rated.

Career Advancement

Impression management might be an interesting field of study from an academic standpoint. However, many readers might also want reassurance that a sensible application of impression management strategies and tactics will help attain the important outcome of career advancement. Otherwise techniques such as personal branding would hardly be worth the effort for people intent on using impression management skills to advance.

In Chapter 6, we described a study indicating that the impression management tactic of ingratiation is an important pathway to the boardroom. The study found that ingratiatory behavior toward executives who control access to board positions can provide an alternative pathway to the boardroom for those who lack the social and educational credentials associated with the power elite.[8] The widely practiced system of patronage in public office demonstrates the same truth about ingratiation. After every election many choice political positions are given to those people who have done favors for the new office holder. Even when the new appointees have bone fide qualifications for the position, the ingratiators are chosen over other well-qualified candidates.

According to another study, ingratiation aimed at a manager may provide a 5% edge to the actor in today's competitive workplace. With so many highly qualified candidates competing for limited organizational resources, including job security, subordinates can distinguish themselves by effective use of ingratiation.[9]

Improved Relationships with Work Associates

Techniques of impression management aimed at enhancing others, similarly to the many other techniques described in this book, have many positive consequences for the actor, the target, and the organization. For positive consequences of other-enhancing techniques to be forthcoming, the actor needs the right skills, such as sensitivity and cognitive ability. Also, the organizational culture has to be appropriate for the use of impression management tactics, as described in Chapter 3.

An illustrative starting point in understanding the positive consequences of making others feel good is recognizing the outcomes of humor. An analysis by Cecily D. Cooper suggests that the effective use of humor may result in the individual enjoying his or her work and attaining organizational rewards. The actor who makes the manager feel good, for example, may receive a more positive performance evaluation and salary increase. Humor may also help the ingratiator alleviate boredom. Humor as an ingratiating tactic can also lead to more rewards for the actor because the humor triggers more positive affect in the target, making the latter more susceptible to persuasion. If the target is in a good mood, he or she might also be more likely to help the actor, leading perhaps to more lenience in granting more money in a budget or a bonus. Also, humor is typically perceived as a positive emotion, and workers who display positive emotion are more likely to receive above-average performance evaluations.[10]

The target of humor as ingratiation also benefits because of an enhanced quality of work relationship with the actor. Research suggests that humor enhances the quality of leader-member exchanges (LMX). In ordinary terms, it is more fun to work with someone who makes you laugh from time to time.[11]

Cooperative Behavior and Satisfaction within Teams

A key advantage of impression management is that it can lead to cordial, pleasant relationships among work associates. People who want to create a positive impression on coworkers are less likely to behave rudely, such as ignoring them or swearing at them. Work associates who engage in self-enhancement as well as enhancing others create a comfortable work environment. In support of this idea, Nhung T. Nguyen conducted a study with student teams working on a class project. The task for the teams was to assume the role of a consulting firm hired to solve a specific organizational problem using management practices and concepts learned in class. The teams were encouraged to interview business managers to come up with realistic problems to work on as consultants. Confidential peer evaluations were conducted at the end of the semester after the student teams had submitted their projects and delivered oral presentations. Project grades were determined by peer evaluation. Questionnaires were used to measure the study variables of ingratiation, self-promotion, altruism, conscientiousness, and team satisfaction.

Several of the study results were relevant to understanding the impact of impression management on cooperative behavior and satisfaction. First, peer ratings of ingratiation were positively and significantly related to self-ratings of team satisfaction. (Ingratiating behaviors by teammates enhance job satisfaction.) Ingratiation was also positively related to altruism and conscientiousness, which, in turn, was correlated with team satisfaction. The findings also suggested that team members were more satisfied with their teams when team members perceived them as engaging in ingratiation. But team satisfaction was not high when team members described themselves as ingratiating or self-promoting. Another finding related to the impact of impression management was that ingratiation, altruism, and conscientiousness were positively related to team members liking their peers. (Although conscientiousness is rarely perceived as a tactic of impression management, displaying conscientiousness creates a good impression.)

Based on these results, Nguyen concluded that impression management is a competency that should be nurtured in organizations. In contrast, many observers tend to regard impression management as a form of negative manipulation.[12]

Enhanced Sales and Stock Price for the Organization

Corporate-level impression management has positive consequences of its own in terms of the company selling more goods and services and the stock price climbing. As described in Chapter 10, corporate-level impression management takes the form of corporate image and reputation. The Economist Intelligence Unit on Corporate Responsibility conducted an extensive study of 1,254 high-level managers to investigate if promoting enlightened social, environmental, and ethical practices has a financial payoff. One finding was that the business community strongly believes that such a relationship exists.

Companies that develop a strong reputation by paying the most attention to sustainability issues, such as climate change or treatment of workers in developing nations, far out-perform those that do not. The companies strong in the areas mentioned experienced a 16% rise in profits in the year studied, and enjoyed stock price growth of 45%. Companies that rated their own environmental performance as poor experienced only 7% profit growth and 12% growth in stock prices. Only 6% of respondents agreed with this statement about working on sustainability: "No benefit expected beyond compliance with regulation."

The study also found evidence that the companies surveyed are strongly concerned about their image. Asked to name the highest priority of their corporate responsibility programs over the upcoming five years, 61% of the executives cited communicating their practices to investors as a "leading" or "major" priority.[13] Nevertheless, being concerned about image does not necessarily mean that the company management teams involved are not interested in sustaining the environment.

Another investigation concluded that a good corporate name can be a company's most important asset and actually boost the stock price. A specific finding was that a company's reputation for being able to deliver growth, attract talented employees, and avoid ethical mishaps has consequences for the value of its stock. The reputation can account for as much as a 30–70% gap between the book value of most companies and the total value of their outstanding stock shares. The book value represents the price that could be obtained by selling off the assets of the company.

Another finding of the investigation under consideration was that public relations alone could move the stock of Southwest Airlines up or down by 3.5%, equal to about $400 million in market value in the current period. The point here is that a positive reputation has an enormous financial consequence for a consumer-oriented company.[14]

A study by Pratima Bansal and Iain Clelland analyzed how corporate image in relation to environmental performance affects the stock price. Positive environmental performance would include the company's efforts at reducing pollution, whereas negative environmental performance would include having a toxic spill into public water. The measure of stock price chosen was *unsystematic risk*, which reflects the variability in a firm's stock price associated with events that primarily affect that firm. Firm-specific events would include a labor strike and an oil spill. *Systematic risk* reflects the variability in stock price associated with larger external economic events such as changes in interest or exchange rates.

An analysis of media reports and stock prices of 100 firms over a five-year period indicated that environmentally legitimate (or friendly) firms incur less systematic risk than environmentally illegitimate (unfriendly) firms. Furthermore, when a company is already environmentally legitimate, more public relations about the issue may not do any good in terms of stock price. The study also showed that a company can soften this effect by expressing commitment to the natural environment. One conclusion reached in the study was that new information about a company's environmental performance has an immediate effect on a firm's stock price. At the same time the information has an enduring impact because it influences investor judgments of a firm's commitment to the environment.[15]

Dysfunctional Consequences of Impression Management

For many people, the term *impression management* is negatively toned because the term connotes dishonesty, deception, and a distorted impression. Here we summarize some of the dysfunctional consequences of impression management, particularly when its strategies and tactics are applied without skill, sensitivity, and ethical reasoning. The dysfunctional consequences are also outlined in Figure 11-3.

Ethical Lapses, Including Faking, Lying, and Stealing

Ethics specialist Dennis Moberg advises that some approaches to impression management can be quite devious, and therefore should be rejected. He cites an example of students concerned about ingratiating themselves with their superiors being advised to uncover their superiors' opinions on an issue, fake a contrary opinion, and then allow the boss to convince them that their original position was incorrect.[16]

An extreme dysfunctional approach to impression management involves a criminal creating the impression of being honest and trustworthy, based on a smooth and suave appearance. In this sense, the impression manager is indeed an actor. Fraudulent impressions are created by some people to influence others to invest money in their dishonest schemes. For example, celebrities and other wealthy people often turn over huge sums of money to a charming person who claims to offer a lucrative investment. One such impression manager is Alfredo Trujillo Fox, who has several lawsuits pending against him, and has filed for bankruptcy. One of the scams of this impression manager proceeded as follows:

> Drew Gordon, a chiropractor, met Fox at the Beverly Hills BMW dealership. Fox was suave, and had an irresistible business offer. He bought two luxury cars on the spot, and introduced himself as the brother of former Mexican President Vicente Fox. "I have a perfect business for you," said Trujillo (Fox). Three weeks later, Gordon signed a contract to invest in a cellphone radiation shield for children, and wrote Fox two checks for $25,000 to be repaid in six months with a sizeable return. Soon after Trujillo received the money, he changed his address and phone number, stopped returning calls and vanished.[17]

Dennis Bromley observes that impression management, particularly ingratiation, reflects an excessive concern to make a good impression and avoid critical evaluation, and a failure to face up to the ethical implications of what a person is doing.[18] Yes-person behavior fits this concern. People who attempt to ingratiate themselves with their superior by always agreeing (an extreme form of opinion conformity) might be

Figure 11-3 Dysfunctional Consequences of Impression Management.

1. Ethical lapses, including faking, lying, and stealing
2. Diversion of mental resources
3. Engendering of mistrust and dislike of the actor
4. Emotional labor and distress
5. Choking under pressure

regarded as unethical because they are withholding professional judgment just to receive approval. Imagine a mechanical engineer who believes that the company's effort to save money on brake linings will result in brake failure. To avoid displeasing the boss, the engineer says the cost-saving idea is sound. Ultimately several highway deaths are attributed to failed brakes because of the inexpensive part.

Similarly, making others feel good in the form of opinion conformity can be destructive when subordinates go along with egregiously wrong decisions. Instead of providing the manager with useful, critical feedback, the subordinate goes along with a bad pending decision just to be liked by the manager.[19] During the events leading up to the financial crisis that surfaced in 2008, many managers and professionals were aware of the pitfalls within the new forms of investments being planned by executives in their firms. Among these investments were securities based on subprime mortgages. Instead of stepping forth and indicating "thumbs down," it appears that many knowledgeable individuals indicated "thumbs up" in order to make top management feel good. (Also, by supporting these risky investments, the opinion conformists hoped to earn large financial payouts for themselves.)

The yes-person technique and not providing critical feedback are different aspects of the same phenomenon of not thinking independently in order to please another person. Instead of arriving at an independent judgment, the organizational actor intent on creating a good impression makes a decision to please the target. In this sense, the non-independent thinker is an extreme self-monitor.

A humorous, yet still unethical, approach to impression management is the use of information technology to fake working. One such approach is to rig a cell phone with the background noise of a busy office, and then call the boss from the beach or ski slope pretending to be working. Another example of faking is a technical support worker who enjoyed taking three-hour lunch breaks. He programmed his hand-held computer to link up to his desktop computer so he could open, close, and move files so it would look as if he had just stepped away from his desk.[20] Another approach to creating a false—and therefore unethical—impression is to fake the time at which an e-mail message is sent to make it appear that the person was working late at night.

Diversion of Mental Resources

A potential problem with workers who engage in frequent other-enhancement is that they focus so much on social relationships that their work suffers. Concentration on work is diminished as the person diverts considerable time to self-presentation. Also, too much time invested in any form of impression management may lower productivity. Mental resources can also be misdirected in another way. Ronald J. Deluga observes that there is an insidious dark side to ingratiation that can have negative outcomes for individuals and the organization. If the manager gives inappropriate rewards to those who flatter him or her, other subordinates may become resentful and perform poorly. The poor performance has come about because of the resentment created by the rewards perceived as unfair.[21]

Engendering of Mistrust and Dislike of the Actor

Organizational actors who engage in excessive impression management are sometimes distrusted, leading to communication breakdowns because their messages are not taken seriously. The actor then faces the complicated problem of attempting to repair trust, including the possibility that targets may not trust the actor in the future.[22] Another communication problem is that in order to create a good impression, some people will not ask for help even if it is needed. To project an air of self-confidence and competence the worker might attempt to tackle a very difficult task alone rather than ask for assistance. Ronald E. Riggio explains that the restricted communication that results may lead to a mismatch between the actor's skills and abilities and the job requirements.[23]

Organizational actors who engage in excessive and transparent attempts to make others feel good run the risk of being viewed negatively by coworkers as well as their targets. Commonly used terms for excessive other-enhancers include apple-polisher, backscratcher, boot-licker, suck-up, toady, yes-man, and yes-woman.

Another problem related to mistrust is that too much ingratiation may lead to a dysfunctional culture whereby rampant ingratiation undermines morale. In such a culture, a widely expressed sentiment is "you can't get anywhere around here without sucking up to management." It has been observed that in some organizations, upward mobility for managers is more related to ingratiating skill than what is best for the organization.[24]

Emotional Labor and Distress

At times it can be emotionally painful to manage one's impression when the management involves suppressing emotion in order please the target. Alicia Grandey defines **emotional labor** as the process of regulating both feelings and expressions to meet organizational goals. Quite often these goals can mean the suppression of emotion in order to create a positive impression. Emotional labor involves both surface acting and deep acting. Surface acting means faking expressions such as smiling, whereas deep acting involves controlling feelings, such as suppressing anger toward a customer whom you perceive to be uncivil. Sales workers and customer service representatives carry the biggest emotional labor among all workers because so often they have to take on facial expressions and feelings to please customers.[25]

Emotional dissonance is a key aspect of emotional labor, referring to the mismatch between felt and expressed emotions. The greater the gap between actual and expressed feelings, the more frequently workers report feeling emotional exhaustion, dissatisfaction with their jobs, and cynicism toward customers.[26] Imagine making a PowerPoint presentation to senior management, and being interrupted with what you perceive to be foolish questions and ridicule. You want to retaliate, but to create a positive impression you instead keep smiling and making comments such as "good question."

A variation of emotional labor can occur when workers create a façade in relation to conforming to corporate values. Façade creation might include conforming to the dress code despite disliking such attire, expressing agreement with one's manager although one thinks the manager is wrong, and going along with a group decision that one thinks is ridiculous. Each of the behaviors just mentioned is an attempt to create a positive impression by pleasing others. Maintaining a façade for a long time can lead to emotional distress, as does emotional labor.[27]

Choking under Pressure

An uncomfortable dysfunction of impression management is that a person might focus so much on looking good (or making a command performance) that his or her performance suffers. According to Roy F. Baumeister, choking under pressure often occurs as the result of focusing attention on oneself. Such a self-focus can easily take place when a person feels others are paying close attention to his or her performance, as in many self-presentational situations.

The dysfunctional pattern of too much self-focus appears to be particularly troublesome when the person is attempting to communicate a desired social identity to the audience, which is the central task of self-presentation.[28] Visualize a company financial manager making a presentation to financial analysts who will be judging the worth of the company for investment purposes. The manager is being observed by his or her immediate manager, who has accompanied the finance manager on the visit to the analysts. Under the pressure of trying to create a strong impression, the manager fumbles a bit, for example confusing a few facts such as misstating the name of the firm listening to the analysis. As is common in choking situations, the finance manager might not be able to think of something creative to say to answer a difficult question.

Although it is possible for impression management to have negative consequences, used with sensitivity, including awareness of the situation, impression management strategies and tactics can be beneficial to individuals, organizations, and their outside stakeholders. Indeed, workers not trying to create a good impression would create many dysfunctions within the organization.

Guidelines for Application and Practice

1. Impression management techniques are of demonstrated value to the individual for purposes such as enhancing performance during a job interview, receiving better performance evaluations, and career advancement. To obtain these good results, the organizational actor should not use such techniques in a blatant and manipulative manner. Good sensitivity and tact should be utilized when managing one's impression, and impression management strategies and tactics should be a supplement to good job performance, not a substitute for it.
2. A highly functional use of impression management strategies and techniques for the organization is for workers to make a conscious attempt to engage in positive impression management techniques. As a result, smoother teamwork and customer relationships are likely to be forthcoming.

3. Top-level management, as well as other workers, can often boost the company's stock price by developing a positive corporate image. Part of this image is attributed to profit performance, yet developing environmentally friendly policies and executing them well will also contribute to an enhanced reputation and stock price.

4. Managers, and other workers, are not helpless in fending off some of the potential negative consequences of other-enhancement, including flattery, opinion conformity, and doing favors. The target can question whether the flattery is overdone, whether too much agreement exists, and whether some of the personal favors are inappropriate. Sample appropriate questions here would be as follows: (1) Do I really deserve all these compliments? (2) Am I really so wise that all my proposals and decisions should receive such accolades? (3) Is it really appropriate for _____ to bring me a gift every time he/she visits Europe on a business trip?

When the target has a strong "no" response to the type of questions just posed, he or she can confront the actor, by saying that overdone compliments are not necessary, that criticism is welcome, and that he or she would prefer that gifts were directed to a charity.

Summary

Strategies and techniques of impression management can have many functional, or positive, consequences for individuals and organizations, including the following: (1) successful outcomes of the employment interview; (2) improved performance evaluation results and supervisory ratings; (3) career advancement; (4) improved relationships with work associates; (5) cooperative behavior and satisfaction within teams; and (6) enhanced sales and stock price for the organization.

Strategies and techniques of impression management can also have dysfunctional, or negative, consequences, as follows: (1) ethical lapses, including faking, lying, and stealing; (2) diversion of mental resources; (3) the engendering of mistrust and dislike of the actor; (4) emotional labor and distress; and (5) choking under pressure.

Although it is possible for impression management to have negative consequences, used with sensitivity, including awareness of the situation, impression management strategies and tactics can be beneficial to individuals, organizations, and their outside stakeholders.

Guidelines for application and practice offered here include: (1) used with sensitivity and tact, impression management techniques can help attain useful outcomes; (2) impression management techniques can help build better work relationships; (3) a positive corporate image can help boost a company's stock price; and (4) insincere attempts at impression management can by confronted by managers and other workers.

Glossary

Alpha executive   An executive, or manager at another level, who is ambitious, self-confident, competitive, and brash.

Balance theory   The explanation that a balance of sentiments (or feelings) is the implicit goal of interpersonal interaction.

Business etiquette   A special code of behavior required in work situations.

Charisma   A special quality of leaders whose purposes, powers, and extraordinary determination differentiate them from others.

Corporate image (or **reputation**)   The manner in which a business firm, its activities, and its products or services are perceived by outsiders.

Corporate social performance   The extent to which a firm responds to the demands of its stakeholders for behaving in a socially responsible manner.

Corporate social responsibility   The idea that business firms have obligations to society beyond their economic obligations to owners or stockholders, and also beyond those prescribed by law.

Damage control   In impression management, taking positive action to make excuses for or repair the negative consequences of having made a serious mistake, and received negative publicity.

Downsizing   Slimming down of operations to focus resources and boost profits or decrease expenses.

Dramaturgy   A process in which actors engage in performances in various settings for particular audiences in order to shape their definitions of the situation.

Emotional dissonance   A key aspect of emotional labor, referring to the mismatch between actual and expressed feelings.

Emotional labor   The process of regulating both feelings and expression to meet organizational goals.

Enhancement of others   Efforts by an actor to increase his or her attractiveness to a target based on the use of favorable evaluations of the target's attributes, behavior, or performance.

Extraversion   A personality trait reflecting the quality or intensity of social interactions, the need for social stimulation, self-confidence, and competition.

Hands-on leader   One who gets directly involved in the details and processes of operations.

Identity enhancement activities   Strategies and behaviors directed toward improving or advancing the actor's social identity as perceived by the target.

Identity protection activities   Strategies and behaviors directed toward the prevention of damage or harm to the actor's social identity as perceived by the target.

Implicit leadership theories   Personal assumptions about the traits and abilities that characterize an ideal organizational leader.

Impression management   The process by which people control the impression others form of them.

Ingratiation   Getting another person to like you by using such tactics as making him or her feel important, acting humbly, praising him or her, asking politely, and pretending to let him or her make decisions which go along with what you want.

Leading by example   A leader acting as a positive role model.

Machiavellianism   The extent to which individuals behave manipulatively, hold cynical views of human nature, and have a generally low regard for conventional standards of morality.

Microinequity   A small, semiconscious message sent with a powerful impact on the receiver.

Opinion conformity   The actor expressing opinions or acting in ways consistent with the target's attitudes, beliefs, and values in order to increase the target's liking of the actor.

Organizational citizenship behavior   Individual behavior that is discretionary, not directly or explicitly recognized by the formal reward system, and that in aggregate promotes the effective functioning of the organization.

Organizational culture   A system of shared values and beliefs that influence worker behavior.

Performance evaluation blip   A surge in performance quantity or quality right before the performance review.

Personal brand   The qualities based on an individual's collection of strengths that make him or her unique.

Personal magnetism   The quality of being captivating, charming, and charismatic.

Political correctness   The act of being careful not to offend or slight anyone, and being extra careful and respectful.

Procrastination   Delaying a task for an invalid or weak reason.

Public self   What the person is communicating about himself or herself, and what others actually perceive about the person.

Reference goal   The actor's desired state of social identity, such as wanting to be a competent international marketing professional.

Rudeness   Insensitive or disrespectful behavior engaged in by a person who displays a lack of regards for others.

Script development   The conscious, active processing of relevant social cues when encountering a situation in which no existing script clearly applies.

Scripts   Mechanisms that allow efficient functioning by simplifying the information processing requirements of routine activities and presenting guidelines for appropriate behavior.

Self-handicapping   An individual's attempt to reduce a threat to self-esteem by actively seeking or creating factors that prevent poor performance itself being perceived as a cause of failure.

Self-management   The ability to control one's emotions and act with honesty and integrity in a consistent and acceptable manner.

Self-monitoring   The observation and control of expressive and self-presentational behaviors.

Self-protection (or **identity protection**) **techniques**   Strategies and tactics directed toward the prevention of damage or harm to the actor's social identity in the perception of the target.

Self-serving bias   In attributing causes, the almost reflexive tendency of individuals to attribute successful outcomes to themselves and failing outcomes to external factors.

Servant leader   A leader who emphasizes integrity and serves constituents by working on their behalf to help them achieve their goals, not the leader's own goals. This behavior derives naturally from a commitment to service.

Social identity   An individual's identification with a particular social category, such as a team member, leader, or free agent.

Spin   Putting a favorable face on a negative situation or person.

Status   A person's rank in a social hierarchy based on the esteem accorded that person by the self and others.

Status characteristic   Any feature of an individual for which expectations and beliefs come to be organized.

Surface-level self-presentation tactics   Those aspects of impression management that focus on readily observable behaviors rather than underlying characteristics.

Trust   A person's confidence in another individual's intentions and motives and in the sincerity of that individual's words.

Whistle blower   An employee who discloses organizational wrongdoing to parties who can take action.

Notes

Chapter 1

1. Mark R. Leary and Robin M. Kowalski, "Impression Management: A Literature Review and Two-Component Model," *Psychological Bulletin*, No. 1, 1990, p. 34.
2. Constant D. Beugré and Patrick R. Liverpool, "Politics as Determinant of Fairness Perceptions in Organizations," in Eran Vigoda-Gadot and Amos Drory, *Handbook of Organizational Politics* (Northampton, MA: Edward Elgar, 2006), p. 124.
3. Edward J. Hegarty, *How to Succeed in Company Politics*, 2nd ed. (New York: McGraw-Hill, 1976), p. 228. The same explanation was presented in the first edition of *How to Succeed in Company Politics*, 1964.
4. Erving Goffman, *The Presentation of Self in Everyday Life* (Garden City, NY: Doubleday Anchor, 1959); Robert A. Giacalone and Paul Rosenfeld, "Impression Management in Organizations: An Overview," in Giacalone and Rosenfeld (Eds.), *Impression Management in the Organization* (Hillsdale, NJ: Lawrence Erlbaum Associates, 1989), p. 2; William L. Gardner and Mark J. Martinko, "Impression Management in Organizations," *Journal of* Management, No. 2, 1988, p. 322; Dennis P. Bozeman and K. Michele Kacmar, "A Cybernetic Model of Impression Management Processes in Organizations," *Organizational Behavior and Human Decision Processes*, March 1997, p. 9.
5. Cited in Jared Sandberg, "The Art of Showing Pure Incompetence at an Unwanted Task," *The Wall Street Journal*, April 17, 2007, B1.
6. Leary and Kowalski, "Impression Management," p. 34.
7. Barry R. Schlenker, *Impression Management: The Self-Concept, Social Identity, and Interpersonal Relations* (Monterey, CA: Brooks/Cole, 1980), p. 6.
8. Leary and Kowalski, "Impression Management," p. 34.
9. Leary and Kowalski, "Impression Management," pp. 34–47.
10. Stephen B. Knouse, book review in *Personnel Psychology* of Paul Rosenfeld, Robert A. Giacalone, and Catherine A. Riordan, *Impression Management in Organizations: Theory, Measurement, Practice* (London: Routledge, 1995).
11. Leary and Kowalski, "Impression Management," p. 34.
12. Bernard M. Bass, *Bass & Stogdill's Handbook of Leadership: Theory, Research, & Managerial Applications*, 3rd ed. (New York: The Free Press, 1990), p. 210. Derived from Barry R. Schlenker, *Impression Management: The Self-Concept, Social Identity, and Interpersonal Relations* (Monterey, CA: Brooks/Cole, 1980).
13. John R. Schermerhorn, Jr., James G. Hunt, and Richard N. Osburn, *Core Concepts of Organizational Behavior* (New York: Wiley, 2004), p. 79.
14. Mark C. Bolino and William H. Turnley, "More than One Way to Make an Impression: Exploring Profiles of Impression Management," *Journal of Management*, No. 2, 2003, p. 141.

15. Bozeman and Kacmar, "A Cybernetic Model of Impression Management Processes in Organizations," p. 9.
16. Barry R. Schlenker and B. A. Pontari, "The Strategic Control of Information: Impression Management and Self-Presentation in Daily Life," in A. Tessler, R. Felson, and J. Suls (Eds.), *Perspectives on Self and Identity* (Washington, DC: American Psychological Association, 2000), p. 199.
17. Lauren Morgan Roberts, "Changing Faces: Professional Image Construction in Diverse Organizational Settings," *Academy of Management Review*, October 2005, p. 205.
18. D. J. Schneider, "Tactical Self-Presentations: Toward a Broader Conception," in J. T. Tedeschi (Ed.), *Impression Management Theory and Social Psychological Research* (New York: Academic Press, 1981), pp. 23–40.
19. Martin M. Chemers, *An Integrative Theory of Leadership* (Mahwah, NJ: Erlbaum, 1997), p. 27.
20. James L. Bowditch and Anthony F. Buono, *A Primer on Organizational Behavior*, 5th ed. (New York: Wiley 2001), p. 4; www.bentley.edu/cbe/, 2009.

Chapter 2

1. This chapter consists largely of an excerpt and adaptation of Dennis P. Bozeman and K. Michele Kacmar, "A Cybernetic Model of Impression Management Processes in Organizations," *Organizational Behavior and Human Decision Processes*, March 1997, pp. 9–30. The research behind the conclusions and findings reported in this chapter was synthesized by Bozeman and Kacmar. Many of the examples provided in the chapter are original from the present author.
2. Rob Goffee and Gareth Jones, "Managing Authenticity: The Paradox of Great Leadership," *Harvard Business Review*, December 2005, p. 88.
3. Elizabeth Wolfe Morrison and Robert J. Bies, "Impression Management in the Feedback-Seeking Process: A Literature Review and Research Agenda," *Academy of Management Review*, July 1991, pp. 522–541.

Chapter 3

1. Mark Snyder and John Copeland, "Self-Monitoring Processes in Organizational Settings," in Robert A. Giacolne and Paul Rosenfeld (Eds.), (Hillsdale, NJ: Lawrence Erlbaum, 1989), p. 7.
2. Mark C. Bolino and William H. Turnley, "More than One Way to Make an Impression: Exploring Profiles of Impression Management," *Journal of Management*, No. 2, 2003, pp. 141–160.
3. William L. Gardner and Mark J. Martinko, "Impression Management in Organizations," *Journal of Management*, No. 2, 1998, p. 330.

4. Richard Christie and F. Geis, *Studies in Machiavellianism* (New York: Academic Press, 1970).

5. Roy J. Lewicki, Daniel McAllister, and Robert J. Bies, "Trust and Distrust: New Relationships and Realities," *Academy of Management Review*, July 1998, p. 439.

6. Robert Glaser, "Paving the Road to Trust," *HRfocus*, January 1997, p. 5; Thomas A. Stewart, "Whom Can You Trust? It's Not So Easy to Tell," *Fortune*, June 12, 2000, p. 334; "4 Keys to Building Trust Quickly," *Manager's Edge*, March 2005, p. 4.

7. Quoted in Faith Chukwudi, "Crisis Management: An Airline Professional Says Establishing Trust Is the First Step in Effective Leadership," *Black Enterprise*, October 2007, p. 69.

8. Remus Ilies and Timothy A. Judge, "On the Heritability of Job Satisfaction: The Mediating Role of Personality," *Journal of Applied Psychology*, August 2003, pp. 750–759; Zak Stambor, "Optimists Have Longer, More Satisfying Relationships, Study Suggests," *Monitor on Psychology*, September 2006, p. 15.

9. Dennis P. Bozeman and K. Michele Kacmar, "A Cybernetic Model of Impression Management Processes in Organizations," *Organizational Behavior and Human Decision Processes*, March 1997, p. 20.

10. Deborah Tannen, *Talking from 9 to 5* (New York: William Morrow, 1994); Tannen, "The Power of Talk: Who Gets Heard and Why," *Harvard Business Review*, September–October 1995, pp. 138–148; Daniel J. Canary and Kathryn Dindia, *Sex Differences and Similarities in Communication* (Mahwah, NJ: Erlbaum, 1998), p. 318; John Gray, *Men Are from Mars, Women Are from Venus* (New York: HarperCollins, 1992).

11. Bolino and Turnley, "More than One Way to Make an Impression," p. 153.

12. Ronnie Kurchner-Hawkins and Rima Miller, "Organizational Politics: Building Positive Political Strategies in Turbulent Times," in Eran Vigoda-Gadot and Amos Drory (Eds.), *Handbook of Organizational Politics* (Northampton, MA: Edward Elgar, 2006), p. 343.

13. Cited in Myeong-Gu Seo, "Overcoming Emotional Barriers, Political Obstacles, and Control Imperatives in the Action-Science Approach to Individual and Organizational Learning," *Academy of Management Learning and Education*, March 2003, p. 11.

14. Shari Caudron, "Don't Mess with Carly," *Workforce Management*, July 2003, pp. 28–33. The quotation is from p. 30.

15. Edgar Schein, "Organizational Culture and Leadership," in *Business: The Ultimate Resource* (Cambridge, MA: Perseus Books Group, 2002), p. 937.

16. Geoffrey Colvin, "A Growth Plan for HP's CEO," *Fortune*, October 16, 2006, p. 70.

17. James L. Bowditch and Anthony F. Buono, *A Primer on Organizational Behavior*, 5th ed. (New York: Wiley, 2001), p. 291.

18. Synthesized from the literature in Amos Drory and Nurit Zaidman, "The Politics of Impression Management in Organizations: Contextual Effects," in Eran

Vigoda-Gadot and Amos Drory (Eds.), *Handbook of Organizational Politics* (Northampton, MA: Edward Elgar, 2006), pp. 77–79.

19. Zoe I. Barsness, Kristina A. Diekman, and Marc-David L. Seidel, "Motivation and Opportunity: The Role of Remote Work, Demographic Dissimilarity, and Social Network Centrality in Impression Management," *Academy of Management Journal*, June 2005, pp. 401–419.

20. Gardner and Martinko, "Impression Management in Organizations," pp. 327, 330.

21. John Brodie, "King of Cool," *Fortune*, September 1, 2008, pp. 50–61.

22. Barsness, Diekman, and Seidel, "Motivation and Opportunity," p. 414. The section about remote work reported here is found on pp. 407 and 408.

Chapter 4

1. E. E. Jones and T. S. Pittman, "Toward a General Theory of Strategic Self-Presentation," in J. Suis (Ed.), *Psychological Perspectives on the Self* (Hillsdale, NJ: Lawrence Erlbaum, 1982), pp. 231–261.

2. Gary Yukl and J. Bruce Tracey, "Consequences of Influence Tactics Used with Subordinates, Peers, and the Boss," *Journal of Applied Psychology*, August 1992, p. 526.

3. Robert B. Cialdini, "Harnessing the Science of Persuasion," *Harvard Business Review*, October 2001, pp. 72–79; Cialdini, *Influence: Science and Practice*, 5th ed. (Boston: Allyn & Bacon, 2008).

4. Cialdini, "Harnessing the Science of Persuasion," p. 79.

5. Erin White, "Art of Persuasion Becomes Key: Managers Sharpen Their Skills as Line of Authority Blurs," *The Wall Street Journal*, May 19, 2008, p. B5.

6. The paraphrased quotation is from Lee Anna Jackson, "The Art of Persuasion: How to Get What You Want from Employers, Clients, and Staff," *Black Enterprise*, July 2006, p. 74.

7. Robert Greene with Joost Elffers, *The 48 Laws of Power* (New York: The Penguin Group, 2000).

8. Robert B. Cialdini, "Indirect Tactics of Impression Management," in Robert A. Giacalone and Paul Rosenfeld (Eds.), *Impression Management in the Organization* (Hillsdale, NJ: Lawrence Erlbaum, 1989), pp. 50–51.

9. Lynn A. McFarland, "An Examination of Impression Management Use and Effectiveness Across Assessment Center Exercises: The Role of Competency Demands," *Personnel Psychology*, Winter 2005, p. 953.

10. Eric J. Romeo and Kevin W. Cruthirds, "The Use of Humor in the Workplace," *Academy of Management Perspectives*, May 2006, pp. 60, 63–64.

11. Christine M. Pearson and Christine L. Porath, "On the Nature, Consequences and Remedies of Workplace Incivility: No Time for 'Nice'? Think Again," *Academy of Management Executive*, February 2005, pp. 7–18.

12. Jared Sandberg, "Office Minstrels Drive the Rest of Us Nuts but Are Hard to Silence," *The Wall Street Journal*, February 14, 2006, p. B1.

13. Quoted in Teresa M. McAleavy, "Managers, Mind Your Manners in the Office," *The Record*, syndicated story, January 18, 2007.

14. Linda Kaplan Thaler and Robin Koval, *The Power of Nice* (New York: Currency Doubleday, 2006).

15. Stephen G. Harrison, "Leadership and Hope Go Hand in Hand," *Executive Leadership*, June 2002, p. 8.

16. Quoted in Vanessa Fuhrmans, "The 50 Women to Watch," *The Wall Street Journal*, November 19, 2007, p. R4.

17. Daniel Goleman, Richard Boyatzis, and Annie McKee, "Primal Leadership: The Hidden Driver of Great Performance," *Harvard Business Review*, December 2001, pp. 42–51.

18. Cited in Sue Shellenbarger, "Read This and Weep: Crying at Work Gains Acceptance," *The Wall Street Journal*, April 26, 2007, p. D1.

19. Dennis W. Organ, *Organizational Citizenship Behavior: The Good Soldier Syndrome* (Lexington, MA: Lexington Books, 1988). The definition is from p. 4.

20. Organ, *Organizational Citizenship Behavior*.

21. Mark C. Bolino, "Citizenship and Impression Management: Good Soldiers or Good Actors?" *Academy of Management Review*, January 1999, pp. 82–98.

22. Adam M. Grant and David M. Mayer, "Good Soldiers and Good Actors: Prosocial and Impression Management Motives as Interactive Predictors of Affiliative Citizenship Behaviors," *Journal of Applied Psychology*, July 2009, pp. 900–912.

23. Bolino, "Citizenship and Impression Management," p. 92.

24. Diane M. Bergeron, "The Potential Paradox of Organizational Citizenship Behavior: Good Citizens at What Cost?" *Academy of Management Review*, October 2007, pp. 1078–1095.

25. Mark C. Bolino and William H. Turnley, "The Personal Costs of Citizenship Behavior: The Relationship between Individual Initiative and Role Overload, Job Stress, and Work-Family Conflict," *Journal of Applied Psychology*, July 2005, pp. 740–748.

26. Andrew J. DuBrin, *Leadership: Research Findings, Practice, and Skills*, 6th ed. (Boston: Houghton Mifflin, 2010), p. 251.

27. Stephen P. Robbins, *Essentials of Organizational Behavior*, 7th ed. (Upper Saddle River, NJ: Prentice Hall, 2003), p. 160.

28. Cheryl Dahle, "Showing Your Worth without Showing Off," *New York Times* (nytimes.com), September 19, 2004, pp. 1–2.

29. Quoted in Dahle, "Showing Your Worth without Showing Off," p. 1.

30. Nanette Byrnes and David Kiley, "Hello, You Must Be Going," *Business Week*, February 12, 2007, pp. 30–32.

31. The scientific information about multitasking is reviewed in Claudia Wallis, "The Multitasking Generation," *Time*, March 27, 2006, pp. 48–55. See also Joshua S. Rubinstein, David E. Meyer, and Jeffrey E. Evans, "Executive Control of Cognitive Processes in Task Switching," *Journal of Experimental*

Psychology—Human Perception and Performance, Vol. 26, January 2000, No. 4, pp. 763–769.

32. Research from the University of Oregon reported in "The Problem with Extreme Multitasking," *The Wall Street Journal*, February 12, 2008, p. B4.

33. Quoted in Claudia Wallis and Sonja Steptoe, "The Case for Doing One Thing at a Time," *Time*, January 16, 2006, p. 76.

34. Interview by Alyssa Danigelis, "Like, Um, You Know," *Fast Company*, May 2006, p. 99.

35. "How to Manage Anger," *Top Health*, May 2005, p. 2.

Chapter 5

1. Joy Peluchette, Katherine Karl, and Kathleen Rust, "Dressing to Impress: Beliefs and Attitudes Regarding Workplace Attire," *Journal of Business Psychology*, Fall 2006, pp. 45–63.

2. Advice presented in Alessandra Galloni and Christina Passariello, "Armani's One-Man Brand," *The Wall Street Journal*, April 10, 2006, p. B1.

3. Cited in Christina Binkley, "Women in Power: Finding Wardrobe Balance," *The Wall Street Journal*, January 24, 2008, p. D7.

4. Christina Binkley, "General Counsel: Fashion Fuels a Friendship," *The Wall Street Journal*, July 31, 2008, p. D8.

5. Quoted and cited in Lorinda Toledo, "What to Wear to Work?" Rochester, New York, *Democrat and Chronicle*, July 27, 2008, p. 5E.

6. Cited in Christina Binkley, "Want to Be CEO? You Have to Dress the Part," *The Wall Street Journal*, January 10, 2008, p. D1.

7. Quoted in Christina Binkley, "Risky Business: Décolletage at Work Dinner," *The Wall Street Journal*, May 8, 2008, p. D10.

8. Binkley, "Want to Be CEO?" pp. D1, D8.

9. Quoted in Victoria E. Freile, "Use Your Clothing to Create the Image that You Want to Project," Rochester, New York, *Democrat and Chronicle*, August 10, 2008, p. 3E.

10. "Reinvent Yourself. Repeat," *Business 2.0*, December 2005, p. 124.

11. Peter Glick, Sadie Larsen, Cathryn Johnson, and Heather Branstiter, "Evaluations of Sexy Women in Low- and High-Status Jobs," *Psychology of Women Quarterly*, December 2005, pp. 389–395.

12. "From Incentives to Penalties: How Far Should Employers Go to Reduce Workplace Obesity?" *Knowledge@Wharton*, January 9, 2008, pp. 1–4.

13. "Leadership Tips," *Executive Leadership*, November 2006, p. 8.

14. Timothy A. Judge and Daniel M. Cable, "The Effect of Physical Height on Workplace Success and Income: A Preliminary Test of a Theoretical Model," *Journal of Applied Psychology*, June 2004, pp. 428–441.

15. Christine L. Porath and Amir Erez, "Does Rudeness Really Matter? The Effects of Rudeness on Task Performance and Helpfulness," *Academy of Management Journal*, October 2007, pp. 1181–1197.

16. Porath and Erez, "Does Rudeness Really Matter?" p. 1191.

17. Paraphrased from "How Not to Make a Fool of Yourself in Public," *Executive Advantage* (Briefings Publishing Group), 2002.

18. Amy Joyce, "Coursework for the Etiquette Prerequisite," *Washington Post* (washingtonpost.com), August 29, 2006, p. 1.

19. Saul Kassin, *Psychology*, 3rd ed. (Upper Saddle River, NJ: Prentice Hall, 2001), p. 219.

20. Edward J. Hegarty, *How to Succeed in Company Politics*, 2nd ed. (New York: McGraw-Hill, 1976), p. 30; "Making a Great First Impression—Communication Skills from MindTools.com," 1995–2008, accessed July 11, 2008.

21. Dana Mattioli, "Next on the Agenda: Kisses from Honey Bunny," *The Wall Street Journal*, June 10, 2008, p. D1.

22. Content and quotations from Joann S. Lublin, "Some Dos and Don'ts To Help You Hone Videoconference Skills," *The Wall Street Journal*, February 7, 2006, p. B1.

23. Dennis P. Bozeman and K. Michelle Kacmar, "A Cybernetic Model of Impression Management Processes in Organizations," *Organizational Behavior and Human Decision Processes*, Vol. 69, 1997, p. 23.

24. Evidence reviewed in Paul Rosenfeld, Robert A. Giacalone, and Catherine Riordan, *Impression Management: Building and Enhancing Reputations at Work* (London: Thomson Learning, 2002), p. 70.

25. Many of these ideas were first synthesized by Michael Argyle, *Bodily Communication*, 2nd ed. (Madison, CT: International Universities Press, 1990).

26. "Body Language for Business Success: 77 Ways to Get Results Using Non-Verbal Communication," National Institute of Business Management, Inc., 1989, p. 4.

27. "Body Language for Business Success," p. 16.

28. Geneviève Coutu-Bouchard, "L'Effet Pygmalion," *Montréal Campus*, April 24, 2002, p. 11.

29. John V. Thill and Courtland L. Bovée, *Excellence in Business Communication*, 5th ed. (Upper Saddle River, NJ: Prentice Hall, 2002), p. 38.

30. Aili McConnon, "You Are Where You Sit: How to Decode the Psychology of the Morning Meeting," *Business Week*, July 23, 2007, pp. 66–67.

31. Kate Ludeman and Eddie Erlandson, "Coaching the Alpha Male," *Harvard Business Review*, May 2004, p. 59; Andrew Park, "Taming the Alpha Executive," *Fast Company*, May 2006, p. 88.

32. Ludeman and Erlandson, "Coaching the Alpha Male," p. 62.

33. Carlin Flora, "Judith Regan on Chutzpah," *Psychology Today*, May/June 2005, p. 96.

34. Peter Montoya and Tim Vandehey, *The Brand Called You* (Tustin, CA: Peter Montoya Publishing, 2005), pp. 11–12, 14.

35. C. R. Snyder, "So Many Selves," *Contemporary Psychology*, January 1988, p. 77.

36. Daniel J. Lair, Katie Sullivan, and George Cheney, "Marketization and the Recasting of the Professional Self," *Management Communication Quarterly*, Vol. 18, No. 3, 2005, pp. 307–343.

37. Judith Sills, "Becoming Your Own Brand," *Psychology Today*, January/February 2008, pp. 62–63.

38. Jeninne Lee-St. John, "It's a Brand-You World," *Time*, November 6, 2006, pp. 60–61.

39. Suzanne Hippough, "Image Doctor," *Forbes*, February 26, 2007, p. 60.

40. Carol Hymowitz, "Some CEOs Advertise the 'Me' Brand—With Limited Success," *The Wall Street Journal*, July 16, 2007, p. B1. The analysis of Branson and Stewart are credited to the same source.

41. Suzette Parmley, "Retailing Trump," *Philadelphia Inquirer* (philly.com), August 4, 2006.

42. Hymowitz, "Some CEOs Advertise the 'Me' Brand," p. B1.

43. Hymowitz, "Some CEOs Advertise the 'Me' Brand," p. B1.

44. Matthew Futterman, "A New Big Play for Alex Rodriguez," *The Wall Street Journal*, July 22, 2008, pp. A1, A16.

45. Alan Hughes, "LeBron James: Professional Athlete," *Black Enterprise*, December 2007, p. 135.

46. Lisa Takeuchi Cullen, "What (Not) to Wear to Work," *Time*, June 9, 2008, p. 49.

47. Lublin, "Some Dos and Don'ts to Help," p. B1.

48. Sills, "Becoming Your Own Brand," p. 63.

49. Susan Gunelius, *Women on Business*, January 7, 2008, p. 1.

50. Keith N. Hampton, cited in Stephanie Rosenbloom, "Putting Your Cyberface Forward," *The New York Times* (nytimes.com), January 3, 2008.

Chapter 6

1. William L. Gardner and Mark J. Martinko, "Impression Management in Organizations," *Journal of Management*, No. 2, 1988, p. 332; Barry R. Schlenker, *Impression Management: The Self-Concept, Social Identity, and Interpersonal Relations* (Monterey, CA: Brooks/Cole, 1980).

2. David Kipnis and Stuart Schmidt, "Intraorganizational Influence Tactics: Exploration in Getting One's Way," *Journal of Applied Psychology*, August 1980, p. 445.

3. Linda Himelstein, "Frank's Life in the Rough," *Business Week*, March 31, 2003, pp. 88–89; "After 4 Years, Last Charges Dropped in Quattrone Case," *Bloomberg News*, August 30, 2007.

4. Amy Cortese, "I'm Humble, I'm Respectful," *Business Week*, February 9, 1998, p. 40.

5. Darren C. Treadway, Gerald R. Ferris, Allison B. Duke, Garry L. Adams, and Jason B. Thatcher, "The Moderating Role of Subordinate Political Skill on Supervisors' Impressions of Subordinate Ingratiation and Ratings of Interpersonal Facilitation," *Journal of Applied Psychology*, May 2007, p. 848.

6. Treadway et al., "The Moderating Role of Subordinate Political Skill," pp. 848–855.

7. James D. Westphal and Ithai Stern, "The Other Pathway to the Boardroom: How Interpersonal Influence Behavior Can Substitute for Elite Credentials and Demographic Majority Status in Gaining Access to Board Appointments," *Administrative Science Quarterly*, No. 2, 2006, pp. 169–204; James D. Westphal and Ithai Stern, "Flattery Will Get You Everywhere (Especially If You Are a Male Caucasian): How Ingratiation, Boardroom Behavior, and Demographic Minority Status Affect Additional Board Appointments at U.S. Companies," *Academy of Management Journal*, April 2007, pp. 267–288.

8. Ronald J. Deluga, "Kissing up to the Boss: What It Is and What to Do about It," *Business Forum*, Fall-Winter 2004, pp. 14–18.

9. David A. Ralston and Priscilla M. Elsass, "Ingratiation and Impression Management in the Organization," in Robert A. Giacalone and Paul Rosenfeld (Eds.), *Impression Management in the Organization* (Hillsdale, NJ: Lawrence Erlbaum, 1989), p. 237.

10. Marshall Goldsmith, "All of Us Are Stuck on Suck-Ups," *Fast Company*, December 2003, p. 117.

11. Research reported in Jeffrey Zaslow, "The Most-Praised Generation Goes to Work," *The Wall Street Journal*, April 20, 2007, p. W7.

12. Dale Carnegie, *How to Win Friends and Influence People* (New York: Simon & Schuster, 1936).

13. Paul Rosenfeld, Robert A. Giacalone, and Catherine Riordan, *Impression Management: Building and Enhancing Reputations at Work* (London: Thomson Learning, 2002), p. 45.

14. Carnegie, *How to Win Friends and Influence People*.

15. Andrew J. DuBrin, "Self-Perceived Technical Orientation and Attitudes toward Being Flattered," *Psychological Reports*, Vol. 96, 2005, pp. 852–854.

16. Rosenfeld, Giacalone, and Riordan, *Impression Management*, p. 35.

17. Deluga, "Kissing up to the Boss," p. 15.

18. Donn Byrne, *The Attraction Paradigm* (New York: Academic Press, 1971), as cited in Rosenfeld, Giacalone, and Riordan, *Impression Management*, p. 35.

19. E. E. Jones, K. I. Gergen, P. Gumpert, and J. W. Thibaut, "Some Conditions Affecting the Use of Ingratiation to Influence Performance Evaluation," *Journal of Personality and Social Psychology*, No. 1, 1965, pp. 613–625, as reported in Rosenfeld, Giacalone, and Riordan, *Impression Management*, p. 114.

20. Cecily D. Cooper, "Just Joking Around? Employee Humor Expression as an Ingratiatory Behavior," *Academy of Management Review*, October 2005, pp. 765–776. The quotation appears on pp. 766–767.

21. Robin J. Ely, Debra E. Meyerson, and Martin N. Davidson, "Rethinking Political Correctness," *Harvard Business Review*, September 2006, p. 80.

22. Gary M. Stern, "Small Slights Bring Big Problems," *Workforce*, August 2002, p. 17; Joann S. Lublin, "How to Stop the Snubs that Demoralize You and Your Colleagues," *The Wall Street Journal*, December 7, 2004, p. B1.

23. Ely, Meyerson, and Davidson, "Rethinking Political Correctness," p. 80.

24. Andrew J. DuBrin, *Personal Magnetism: Discover Your Own Charisma and Learn to Charm, Inspire, and Influence Others* (New York: Amacom, 1997), pp. 77–92.

Chapter 7

1. Dennis P. Bozeman and K. Michele Kacmar, "A Cybernetic Model of Impression Management Processes in Organizations," *Organizational Behavior and Human Decision Processes*, March 1997, p. 18.

2. Edward R. Hirt, Sean M. McCrea, and Hillary I. Boris, "I Know You Self-Handicapped the Last Exam: Gender Differences in Reactions to Self-Handicapping," *Journal of Personality Social Psychology*, January 2003, pp. 177–193.

3. Steven Berglas, "Self-Handicapping Behavior and the Self-Defeating Personality Disorder: Toward a Refined Clinical Perspective," in Rebecca C. Curtis, *Self-Defeating Behaviors: Experimental Research, Clinical Impressions, and Practical Implications* (New York: Plenum Press, 1989), pp. 261–288. This section about self-esteem and self-handicapping is derived from Berglas.

4. Jeffrey W. Lucas and Michael J. Lovaglia, "Self-Handicapping: Gender, Race, and Status," *Current Research in Social Psychology*, Vol. 10, No. 16, July 2005, pp. 234–249.

5. Berglas, "Self-Handicapping Behavior and the Self-Defeating Personality Disorder," p. 269.

6. S. Bennett, T. A. Pychyl, M. J. A. Wohl, and Z. Kovaltchouk, "Self-Forgiveness for Task-Specific Procrastination," paper presented at the Eastern Psychological Association Conference, Boston, 2008.

7. Kerry Sulkowicz, "Your Procrastinatin' Heart," *Business Week*, March 12, 2007, p. 18.

8. Hirt, McCrea, and Boris, "I Know You Self-Handicapped the Last Exam," pp. 177–193; Richard Doty, "Self-Handicapping: Factors Identified as Interfering with Performance Are Gender Related," www.homepages.indiana.edu/021403/text/handicapping.html, February 13, 2003, pp. 1–2.

9. Lucas and Lovaglia, "Self-Handicapping: Gender, Race, and Status," pp. 237, 239, 241–242.

10. Quoted in Tamara E. Holmes, "Admitting When You're Wrong," *Black Enterprise*, May 2007, p. 124.

11. "What Should You Do When an Employee Tells You—Nicely—that You Suck at Communicating?" *Communication Solutions*, sample issue, distributed in 2007.

12. J. T. Tedeschi and M. Reiss, "Verbal Strategies in Impression Management," in C. Antaki (Ed.), *The Psychology of Ordinary Explanations of Social Behavior* (London: Academic Press, 1981).

13. William L. Gardner and Mark J. Martinko, "Impression Management in Organizations," *Journal of Management*, No. 2, 1988, p. 332.

14. Paul Rosenfeld, Robert A. Giacalone, and Catherine Riordan, *Impression Management: Building and Enhancing Reputations at Work* (London: Thomson Learning, 2002), pp. 90–92.
15. Research cited in Robert M. Arkin and James A. Shepperd, "Self-Presentation Styles in Organizations," in Robert A. Giacalone and Paul Rosenfeld (Eds.), *Impression Management in the Organization* (Hillsdale, NJ: Erlbaum, 1989), p. 130.
16. M. Thomas, *A New Attitude* (Franklin Lakes, NJ: Career Press, 2005).
17. Zobra Paster, "How to Manage Anger," *Top Health: The Health Promotion and Wellness Newsletter* (Birmingham, AL: Oakstone Publishing, LLC, 2006).
18. Holmes, "Admitting When You're Wrong," p. 124.

Chapter 8

1. Chris Fletcher, "Impression Management in the Selection Interview," in Robert A. Giacalone and Paul Rosenfeld (Eds.), *Impression Management in the Organization* (Hillsdale, NJ: Erlbaum, 1989), p. 269.
2. Esther Dedrick Long and Gregory H. Dobbins, "Self-Monitoring, Impression Management, and Interview Ratings: A Field and Laboratory Study," *Academy of Management Proceedings*, 1992, p. 274.
3. Fletcher, "Impression Management in the Selection Interview," pp. 269–270.
4. Fletcher, "Impression Management in the Selection Interview," pp. 270–272; Aleksander P. J. Ellis, Bradley West, Ann Marie Ryan, and Richard P. DeShon, "The Use of Impression Management Tactics in Structured Interviews: A Function of Question Type?" *Journal of Applied Psychology*, December 2002, p. 1202.
5. Cynthia Kay Stevens and Amy L. Kristof, "Making the Right Impression: A Field Study of Applicant Impression Management during Job Interviews," *Journal of Applied Psychology*, October 1995, pp. 587–606.
6. Joy Pelluchette, Katherine Karl, and Kathleen Rust, "Dressing to Impress: Beliefs and Attitudes Regarding Workplace Attire," *Journal of Business & Psychology*, Fall 2006, pp. 45–63.
7. The meta-analysis about hiring is from Megumi Hosoda, Eugene F. Stone-Romero, and Gwen Coats, "The Effects of Physical Attractiveness on Job-Related Outcomes: A Meta-Analysis of Experimental Studies," *Personnel Psychology*, Summer 2003, pp. 431–462. The two other meta-analyses mentioned are reported in the same source.
8. Fletcher, "Impression Management in the Selection Interview," pp. 272–275.
9. Research about differences in dimensions of cultural values is presented in Mansour Javidan, Peter W. Dorfman, May Sully de Luque, and Robert J. House, "In the Eye of the Beholder: Cross Cultural Lessons in leadership from Project GLOBE," *Academy of Management Perspectives*, February 2006, pp. 69–70.
10. Fletcher, "Impression Management in the Selection Interview," p. 275.
11. Long and Dobbins, "Self-Monitoring, Impression Management, and Interview Ratings," pp. 274–278.

12. David C. Gilmore and Gerald R. Ferris, "The Effects of Applicant Impression Management Tactics on Interviewer Judgments," *Journal of Management*, No. 4, 1989, pp. 557–564.

13. Filip Lievens and Helga Peeters, "Interviewers' Sensitivity to Impression Management Tactics in Structured Interviews," *European Journal of Psychological Assessment*, No. 3, 2008, pp. 174–180.

14. Wei-Chi Tsai, Chien-Cheng Chen, and Su-Fen Chiu, "Exploring the Boundaries of the Effects of Applicant Impression Management Tactics in Job Interviews," *Journal of Management*, February 2005, pp. 108–125.

15. Sara E. Needleman, "Thx for the IView! I Wud ♥ to Work 4U!!, *The Wall Street Journal*, July 29, 2008, pp. D1, D4.

16. Peg Thoms, Rosemary McMasters, Melissa R. Roberts, and Douglas A. Dombkowski, "Résumé Characteristics as Predictors of an Invitation to Interview," *Journal of Business and Psychology*, Spring 1999, pp. 339–356.

17. The quotation as well as the other facts listed in this section are from Lisa Takeuchi Cullen, "Getting Wise to Lies," *Time*, May 1, 2006, p. 59.

18. Abby Ellin, "Auditioning in a Video Résumé," *New York Times* (nytimes.com), April 21, 2007, p. 3.

19. Lisa Takeuchi Cullen, "It's a Wrap. You're Hired," *Time*, March 5, 2007, p. 51.

20. Peter Villanova and H. John Bernardin, "Impression Management in the Context of Performance Appraisal," in Giacalone and Rosenfeld (Eds.), *Impression Management in the Organization*, p. 305.

21. Paul Rosenfeld, Robert A. Giacalone, and Catherine A. Riordan, *Impression Management Building and Enhancing Reputations at Work* (London: Thomson Learning, 2002), p. 166.

22. Sandy J. Wayne and Gerald R. Ferris, "Influence Tactics, Affect, and Exchange Quality in Supervisor-Subordinate Interactions: A Laboratory Experiment and Field Study," *Journal of Applied Psychology*, October 1990, p. 494.

23. Sandy J. Wayne and Robert C. Liden, "Effects of Impression Management on Performance Ratings: A Longitudinal Study," *Academy of Management Journal*, February 1995, pp. 232–260.

24. "First Impression Management: How to Handle the 30 Seconds that Set the Tone for Your Entire Interview," www.hcareers.com/us/resourcecenter/tabid/306/articleid/445/default.aspx, accessed July 11, 2008.

25. "Impression Management," http://changingminds.org/disciplines/job-finding/impression_management.htm, © Syqe 2002–2007, accessed July 11, 2008.

26. Quotation and citation from Nina Jamal and Judith Lindenberger, "How to Make a Great First Impression," www.businessknowhow.com/growth/dress-impression.htm, p. 2, accessed July 7, 2008.

27. "Be Nice to Receptionist; There's Real Power There," Rochester, New York, *Democrat and Chronicle*, September 25, 2006, p. 12D.

28. Quoted in Needleman, "Thx for the IView!" p. D4.
29. Fletcher, "Impression Management in the Selection Interview," p. 278.

Chapter 9

1. Bernard M. Bass with Ruth Bass, *The Bass Handbook of Leadership: Theory, Research, & Managerial Applications*, 4th ed. (New York: The Free Press, 2008), p. 614.
2. George P. Hollenbeck and Douglas T. Hall, "Self-Confidence and Leader Performance," *Organizational Dynamics*, No. 3, 2004, p. 254.
3. Thomas E. Cronin, " 'All the World's a Stage . . .' Acting and the Art of Political Leadership," *Leadership Quarterly*, August 2008, pp. 459–468.
4. Jeffrey Pfeffer, *Managing with Power: Politics and Influence in Organizations* (Boston, MA: Harvard Business School Press, 1992), pp. 279–298.
5. Garry Willis, "What Makes a Good Leader?" *Atlantic Monthly*, April 1994, p. 67. As quoted in Cronin, " 'All the World's a Stage . . .', " p. 463.
6. Joann S. Lublin, "How You Can Ensure a Newly Created Job Has Staying Power," *The Wall Street Journal*, June 5, 2007, p. B1.
7. " 'Making the Rounds' Like a Physician," *Manager's Edge*, February 2006, p. 8.
8. Martin M. Chemers, *An Integrative Theory of Leadership* (Mahwah, NJ: Lawrence Erlbaum, 1997), p. 153.
9. Olga Epitropaki and Robin Martin, "Implicit Leadership Theories in Applied Settings: Factor Structure, Generalizability, and Stability over Time," *Journal of Applied Psychology*, April 2004, pp. 297–299.
10. Olga Epitropaki and Robin Martin, "From Real to Ideal: A Longitudinal Study of Implicit Leadership Theories in Leader-Member Exchanges and Employee Outcomes," *Journal of Applied Psychology*, July 2005, pp. 659–676.
11. Jeffrey Pfeffer, *Managing with Power: Power and Influence in Organizations* (Boston, MA: Harvard Business School Press, 1992), p. 224.
12. Cited in "Choose Words that Inspire," *Executive Leadership*, March 2001, p. 2.
13. Gary Yukl, *Skills for Managers and Leaders: Texts, Cases, and Exercises* (Upper Saddle River, NJ: Prentice Hall, 1990), p. 65.
14. George Anders, "Tough CEOs Often Most Successful, a Study Finds," *The Wall Street Journal*, November 19, 2007, p. B3.
15. Robert K. Greenleaf, *The Power of Servant Leadership* (San Francisco: Berrett-Koehler Publishers, 1998).
16. Based on Robert K. Greenleaf, *Servant Leadership: A Journey into the Nature of Legitimate Power and Greatness* (Mahwah, NJ: Paulist Press, 1997); Robert C. Liden, Sandy J. Wayne, Hao Zhao, and David Henderson, "Servant Leadership: Development of a Multidimensional Measure and Multi-Level Assessment," *Leadership Quarterly*, April 2008, pp. 161–177.
17. "Be a Leader, Not a Pal," *Manager's Edge*, March 2007, p. 3.

18. Jay A. Conger and Rabindra N. Kanungo, *Charismatic Leadership in Organizations* (Thousand Oaks, CA: Sage, 1998).

19. Several of these definitions stem from the literature review found in B. M. Bass, *The Bass Handbook of Leadership*, pp. 575–576. In order of their presentation here, the original citations are as follows: (1) Max Weber, *The Theory of Social and Economic Organization* (New York: The Free Press, 1924/1947), p. 358; (2) Gary A. Yukl, *Leadership in Organizations*, 3rd ed. (Upper Saddle River, NJ: Prentice Hall, 1994), p. 207; (3) James M. Kouzes and Barry Z. Posner, *The Leadership Challenge: How to Get Extraordinary Things Done in Organizations* (San Francisco, Jossey-Bass, 1987), p. 123; (4) Max Weber, *The Sociology of Religion* (Boston, MA: The Beacon Press, 1922/1963); (5) Robert J. House, "A 1976 Theory of Charismatic Leadership," in J. G. Hunt and L. L. Larson (Eds.), *Leadership: The Cutting Edge* (Carbondale, IL: Southern Illinois University Press, 1977); (6) Eric Fromm, *Escape from Freedom* (New York: Farrar & Rinehart, 1941); (7) C. J. Friedrich, "Political Leadership and the Problem of the Charismatic Power," *Journal of Politics*, Vol. 23, 1961, pp. 3–24; (8) D. E. Berlew, "Leadership and Organizational Excitement," in D. A. Kolb, M. Rubin, and J. M. McIntyre (Eds.), *Organizational Psychology* (Englewood Cliffs, NJ: Prentice-Hall, 1974).

20. Jay Conger and Ranbindra N. Kanungo, "Toward a Behavioral Theory of Charismatic Leadership in Organizational Settings," *Academy of Management Review*, 1987, pp. 637–647.

21. William L. Gardner and Bruce J. Avolio, "The Charismatic Relationship: A Dramaturgical Perspective," *Academy of Management Review*, January 1998, pp. 32–58.

22. "You Scratch My Back . . . Tips on Winning Your Colleague's Cooperation," *Working Smart*, October 1999, p. 1.

23. Andrew J. DuBrin, *Leadership: Research Findings, Practice, and Skills* (Mason, OH: South-Western Cengage Learning, 2010), pp. 81–83.

Chapter 10

1. "Corporate Image," Answers.com, accessed July 27, 2008, pp. 1–5.

2. "Corporate Image," pp. 2–4.

3. Anne Fisher, "America's Most Admired Companies," *Fortune*, March 17, 2008, pp. 65–67, 122; Anne Fisher, "America's Most Admired Companies," *Fortune*, March 19, 2007, pp. 88–94.

4. Kerry Capell, "IKEA: How the Swedish Retailer Became a Global Brand," *Business Week*, November 14, 2005, pp. 96–104.

5. Thomas Hoffman, "Online Reputation: Cleaning up Your Image Is Hot, but Is It Ethical?" *Computer World*, March 17, 2008, pp. 22–26; John Tozzi, "Do Reputation Services Work?" *Business Week*, May 1, 2008, p. 11.

6. Pallavi Gorgoi, "Why Avon Is Going Hollywood," *Business Week*, July 28, 2008, p. 58.

7. Emily Thornton, "Carlyle Changes Its Stripes," *Business Week*, February 12, 2007, pp. 46–59.

8. Lee Gomes, "Vendors Still Paying for IT Research that Flatters Them," *The Wall Street Journal*, January 30, 2008, p. B1.

9. Gomes, "Vendors Still Paying for IT Research that Flatters Them," p. B1.

10. Miriam Hill, "J&J Gave Money in Return for Positive Drug Studies," *Philadelphia Inquirer* (philly.com), November 24, 2008, p. 1.

11. Peter Engardio and Michael Arndt, "What Price Reputation?" *Business Week*, July 9 and 16, 2007, pp. 70–84.

12. Robert A. Guth and Jessica E. Vasacellaro, "Microsoft Makes Case for Online Push," *The Wall Street Journal*, July 25, 2008, p. B7.

13. Barnaby Wickham, "Voice of Reason," *Entrepreneur*, March 2007, p. 83.

14. Pratima Bansal and Iain Clelland, "Talking Trash: Legitimacy, Impression Management, and Unsystematic Risk in the Context of the Natural Environment," *Academy of Management Journal*, February 2004, p. 94.

15. "Corporate Social Responsibility: Good Citizenship or Investor Rip-off?" *The Wall Street Journal*, January 9, 2006, p. R6; Dirk Matten and Jeremy Moon, " 'Implicit' and 'Explicit' CSR: A Conceptual Framework for a Comparative Understanding of Corporate Social Responsibility," *Academy of Management Review*, April 2008, pp. 404–424; Peter Edward and Hugh Willmott, "Corporate Citizenship: Rise or Demise of a Myth?" *Academy of Management Review*, July 2008, pp. 771–775.

16. "Corporate Social Responsibility," p. R6.

17. Michael E. Porter and Mark R. Kramer, "Strategy and Society: The Link between Competitive Advantage and Corporate Social Responsibility," *Harvard Business Review*, December 2006, p. 78.

18. The sources in order of use are: Tyler Hamilton, "Branson's $3B Pledge," *Toronto Star* (www.thestar.com), September 22, 2006; Laura Blue, "Let's Talk Trash," *Time*, October 9, 2006, p. A37; Lee Gomes, "Prodded by Consumers, the Computer Industry Slowly Grows Greener," *The Wall Street Journal*, June 14, 2006, p. B1; Richard Gibson, "Companies Opt for Paperless Route," *The Wall Street Journal*, September 27, 2006, p. B5A.

19. Ben Elgin, "The Fuzzy Math of Eco-Accolades," *Business Week*, October 29, 2007, p. 049.

20. www.PrudentialFoundation.com, accessed November 26, 2008.

21. Erin McClam, "*Time* Names Whistleblowers Persons of Year," Associated Press, December 2002; "Former Enron Vice President Sherron Watkins on the Enron Collapse," *Academy of Management Executive*, November 2003, p. 119.

22. Study cited in Louis Aguilar, "Cutbacks to Ripple through Economy," *Detroit News* (detnews.com), September 16, 2006.

23. Marlene Piturro, "Alternatives to Downsizing," *Management Review*, October 1999, p. 38; Daniel Eisenberg, "Where People Are Never Let Go," *Time*, June 18, 2001, p. 40.

24. Information and quotation from Karen E. Klein, "Dissed Online? How to Fix Your Company's Brand Rep," *Business Week*, May 20, 2008, p. 15.

25. Porter and Kramer, "Strategy and Society," p. 78.

Chapter 11

1. Stephen P. Robbins, *Essentials of Organizational Behavior*, 7th ed. (Upper Saddle River, NJ: Prentice Hall, 2003), p. 161.

2. D. C. Gilmore and Gerald R. Ferris, "The Effects of Applicant Impression Management Tactics on Interviewer Judgments," *Journal of Management*, December 1989, pp. 557–564.

3. Chad A. Higgins and Timothy A. Judge, "The Effect of Applicant Influence Tactics on Recruiter Perceptions of Fit and Hiring Recommendations: A Field Study," *Journal of Applied Psychology*, August 2004, pp. 622–632.

4. Cynthia Kay Stevens and Amy L. Kristof, "Making the Right Impression: A Field Study of Applicant Impression Management during Job Interviews," *Journal of Applied Psychology*, October 1995, pp. 587–606.

5. Sandy J. Wayne and Robert C. Liden, "Effects of Impression Management on Performance Ratings: A Longitudinal Study," *Academy of Management Journal*, February 1995, pp. 232–260.

6. Suzanne Zivnuska, Michelke K. Kacmar, L. A. Witt, Dawn S. Carlson, and Virginia K. Bratton, "Interactive Effects of Impression Management and Organizational Politics on Job Performance," *Journal of Organizational Behavior*, August 2004, Issue 5, pp. 627–640.

7. Yei-Yi Chen and Wen Chang Fang, "The Moderating Effect of Impression Management on the Organizational Politics-Performance Relationship," *Journal of Business Ethics*, May 2008, pp. 263–277.

8. James D. Westphal and Ithai Stern, "The Other Pathway to the Boardroom: How Interpersonal Influence Behavior Can Substitute for Elite Credentials and Demographic Majority Status in Gaining Access to Board Appointments," *Administrative Science Quarterly*, No. 2, 2006, pp. 169–204.

9. Ronald Deluga and J. T. Perry, "The Role of Subordinate Performance and Ingratiation in Leader-Member Exchanges," *Group & Organization Management*, Vol. 19, 1994, pp. 67–86. Although this research was conducted in 1994, the conclusions are even truer today.

10. Cecily D. Cooper, "Just Joking Around? Employee Humor Expression as an Ingratiatory Behavior," *Academy of Management Review*, October 2005, pp. 765–776.

11. Cooper, "Just Joking Around?" pp. 772–773.

12. Nhung T. Nguyen, "Putting a Good Face on Impression Management: Team Citizenship and Team Satisfaction," *Journal of Behavioral and Applied Management*, January 2008, pp. 1–13.

13. Pratima Bansal and Iain Clelland, "Talking Trash: Legitimacy, Impression Management, and Unsystematic Risk in the Context of the Natural Environment," *Academy of Management Journal*, February 2004, p. 94.

14. Study reported in Pete Engardio, "Nice Guys Don't Finish Last," *Business Week*, February 13, 2008, p. 15.

15. Study reported in Pete Engardio and Michael Arndt, "What Price Reputation?" *Business Week*, July 9, 2007, pp. 70–79.

16. Dennis J. Moberg, "The Ethics of Impression Management," in Robert A. Giacalone and Paul Rosenfeld (Eds.), *Impression Management in the Organization* (Hillsdale, NJ: Lawrence Erlbaum, 1989), p. 172. The example is attributed to E. E. Jones and C. Wortman, *Ingratiation: An Attributional Approach* (Morristown, NJ: General Learning Press, 1973).

17. Victoria Kim, "Investors Say They Were Duped by an Irresistible Pitch," *Los Angeles Times*, November 11, 2008.

18. Dennis Bromley, book review appearing in *Psychology Learning & Teaching*, Autumn 2002, p. 142. The book under review was Paul Rosenfeld, Robert Giacalone, and Catherine Riordan (Eds.), *Impression Management: Building and Enhancing Reputations at Work* (London: Thomson Learning, 2002).

19. Ronald J. Deluga, "Kissing up to the Boss: What It Is and What to Do about It," *Business Forum*, Fall-Winter 2004, p. 17. The idea about confronting the problem of too much ingratiation is also from the same source.

20. J. Spencer, "Shirk Ethic: How to Fake a Hard Day at the Office—White Collar Slackers Get Help from New Gadgets: The Faux 4 a.m. E-Mail," *The Wall Street Journal*, May 15, 2003, p. D1.

21. Deluga, "Kissing up to the Boss," p. 18.

22. Peter H. Kim, Kurt T. Dirks, and Cecily D. Cooper, "The Repair of Trust: A Dynamic Bilateral Perspective and Multilevel Conceptualization," *Academy of Management Review*, July 2009, p. 403.

23. Ronald E. Riggio, *Introduction to Industrial/Organizational Psychology*, 4th ed. (Upper Saddle River, NJ: Prentice Hall, 2003), p. 294.

24. Deluga, "Kissing up to the Boss," p. 18.

25. Alicia A. Grandey, "Emotion Regulation in the Workplace: A New Way to Conceptualize Emotional Labor," *Journal of Occupational Health Psychology*, Vol. 5, No. 1, 2000, pp. 95–110; Alicia A. Grandey, "When the 'Show Must Go On': Surface Acting and Deep Acting as Determinants of Emotional Exhaustion and Peer-Related Service Delivery," *Academy of Management Journal*, February 2003, pp. 86–96.

26. Reported in review of Neal M. Ashkanasy, Charmine E. J. Härtel, and Wilfred J. Zerbe (Eds.), *Emotions in the Workplace: Research, Theory, and Practice* (Westport, CT: Quorum Books/Greenwood, 2000) in *Contemporary Psychology*, April 2002, p. 165.

27. Patricia Faison Hewlin, "And the Award for Best Actor Goes to . . .: Facades of Conformity in Organizational Settings," *Academy of Management Review*, October 2003, pp. 633–642.

28. Roy F. Baumeister, "Motives and Costs of Self-Presentation in Organizations," in Giacalone and Rosenfeld, *Impression Management in the Organization*, pp. 67–68.

Index

Page numbers in **Bold** denotes a figure/table

A

Aberdeen Group 183
Accenture 182
acclaiming 72–3
acting skills: and leaders
    159–64
actor implementation 31–3, 37
actor perception 25, 36
Adobe Systems Inc. 74
affiliative citizenship 70
aggressives 44, 45, 50, 58
airport delays: used for self-
    handicapping 120
Allstate 179
alpha personality 92–4, 98,
    100
altruism 69
Angel.com 184–5
anger control 67–8, 78, 132,
    134–5
apologizing: and damage control
    129, 134; and job interviews
    142–3
appeal: making an inspirational
    166
appearance 81, 91; and
    charismatic leaders 173; and
    first impressions 90, 99; and
    height 86–7, 99; and job
    interviews 144, 154, 155;
    obesity and health complaints
    85–6, 99; and performance
    evaluation 152; see also
    clothing/dress
approval, need for 44, 56–7, 58
Armani, Giorgio 82
Arruda, William 95
assertiveness: and job interviews
    137
attraction, law of 111
authenticity 18, 95, 162, 195
authority 62
Avolio, Bruce J. 171, 172
Avon Products 182

B

Bacon, Terry 66–7
Bains, Gurnek 96
balance theory: and ingratiation
    104–5, 116
Baldrige, Letitia 87, 99
Ballmer, Steve 184
Bansal, Pratima 185–6, 201
basking in reflected glory 140–1,
    182
Bass, Bernard M. 158
Baumeister, Roy F. 205
Bergeron, Diane M. 71
Berglas, Steven 119, 120
blip approach 153
blogs 98, 181, 193
body language 91, 143 see also
    nonverbal behavior
body mass index 85–6
Bogusky, Alex 84
Bolino, Mark 42, 69, 70–2
Borden, Rob 95
Bozeman, Dennis P. 17, 23, 48,
    90
branding see personal branding
Branson, Richard 96, 188
Bridges, Shirley W. 46–7
Brinkley, Amy Woods 67
Bromley, Dennis 202
Bush, President George H.W.
    182
business etiquette see etiquette
Byrne, Donn 111

C

Cable, Daniel M. 86
career advancement 198–9
Carlyle Group 182
Carnegie, Dale: *How to Win
    Friends and Influence People*
    109, 110
celebrities: corporate image
    and association with 182,
    193

cell phones 48, 74–5, 84, **88**
Center for Business Ethics
    (Bentley University) 12–13
ceremonies 161
certification 62
Chambers, John 172
characteristics and behaviors:
    self-presentation of 60–8, **61**,
    76–7, 79
charismatic leadership/leaders
    169–74, 175–6; definitions
    169–70, 175; desired identity
    images 172, 176; employment
    of specific impression
    management behaviors 172–4,
    176; enhancement methods
    175; and framing 172–3; and
    performing 173–4; role of high
    self-esteem and self-
    monitoring 171–2, 175–6; and
    scripting 173; and staging 173;
    use of impression management
    in creating and maintaining
    170–2, 175
Cheesecake Factory 191
Chemers, Martin 163
Chin, Cathy 155
choking under pressure 205
chutzpah 93, 100
Cialdini, Robert B. 61, 65
Cisco Systems 172
citizenship behaviors see
    organizational citizenship
    behavior
civic virtue 69
civility 66–7, 78, 79
Clark, Jerome 63
Clelland, Iain 185–6, 201
clothing/dress 80, 81–5, 87, **88**,
    90, 91, 99; and creating a
    positive image 82–4, 97; and
    job interviews 144, 154;
    perceptions of sexiness based
    on 83, 84–5, 97, 99; and

performance evaluation 152; and videoconferencing 97
coaching: and personal branding 95
cognitive skills 48, 56, 57
collective culture 52, 64
communication: corporate 180; gender differences in patterns of 48–50, 59
communication style 56; direct 93
community redevelopment projects 189–90
comparator 17, 18, 25–8, 34, 35, 36
compliments 109, 114–15 *see also* flattery
computer industry: environmental protection initiatives 188
Computershare Ltd 188
confidence: and leadership image projection 158, 163
Conger, Jay 170–1
connections: publicizing personal 65
conscientiousness 200
consistency 62
consultation: and leader image projection 166
content-oriented messages 31–2, **31**, 37
contextual variables 53–4, 59
conversation: use of to build rapport 48–9
Cooper, Cecily D. 112, 199
cooperative behavior: impact of impression management on 199–200
corporate communication 180
corporate culture 179
corporate identity 179
corporate image 177–84, 192–3, 200, 201; association with celebrities 182, 193; construction of 180–1, 192, 193; factors essential in managing 179–80, 193; guidelines for application and practice 191–2; and online reputation 181–2, 192, 193; and social responsibility initiatives 187; and sponsored research 182–4, 192, 193; and stock price 201, 206; theory of 179–80, 193
corporate social performance 187

corporate social responsibility 185–91, 192, 193–4; community redevelopment projects 189–90; compassionate downsizing 190–1; and environmental protection 186, 188–9; meaning of 186–7; and whistle blowers 190; work-life programs 189
corporate strategy 180
courtesy 69, 87
Crawley, Steven 4
credit, taking 72–3, 78
criticism: mixing with flattery 109, 117
Cronin, Thomas E. 159
cross-cultural relations **89**
crying 68
cubicles **89**
cultural factors 20; and interviews 145–6; and persuasiveness 63
culture: corporate 179; cross-cultural relations 89; organizational *see* organizational culture
culture-specific codes 54
cybernetic model 4–5, 16–37; actor implementation 31–3, 37; actor perception 25, 36; and comparator 17, 18, 25–8, 34, 35, 36; components 18–33, *19*, 35; and desired social identity (reference goal) 18, 20–4, 36; feedback from target 16, 17, 18, 20, 24–5, 33, 34–5, 36; guidelines for application and practice 34–5; impact on target 33; and job interviewees 19–20; outcome processing 28–31, 37; practical implications of 33–4
cybernetic theory 17–18, 33

D
Dahle, Cheryl 73
damage control 118, 128–32, 134; admitting mistakes 128, 134; and anger control 132, 134–5; apologizing and pardon seeking 129, 134; excuses and the self-serving bias 129–31, 134; recovering from a major error on the job 131–2, 134
deep acting 204

Defend My Name 192
Deluga, Ronald J. 108, 111, 203
direct communication style 93
DiResta, Diane 76
disabilities: interaction with people with 89
discipline 93
distance from the other person 91
Dobbins, Gregory H. 147
downsizing 190–1
dramaturgy 171, 175
dress *see* clothing/dress
Drexler, Mickey 56
DuBrin, Andrew J. 110
dysfunctional consequences (of impression management) 201–5, **202**, 206; choking under pressure 205; diversion of mental resources 203; emotional labor and distress 204–5; engendering of mistrust and dislike of actor 204; ethical lapses 202–3

E
e-mails 150
Economist Intelligence Unit on Corporate Responsibility 200
effector 17, 35
electronic devices *88*; dangling from your clothing 84, 99; and interviews 154; use of during business meetings 74, 75
emotional dissonance 204
emotional labor 204–5
empathy 68
employment interview *see* job interviews
English, Paul 184
enhancement 19–20
enhancement of others 101–17, *101*; and flattery *see* flattery; guidelines for application and practice 114–16; and humor 112, 116, 117; and ingratiation *see* ingratiation; and opinion conformity 111–12, 115–16, 117; and political correctness 113–14, 116, 117
Enron Corporation 51, 190
entitlement 19, 20, 140
environmental performance: impact on sales and stock price 201–2

environmental protection 186, 188–9, 201
Erlandson, Eddie 92
ethics 12–13, 14, 62, 63; lapses in 202–3
etiquette 80, 87–8, 88–9, 97–8, 99, 101
evaluation 22
excuses 32, 133, 134; characteristics of effective 130–1; and damage control 129–31, 134; and job interviews 141
exemplification 42, **42**, **43**; and charismatic leaders 173–4
expectancy theory of motivation 22
expert knowledge 72, 78
extraversion/extraverts 47, 57, 58, 145
eye contact 91, 97

F
façade creation 204–5
Facebook 98, 181, 191
facial expressions 91
faking 202–3
falsification: and job interviews 143; and job résumés 151, 156–7
favors, exchanging of 166
fawning, extreme 105
fear 51, 59
feedback 57; and corporate image 180; and cybernetic model 16, 17, 18, 20, 24–5, 33, 34–5, 36; discrepancies between goals and 23–4, 36; giving positive 115; verbal and nonverbal 24–5, 35
Feldon, Diane 82
Ferris, Gerald R. 148
financial crisis (2008) 203
Fiorina, Carly 51, 52
first impressions 89–90, 98, 99; and videoconferencing 97
flattery 32, 56, 105, 106, 108–11, 116–17, 206; guidelines for skilful use of 114–15; making other people feel important as form of 109, *110*, 117; mixing mild criticism to increase effectiveness of 109, 117; self-perceived technical orientation as a variable that influences 110–11, 117

Fletcher, Clive 136, 145, 147
flexitime 189
follow-up correspondence: after job interviews 150, 156
Fortune list 179
Fox, Alfredo Trujillo 202
framing: and charismatic leadership 172–3
Friedman, Karen 152
functional consequences (of impression management) 195–201, **196**, 205–6; career advancement 198–9; cooperative behavior and satisfaction within teams 199–200; enhanced sales and stock price 200–1; and job interview 195–7; and performance evaluation 197–8

G
Gardner, William L. 56, 171, 172
Gates, Bill 102
gender differences: and communication patterns 48–50, 59; and dress 82; and ingratiation 106; and profiles of impression management 50; and self-handicapping 126–7, 134
General Electric (GE) 163, 173, 179
generalized compliance 69
Gerstner, Louis V. 182
gethuman.com 184
Ghosn, Carlos 74
Gilmore, David C. 148
goal-based interpretation 22–3
goal-directed motivation 23–4
goal(s): activation of identity 21–2; adjustment of reference 30–1; discrepancies between feedback and 23–4, 36; relevance of impression management 8–9; value of desired 9
Goffman, Erving 2–3, 14–15
Google 173, 179, 184
Gostanian, Greg 155
Grandey, Alicia 204
Grant, Adam M. 70
Green, Robert: *The 48 Laws of Power* 63
Greenleaf, Robert K. 167

H
hand gestures 91
handshakes 80, 155
hands-on leadership 167
handwritten thank-you notes 39
Harrison, Stephen G. 67
health 85–6
Hegarty, Edward J. 1
height 86–7, 99
heroic figures 52
Hewlett-Packard (HP) 51, 52, 163
Higgins, Chad A. 197
high-status workers 54, 66, 85, 99, 121–2, 133–4, 138, 140
Hirt, Edward R. 119, 127
honesty 128, 134, 163–4
humility 66–7
humor 65–6, 112, 116, 117, 199
Hurd, Mark 52, 163

I
IBM 179
ideal image 7
identity: creating an 7–8; cybernetic model and desired social 20–4, 36
identity adjustment 27–8, **31**, 32, 35, 36
identity enhancement 26–7, **31**, 32, 33, 35, 36–7
identity goals, activation of 21–2
identity images 6; charismatic leadership and desired 172, 176; desired and undesired 10
identity maintenance 28, 35, 36, 37
identity protection 26–7, **31**, 32, 35, 36, 37 *see also* self-protection techniques
idiosyncrasy credits 12
Ikea 180–1, 192, 193
image: current/potential social 11–12; discrepancy between desired and current 9
Immelt, Jeffrey R. 163, 173
implicit leadership theory: and leadership image projection 164–5, *165*, 174
important: making other people feel 109, *110*
impression construction 5, 6, *6*, 9–12, 15; and current image 11–12; desired and undesired identity images 10; guidelines for application and practice 14;

and role constraints 10–11; and self-concept 10; and target values 11

impression management: definitions of 1, 3–4, 5, 15; individual factors contributing to 38–50, *39*; misconceptions about 1; motives for *see* impression motivation; negative consequences of 201–5, 206; origins of modern study of 2–3, 14–15; positive consequences of 195–201, 206; situational factors contributing to 53–8; two-component model of 4–12, 15

impression motivation 4–9, **6**, 15, 34; discrepancy between desired and current image 9; factors determining 5–6, 8–9, 15; and goal relevance of impressions 8–9; guidelines for application and process 14; types of 6–8, 15; and value of desired goals 9

improvising: and leadership image projection 162

incivility 66, 78, 79, 87

individualistic culture: versus collective culture 52

influence tactics: and leadership image projection 165–7

InfoLink Screening Systems 151

information filtering: and job interviews 143

ingratiation 32, 42, **42**, **43**, 51, 57, 102–13, 198–9; and balance theory 104–5, 116; and ethical lapses 202–3; executive-level study on effectiveness of 106–8, **107**, 116, 198; flattery as a method of 108–11; and humor 112, 116, 117, 199; and job interviews 138–40, 197; opinion conformity as a method of 111–12, 115–16, 117; and performance evaluation 153–4, 157, 197; and political skill 105–6, 116; quiz measuring 102, **103–4**; reasons for importance 102, 104–6; tactics 102; and team satisfaction 200; undermining of morale 204

instant messaging **88**

integrity 10, 35, 46, 67, 167

intelligence 93

interaction, human 52, 59

interactive voice response (IVR) industry 184–5

Internet 95; and online reputation 181–2, 192, 193

interpersonal influence behavior 108

interviews, job *see* job interviews

intimidation 42, **42**, **43**, 57, 69

introductions to people **88**

introverts 47

J

Jamal, Nina 155

James, LeBron 97, 100

Jedinak, Michaela 82

job competencies: versus impression management in job interviews 148–9, 156

job interviews 19–20, 136–50, **137**, 156, 195–7; and apologies 142–3; appearance and dress 144, 154, 155; and assertiveness 137; attributes of interviewee 145–6; attributes of the interviewer 146; basking in reflected glory 140–1; candidate self-monitoring and interview ratings 147; entitlements and enhancements 140; and excuses 141; falsification and information filtering 143; and follow-up correspondence 150, 156; guidelines for application and practice 154–5, 157; impression management tactics used 137–44, 156; impression management versus job competencies 148–9, 156; and ingratiation 138–40, 197; and justifications 141–2; and nonverbal behavior 143–4, 146, 154; and opinion conformity 140, 141; and self-promotion 137–8, **138–9**, 140, 197; situational attributes that influence choice of tactics 145–7, 156

job résumés 150–2, 156–7; traditional 151; video 151–2, 157

Jobs, Steve 72, 167, 169

Johnson & Johnson 183

Joyce, Amy 88

Judge, Timothy A. 86, 197

Jung, Andrea 173

justifications: and job interviews 141–2

K

Kacmar, K. Michele 17, 23, 48, 90

Kanungo, Rabindra N. 170–1

Kidwell, Roland 151

Klaus, Peggy 73, 90

Koval, Robin 67

Kowalski, Robin M. 4, 6, 9, 15

Kramer, Mark R. 192

Kristof, Amy L. 140, 197

Kuczmarski, Tom 96

L

Lafarge 189

Lafley, A.G. 172

leaders/leadership 46, 67, 158–76, **159**; charismatic *see* charismatic leadership; perceived competence of 158

leadership antiprototypes 164, **165**

leadership image projection 158–69, **160**, 175; acting skills required 159–64; being a team player 167; and confidence 163; connecting with the audience 159; consultation with others 166; discipline and toughness 163; exchanging favors and bargaining 166; guidelines for application and practice 174; and hands-on leadership 167; and honesty 163–4; and implicit leadership theories 164–5, **165**, 174; improvising 162; influence tactics 165–7; leading by example and respect 165–6; and listening 161–2, 168; making an inspirational appeal 166; and servant leader 167–9; understanding and exploiting symbols 160–1

leadership prototypes 164, **165**

leading by example 165–6

Leary, Mark R. 4, 6, 9, 15

Liden, Robert C. 197

Lievens, Filip 149

liking 62

Lincoln Electric 191
Lindenberger, Judith 155
listening: and leadership image projection 161–2, 168; as powerful form of flattery 115
listening tour 162
Long, Esther Dedrick 147
Lovaglia, Michael J. 121, 122, 127
low-status workers 54, 85, 99, 121, 133
Lucas, Jeffrey W. 121, 122, 127
Ludeman, Kate 92
lying 10, 41–2, 202–3; and job interviews 143; and job résumés 151

M
McDonald's 188
Machiavellianism 44–5, 57, 58
Madoff, Bernard 45
magnetism 166
Major, John 182
manners 87, 97 see also etiquette
Marchionne, Sergio 161
Martinko 55
Mayer, David M. 70
meetings: seating placement during 92; use of electronic devices during 74, 75
Men's Warehouse 173
Merck 179
Merkle, George 68
Meyer, David E. 75
microinequity 114, 117
Microsoft Corp. 102, 179, 184
mistakes 46; admitting of and damage control 128, 134; apologizing for 129; recovering from a major error on the job 131–2
Moberg, Dennis 202
Montoya, Peter 94
motivation: goal-directed 23–4; valance-instrumentality-expectancy theory of 22; see also impression motivation
Mulcahy, Anne M. 75
Mullaly, Alan 75
multitasking 74–5
MySpace 181

N
name dropping 65
names, remembering 115, 175

Nardelli, Bob 92
negative discrepancies 7, 17–18, 26, 27, 34, 35, 36–7
negative impressions, creating 3, 75–6, **76–7**, 78–9
Nguyen, Nhung T. 199–200
Nike 189
nonverbal behavior 32–3, 34, 37, 90–2, 98, 100; and charismatic leaders 173; and feedback 24, 35; and insincere flattery 109, 117; and job interviews 143–4, 146, 154
norm conformance: and effective excuses 131

O
obesity 85–6, 99
occupational status 54 see also high-status workers; low-status workers
online reputation 181–2, 192, 193
opinion conformity 203; and ingratiation 111–12, 115–16, 117; and job interviews 140, 141
opinionated, being 93
optimism 47, 58
organizational citizenship behavior 68–72, 78; dimensions of 69, 79; downsides of 71–2, 79; and image concerns 69–70; impression- management-relevant characteristics of 70–1
organizational culture 50–4, 58–9, 64, 199; fear 51, 59; heroic figures 52; human interaction 52; influence on tactics used in interviews 146; power struggling 51, 58; trust and respect for the individual 52
organizational politics 197–8
organizations 177–94, 178; corporate image and reputation 177–84, 192–3, 200, 201; impact of impression management on sales and stock price 200–1; and social responsibility 185–91, 192, 193–4; and spin 184–5, 192, 193
Orman, Suzie 75
other-enhancement see enhancement of others

outcome processing: cybernetic model 28–31, 37; and scripts 29–30

P
Pachter, Barbara 97
paraphrasing 115
pardon seeking 129, 134
passives 44, 45, 50, 58
patronage 198–9
Paychex Inc. 53
Pearlstine, Norman 182
Peeters, Helga 149
perceived adequacy: and effective excuses 130
perceived sincerity: and effective excuses 131
perfectionism: and procrastination 124, **125–6**, 133, 134
performance evaluation 152–4, 156, 157, 197–8; and ingratiation 153–4, 157, 197; performance blips and ingratiation during 153–4, 157, 197; and supervisory ratings 197–8; variables influencing impression management for 153, 157
performance evaluation blip 153, 157
performing: and charismatic leadership 173–4
perfume, use of 83
Perrow, Charles 51
personal branding 80, 94–7, 98, 100; coaching assistance with 95; as a professional identity 94–5; strong brands for businesspeople and athletes 95–7
personality factors 38–50
persuasiveness 60–3
pessimism 47
Pfeffer, Jeffrey 51, 160, 166
physical attractiveness: and job interviews 144
politeness 68–9, 78, 79, 87, 90, 145
political correctness: and enhancement of others 113–14, 116, 117
political language 161
political skill: and ingratiation 105–6, 116
Political Skill Inventory 105–6

Porter, Michael E. 192
positive discrepancies 17–18,
    27–8, 30, 32, 35, 37
positives 44, 45, 50, 58
post-interviews 150
posture 91, 99
power relations/struggles 51,
    53–4, 57, 58
praise 62, 106, 108, 111, 115 *see
    also* flattery
primacy 89, 99
private self 94
problem solving 46
procrastination 123–6, **123**, 133,
    134
Procter & Gamble 172
professional identity: personal
    brand as 94–5
profiles of impression
    management 44 *see also*
    aggressives; passives; positives
progress reports, providing timely
    73
Project Management Professional
    62
prosocial 70
Prudential Foundation 189
public self 7, 94
punishments, minimizing 6–7

Q
Quattrone, Frank P. 102

R
rapport 48–9
Ready to Work program 189
recency 153
receptionists: creating favorable
    impression on 155
reciprocity 62
recycling 188
reference goal 18, 20–4;
    adjustment of 30–1
Reiss, M. 129
relation-oriented messages 32,
    37
relationships: between men and
    women 88; building good 64;
    impact of impression
    management on improving
    199–200, 205
remote work 56, 58, 59
reputation 94; corporate 179, 201;
    developing a positive 63–4, *64*;
    online 181–2, 193; sponsored

research to enhance a company
    182–4; *see also* corporate
    image
respect 52
ResumeDoctor.com 151
résumés *see* job résumés
rewards, maximizing of 6–7
Riggio, Ronald E. 204
Robbins, Stephen P. 72
Rodriguez, Alex 96–7
role constraints 6, 10–11
Rosenfeld, Paul 130
rounding 162
rudeness 66, 78, 79, 87, 145
Russo, Rob 192

S
sales 200–1
Scale of Upward Influence 106
scarcity 62
Schlenker, Barry 4
script/scripting 29–30, 35, 37, 48,
    173
search engine optimization (SEO)
    181, 193
Sears Holdings Corp. 74
self-beliefs 10, 14
self-concept 6, 10, 14, 21, 36
self-confidence 93
self-disclosure: and job interviews
    145
self-enhancement 21, 36
self-esteem 7, 36; charismatic
    leaders and high 171, 175–6
self-esteem protection 119–21,
    133
self-evaluation 7
self-handicapping 32, 118,
    119–27, 132–3; definition 119;
    effects of status on 121–3,
    133–4; and gender differences
    126–7, 134; goals of 119;
    procrastination as 123–6, *123*,
    133, 134; self-esteem
    protection 119–21, 133
self-monitoring 22, 39–44, **40–1**,
    57, 58; charismatic leaders and
    high 171–2, 176; and job
    interviews 147; reasons for 44;
    scale **40–1**
self-perceived technical
    orientation: and flattery
    110–11
self-presentation 3, 4, 13, 15;
    avoiding unfavourable 75–6,

76–7; of characteristics and
    behaviors 60–8, **76–7**; motives
    for 6–8; substantive
    approaches to 60–79; surface-
    level approaches to 80–100; of
    work accomplishments 68–75,
    68, 77, 79
self-promotion 32, 42, **42**, **43**; and
    charismatic leaders 174; during
    job interview 137–8, **138–9**,
    140, 197
self-protection techniques 118–35,
    118; damage control *see*
    damage control; guidelines for
    application and practice 132–3;
    self-handicapping *see* self-
    handicapping
self-serving bias 130, 134
servant leader 167–9
sexiness: perceptions of based on
    clothing/dress 83, 84–5, 97, 99
Shields, Stephanie 68
showing, making a quick 74, 78
Sills, Judith 94, 95, 98
Simon, Kim 162
situational factors 22, 53–6, **53**;
    characteristics of the target 56;
    contextual variables 53–4; and
    job interviews 145–7, 156; and
    remote working 56; social
    network centrality 54–5
slight 114
Smackum, Rhoda 128
smiling 80
social identity 34; cybernetic
    model and desired 20–4, 36
social network centrality 55, 56,
    58, 59
social networking sites 98
social proof 62
social responsibility, corporate *see*
    corporate social responsibility
Sony 189
Southwest Airlines 201
speech: and creating a negative
    impression 76
spin 184–5, 192, 193
sponsored research: and
    enhancing of company
    reputation 182–4, 192, 193
sports celebrities: and branding
    96–7
sportsmanship 69
staging: and charismatic
    leadership 173

status: effects of on self-handicapping 121–3, 133–4; *see also* occupational status
status characteristics theory 121–2, 133–4
stealing 202
Stern, Ithai 106
Stevens, Cynthia Kay 140, 197
Stewart, Martha 95–6
stock price 200–1, 206
storytelling 73
strategic incompetence 3–4
stress, job 72
subject matter expert 72, 78
substantive approaches 60–79
Sulkowicz, Kerry 124, 126
supplication 42, *42*, *43*, 57, 69, 152
surface acting 204
surface-level self-presentation tactics 80–100, *81*
sustainability issues 200–1
symbols: understanding and exploiting of by leaders 160–1
synchrony 175

T
target: characteristics of 56, 57, 59; focusing on needs of 63, 78
team player, being a 167
team satisfaction: impact of impression management on 199–200

Tedeschi, J.T. 129
textspeak 88, 150, 156
Thaler, Linda Kaplan 67
Tiffany & Co. 180
tobacco industry 183
touching behavior 91–2
toughness: and leadership image projection 163
Treadway, Darren C. 104
Trump, Donald J. 96
trust 46, 52, 204
trustworthiness 45–7, 57, 58; and charismatic leaders 172; and leadership image projection 163–4; and servant leadership 168
Turnley, William H. 42, 71–2

V
valance-instrumentality-expectancy (VIE) theory 22, 36
values, target 11, 14
verbal tactics 31–2, 31, 37
video résumés 151–2, 157
videoconferencing 90, 97, 99
Virgin 96
Virgin Fuels 188
visibility 95
visions, creating 46, 159, 175
voice inflection 32–3
voice quality 91

W
Wal-Mart 160, 177–8

Waldt, Dorothy 83
walking around, management by 162
Walton, Sam 160
Watkins, Sherron 190
Wayne, Sandy J. 197
webcasts 90
websites, personal 10
weight 85–6, 99
Welch, Jack 93
Westphal, James D. 106
whistle blowers 190
White, Erin 63
Willis, Gary 161
Witherspoon, Reese 182
women: and communication 48–50, 59; and dress 82; and ingratiation 106; and job interviews 145; and self-handicapping 126–7, 134
Woods, Tiger 182
work accomplishments: self-presentation of 68–75, *68*, *77*, 79
work-life programs 189
World Wildlife Fund 189

Y
Yahoo 184
yes-person technique 203

Z
Zimmer, George A. 173
Zirngibl, Michael 1845